The Essential Ninja Foodi Cookbook UK 2023 for Beginners

1000 Days Healthy, Hands-Off, Amazing Mouthwatering and Budget-Friendly Ninja Foodi Recipes. Grill, Pressure Cook, Air Fry, Bake,Dehydrate, and More

Lloyd Rogahn

Warning-Disclaimer

The purpose of this book is to educate and entertain. The author or publisher does not guarantee that anyone following the techniques, suggestions, tips, ideas, or strategies will become successful. The author and publisher shall have neither liability or responsibility to anyone with respect to any loss or damage caused, or alleged to be caused, directly or indirectly by the information contained in this book.

Table of Contents

Chapter 4 Snacks and Appetisers   29

Chapter 5 Fish and Seafood   39

Chapter 8 Desserts   74

Chapter 9 Staples, Sauces, Dips, and Dressings   84

INTRODUCTION

Today's kitchens are losing space on countertops with separate appliances like air fryers, bread makers, rice makers, and pressure cookers, just to name a few. Forget hoarding separate units for each function and enter Ninja's latest do-it-all appliance: the 9-in-1 versatility Pressure Cooker and Air fryer Combo.

This single pot can pressure cook, air crisp, bake, dehydrate, roast, slow cook, steam, sear, or even make yoghurt. This countertop-friendly machine has replaced all other appliances in many kitchens because of its extreme versatility, electricity savings, and 70% faster cooking than traditional ovens, pressure cookers and air fryers.

We bought this pot when it was a new thing for people and they were afraid to use it. Also, there were NO recipes to try in this combo pot. So, we started figuring it out and tried different recipes every day and now we have a list of recipes to show for it. This appliance has now become the mainstay of our kitchen. From porridge to roast chicken, soups and pies - the possibilities are endless. We also made bulk stews from raw ingredients in just 55 minutes, with beef falling apart. But for us, the absolute joy was our roast potatoes - they came out perfectly crispy with a golden brown texture and fluffy from the inside.

So far we've used this pressure cooker and air fryer combo with different recipes and ingredients and they all turned out perfectly. Therefore, based on our experience we have created this cookbook for those who haven't yet tried this appliance or are using it for months. Each recipe has simple ingredients that you can easily find in your kitchen or buy from your nearest market. Plus, all recipes have easy step-by-step instructions with correct cooking time and temperature settings to eliminate any confusion. Now you can take your family meal time to the max with our list of scrumptious recipes that require you to spend less time in the kitchen.

You can also try these recipes and share this cookbook with your loved ones who want to make a variety of meals with simple ingredients in under 30 to 45 minutes. We have created this cookbook with love and want to pass this love to your kitchen so you can also create memories on your dinner table with your loved ones.

Let's uncover the delicacies that are soon to be served on your table!

Chapter 1: The Perfect Ninja Foodi Pressure Cooker & Air Fryer Combo!

Fancy a Sunday dinner that's prepared in less than an hour so you can have more family time? The Ninja Foodie Pressure Cooker and Air Fryer Combo is exactly the one that fits your lifestyle. You can use it for a range of different cooking options: steam, slow cook, air fry, pressure cook, roast, bake or make homemade yoghurt. From juicy steaks, slow-cooked veggies, roasted chicken, and bubbling pasta to steamed fish, you can cook an entire three-course meal, roast a complete chicken, and bake dessert in the same unit after your main. Explore more about this miracle appliance in this cookbook before you jump on to the recipes section.

How Does the Ninja Foodi Pressure Cooker and Air Fryer Combo Work?

You might be wondering how a single appliance operates as an air fryer and an electric pressure cooker. The miracle happens with its two-lid design. The pressure lid is for the pressure cooker portion which is removable and the Crisping lid is for the air fryer that's attached to it by a hinge. You can cook and crisp in the same pot by simply switching between the lids. The appliance works using TenderCrisp technology that traps steam and increases the pressure inside so you can prepare the food 70% faster than the standard cooking time. Plus, the air frying feature will give your meals a crispy, golden finish that couldn't be achieved with typical pressure cookers.

With Ninja Pressure Cooker and Air Fryer Combo, you can cook an entire meal in one pot. You don't have to move hot food from a pressure cooker to an air fryer for a golden crispy texture. Moreover, the appliance also has a steamer and slow cooker for busy people. Just put the ingredients in the pot for overnight cooking and enjoy a homemade meal even after a hectic day at work.

Now you can roast the perfect chicken, sear juicy steaks, steam bake cakes, slow cook stews, and sous vide seafood - everything you could have ever wished to cook but couldn't prepare due to your busy routine. Your life's now sorted!

9-In-1 Versatility to Ensure No Sweat Cooking at Home

Although Ninja combo is beasty, we love it for its 9-in-1 versatility through which we can make moist and yummy cakes, juicy and tender chicken, crisp and flavourful veggies, wonderfully creamy yoghurt, fluffy rice, and whatnot.

Pressure Cook

The pressure cook feature allows you to make tender, juicy meat in less time. Superheated pressurised steam infuses moisture into ingredients and quickly cooks food from the inside out. While the leftover juice from the meat can be used to steam the veg or to make gravy. So no waste at all.

Air Crisp

Get that restaurant-style crispy, golden, texture to your fries and chicken or veggies with 75% less fat and oil than traditional methods. The air crisp feature will help you make crispy bacon, chips, fish fingers, chicken wings, etc without drying out.

Steam

If you want to steam cook your sea bass, rice, vegetables, and more to perfection then use the steam function. You'll get soft and fluffy rice and juicy veggies and meat because steam seals in flavour while maintaining the texture of food.

Slow Cook

The Ninja combo pot can slow cook food for up to 12 hours. You can make casseroles, zesty risottos, your favourite chilis and stews without any effort. Just leave the ingredients on slow cooking mode and arrive home to a delicious meal.

Yoghurt

Making homemade yoghurt is now easy with just a touch of a button. Just put the ingredients in the pot and set the digital timer to Yoghurt and wait for creamy yoghurt to be ready - exactly as you like it.

Sear/Sauté

Searing and sauteing like your favourite restaurant is now achievable at home. The ninja air fryer and pressure cooker combo will reward you with beautifully tender, succulent cuts quickly with minimum effort.

Bake/Roast

Ninja pressure cooker and air fryer pot will outcompete your bread maker. From fresh homemade bread, sourdough, and rich nut roasts, to cookies, cakes and brownies, you can make anything to delight your sweet tooth.

Grill

The grill function will enable you to grill your favourite salmon fillets with just the right amount of caramelisation or crispiness.

Dehydrate

The dehydrator operates from 26 degrees Celsius to 90 degrees Celsius to dehydrate fresh herbs, beef for jerky, banana, apple, and vegetables - the only limit is your imagination.

Effortless Cooking With Handy Parts and Accessories

Since we've been creating pressure cooker and air fryer recipes for quite some time we've found the Ninja combo pot an absolute game-changer for us. You'll not just love its versatile features but also embrace its parts and accessories.

Pressure Lid

A chic pressure cooking lid makes this pot the ultimate pressure cooker that quickly transforms the toughest ingredients into tender, juicy, and flavorful meals. You can detach the lid from the main unit by moving it counterclockwise. You can either let the unit release steam naturally for up to 20 minutes or go for a quick pressure release (if your recipe calls for it). To do this, turn the pressure release valve to the VENT position and steam will release quickly.

Crisping Lid

The pot has a fitted crisper lid that's always attached to it at 90 degrees. Drop this lid when you want to crisp and caramelise your food to golden-brown perfection. You can open the lid during the cooking process to check on your food. The timer will automatically pause and the heating element will turn off. When you close the lid, the timer will resume cooking and counting down.

Cooking Pot

The removable cooker pot is a bit shallower and wider and has a non-stick coating that creates a barrier between the food and heating element to avoid dreaded burn notice. You can try juicy steaks, caramelise onions, toast seeds, and prepare sauce bases in the same pot.

Cook and Crisp Basket

We all love to munch on crispy snacks whenever we get the chance. The 'cook and crisp' basket is large enough to hold 4.7 litres to satisfy your hunger. You can air fry anything you want in one setting to feed a family of 4 to 6 people. During cooking, you can lift out the basket to shake or toss ingredients to ensure even browning.

Reversible Rack

Using the 2-tier reversible rack you can easily layer ingredients on it. You can also place the top tier rack over the reversible rack to cook sides and mains at the same time.

Cleaning Your Ninja Foodie Is a Breeze

It takes a little effort to clean your appliance, but you must do this to ensure it functions at its best. You can disassemble the majority of parts which makes cleanup a breeze and your Ninja Foodi will smell fresh for a long time.

♦ Use a clean damp cloth to clean the cooker base and the control panel.

♦ Put the pressure lid, cooking pot, reversible rack, crisp basket, and silicone ring in the dishwasher for easy cleaning.

♦ You can also hand wash the removable parts with warm, soapy water. But don't use metal scouring pads or if scrubbing is required, use a non-abrasive sponge to clean the pot. Air-dry all parts after cleaning and reassemble the appliance for the next use.

♦ If you want to deep clean the appliance in one setting, put 250ml hot water and 250ml lemon juice in the pot and pressure cook for 10 mins. Quickly release the pressure, open the pressure lid, and put down the air fryer lid for at least 5 mins to steam clean the grill area. Open the lid, use a damp cloth to wipe the grill lid then dry the appliance with a microfibre cloth or kitchen towels.

Chapter 2 Breakfasts

Hole in One

Prep time: 5 minutes | Cook time: 6 to 7 minutes | Serves 1

1 slice bread
1 teaspoon soft butter
1 egg
Salt and pepper, to taste
1 tablespoon shredded Cheddar cheese
2 teaspoons diced ham

1. Place a baking dish inside cook & crisp basket and Preheat the Ninja Foodi cooker to 165°C. 2. Using a 2½-inch-diameter biscuit cutter, cut a hole in center of bread slice. 3. Spread softened butter on both sides of bread. 4. Lay bread slice in baking dish and crack egg into the hole. Sprinkle egg with salt and pepper to taste. 5. Cook for 5 minutes. 6. Turn toast over and top it with shredded cheese and diced ham. 7. Cook for 1 to 2 more minutes or until yolk is done to your liking.

Pizza Eggs

Prep time: 5 minutes | Cook time: 10 minutes | Serves 2

235 ml shredded Mozzarella cheese
7 slices pepperoni, chopped
1 large egg, whisked
¼ teaspoon dried oregano
¼ teaspoon dried parsley
¼ teaspoon garlic powder
¼ teaspoon salt

1. Place Mozzarella in a single layer on the bottom of an ungreased round nonstick baking dish. Scatter pepperoni over cheese, then pour egg evenly around baking dish. 2. Sprinkle with remaining ingredients and place into cook & crisp basket. Adjust the temperature to 165°C and bake for 10 minutes. When cheese is brown and egg is set, dish will be done. 3. Let cool in dish 5 minutes before serving.

Potatoes Lyonnaise

Prep time: 10 minutes | Cook time: 31 minutes | Serves 4

1 sweet/mild onion, sliced
1 teaspoon butter, melted
1 teaspoon brown sugar
2 large white potatoes (about 450 g in total), sliced ½-inch
thick
1 tablespoon vegetable oil
Salt and freshly ground black pepper, to taste

1. Preheat the Ninja Foodi cooker to 190°C. 2. Toss the sliced onions, melted butter and brown sugar together in the cook & crisp basket. Air crisp for 8 minutes, shaking the basket occasionally to help the onions cook evenly. 3. While the onions are cooking, bring a saucepan of salted water to a boil on the stovetop. Par-cook the potatoes in boiling water for 3 minutes. Drain the potatoes and pat them dry with a clean kitchen towel. 4. Add the potatoes to the onions in the cook & crisp basket and drizzle with vegetable oil. Toss to coat the potatoes with the oil and season with salt and freshly ground black pepper. 5. Increase the Ninja Foodi cooker temperature to 205°C and air crisp for 20 minutes, tossing the vegetables a few times during the cooking time to help the potatoes brown evenly. 6. Season with salt and freshly ground black pepper and serve warm.

Bunless Breakfast Turkey Burgers

Prep time: 5 minutes | Cook time: 15 minutes | Serves 4

450 g turkey sausage meat, removed from casings
½ teaspoon salt
¼ teaspoon ground black pepper
60 ml seeded and chopped green
pepper
2 tablespoons mayonnaise
1 medium avocado, peeled, pitted, and sliced

1. In a large bowl, mix sausage meat with salt, black pepper, bell pepper, and mayonnaise. Form meat into four patties. 2. Place patties into ungreased cook & crisp basket. Adjust the temperature to 190°C and air crisp for 15 minutes, turning patties halfway through cooking. Burgers will be done when dark brown and they have an internal temperature of at least 75°C. 3. Serve burgers topped with avocado slices on four medium plates.

Wholemeal Banana-Walnut Bread

Prep time: 10 minutes | Cook time: 23 minutes | Serves 6

Olive oil cooking spray
2 ripe medium bananas
1 large egg
60 ml non-fat plain Greek yoghurt
60 ml olive oil
½ teaspoon vanilla extract
2 tablespoons honey
235 ml wholemeal flour
¼ teaspoon salt
¼ teaspoon baking soda
½ teaspoon ground cinnamon
60 ml chopped walnuts

1. Preheat the Ninja Foodi cooker to 180°C. Lightly coat the inside of a 8-by-4-inch loaf pan with olive oil cooking spray. (Or use two 5 ½-by-3-inch loaf pans.) 2. In a large bowl, mash the bananas with a fork. Add the egg, yoghurt, olive oil, vanilla, and honey. Mix until well combined and mostly smooth. 3. Sift the wholemeal flour, salt, baking soda, and cinnamon into the wet mixture, then stir until just combined. Do not overmix. 4. Gently fold in the walnuts. 5. Pour into the prepared loaf pan and spread to distribute evenly. 6. Place the loaf pan in the cook & crisp basket and bake for 20 to 23 minutes, or until golden brown on top and a toothpick inserted into the center comes out clean. 7. Allow to cool for 5 minutes before serving.

Breakfast Calzone

350 ml shredded Mozzarella cheese
120 ml blanched finely ground almond flour
30 g full-fat cream cheese
1 large whole egg

4 large eggs, scrambled
230 g cooked sausage meat, removed from casings and crumbled
8 tablespoons shredded mild Cheddar cheese

1. In a large microwave-safe bowl, add Mozzarella, almond flour, and cream cheese. Microwave for 1 minute. Stir until the mixture is smooth and forms a ball. Add the egg and stir until dough forms. 2. Place dough between two sheets of parchment and roll out to ¼-inch thickness. Cut the dough into four rectangles. 3. Mix scrambled eggs and cooked sausage together in a large bowl. Divide the mixture evenly among each piece of dough, placing it on the lower half of the rectangle. Sprinkle each with 2 tablespoons Cheddar. 4. Fold over the rectangle to cover the egg and meat mixture. Pinch, roll, or use a wet fork to close the edges completely. 5. Cut a piece of parchment to fit your cook & crisp basket and place the calzones onto the parchment. Place parchment into the cook & crisp basket. 6. Adjust the temperature to 190°C and air crisp for 15 minutes. 7. Flip the calzones halfway through the cooking time. When done, calzones should be golden in color. Serve immediately.

Streusel Pumpkin Cake

Streusel Topping:
60 ml granulated sweetener
60 ml almond flour
2 tablespoons coconut oil or unsalted butter, softened
½ teaspoon ground cinnamon
Cake:
2 large eggs, beaten
480 ml almond flour

240 ml pumpkin purée
180 ml granulated sweetener
2 teaspoons pumpkin pie spice
2 teaspoons vanilla extract
½ teaspoon fine sea salt
Glaze:
120 ml granulated sweetener
3 tablespoons unsweetened almond milk

1. Set a reversible rack in the Ninja Foodi cooker and pour in 240 ml water. Line a baking pan with baking paper. 2. In a small bowl, whisk together all the ingredients for the streusel topping with a fork. 3. In a medium-sized bowl, stir together all the ingredients for the cake until thoroughly combined. 4. Scoop half of the batter into the prepared baking pan and sprinkle half of the streusel topping on top. Repeat with the remaining batter and topping. 5. Place the baking pan on the reversible rack in the Ninja Foodi cooker. 6. Lock the lid, Set the cooking time for 30 minutes on High Pressure. 7. Meanwhile, whisk together the granulated sweetener and almond milk in a small bowl until it reaches a runny consistency. 8. When the timer goes off, do a natural pressure release for 10 minutes, then release any remaining pressure. Open the lid. 9. Remove the baking pan from the pot. Let cool in the pan for 10 minutes. Transfer the cake onto a plate and peel off the baking paper. 10. Transfer the cake onto a serving platter. Spoon the glaze over the top of the cake. Serve immediately.

Bacon and Spinach Eggs

2 tablespoons unsalted butter, divided
120 ml diced bacon
80 ml finely diced shallots
80 ml chopped spinach, leaves only
Pinch of sea salt

Pinch of black pepper
120 ml water
60 ml heavy whipping cream
8 large eggs
1 tablespoon chopped fresh chives, for garnish

1. Set the Ninja Foodi cooker on the Sauté mode and melt 1 tablespoon of the butter. Add the bacon to the pot and sauté for about 4 minutes, or until crispy. Using a slotted spoon, transfer the bacon bits to a bowl and set aside. 2. Add the remaining 1 tablespoon of the butter and shallots to the pot and sauté for about 2 minutes, or until tender. Add the spinach leaves and sauté for 1 minute, or until wilted. Season with sea salt and black pepper and stir. Transfer the spinach to a separate bowl and set aside. 3. Drain the oil from the pot into a bowl. Pour in the water and put the reversible rack inside. 4. With a paper towel, coat four ramekins with the bacon grease. In each ramekin, place 1 tablespoon of the heavy whipping cream, reserved bacon bits and sautéed spinach. Crack two eggs without breaking the yolks in each ramekin. Cover the ramekins with aluminium foil. Place two ramekins on the reversible rack and stack the other two on top. 5. Lock the lid. Set the cooking time for 2 minutes at Low Pressure. When the timer goes off, use a natural pressure release for 5 minutes, then release any remaining pressure. Carefully open the lid. 6. Carefully take out the ramekins and serve garnished with the chives.

Southwestern Frittata with Avocados

2 tablespoons coconut oil
60 ml diced onion
60 ml diced green chilies
½ green bell pepper, diced
8 eggs
1 teaspoon salt
½ teaspoon chili powder
¼ teaspoon garlic powder

¼ teaspoon pepper
60 ml double cream
4 tablespoons melted butter
120 ml shredded Cheddar cheese
240 ml water
2 avocados
60 ml sour cream

1. Press the Sauté button and add coconut oil to Ninja Foodi cooker. Add onion, chilies, and bell pepper. Sauté until onion is translucent and peppers begin to soften, approximately 3 minutes. While sautéing, whisk eggs, seasoning, double cream, and butter in large bowl. Pour into 7-inch round baking pan. 2. Press the Start/Stop button. Add onion and pepper mixture to egg mixture. Mix in Cheddar. Cover pan with aluminium foil. 3. Pour water into Ninja Foodi cooker, and scrape bottom of pot if necessary to remove any stuck-on food. Place steam rack into pot and put in baking dish with eggs on top. Click lid closed. 4. Set time for 25 minutes. 5. While food is cooking, cut avocados in half, remove pit, scoop out of shell and slice thinly. When timer beeps, quick-release the pressure. Serve with avocado slices and a spoonful of sour cream.

Egg in a Hole

Prep time: 5 minutes | Cook time: 5 minutes | Serves 1

1 slice bread
1 teaspoon butter, softened
1 egg
Salt and pepper, to taste

1 tablespoon shredded Cheddar cheese
2 teaspoons diced ham

1. Preheat the Ninja Foodi cooker to 165ºC. Place a baking dish in the cook & crisp basket. 2. On a flat work surface, cut a hole in the center of the bread slice with a 2½-inch-diameter biscuit cutter. 3. Spread the butter evenly on each side of the bread slice and transfer to the baking dish. 4. Crack the egg into the hole and season as desired with salt and pepper. Scatter the shredded cheese and diced ham on top. 5. Bake in the preheated Ninja Foodi cooker for 5 minutes until the bread is lightly browned and the egg is cooked to your preference. 6. Remove from the basket and serve hot.

Egg and Bacon Muffins

Prep time: 5 minutes | Cook time: 15 minutes | Serves 1

2 eggs
Salt and ground black pepper, to taste
1 tablespoon green pesto

85 g shredded Cheddar cheese
140 g cooked bacon
1 spring onion, chopped

1. Preheat the Ninja Foodi cooker to 175ºC. Line a cupcake tin with parchment paper. 2. Beat the eggs with pepper, salt, and pesto in a bowl. Mix in the cheese. 3. Pour the eggs into the cupcake tin and top with the bacon and spring onion. 4. Bake in the preheated Ninja Foodi cooker for 15 minutes, or until the egg is set. 5. Serve immediately.

Slow-Cooked Granola with Nuts

Prep time: 5 minutes | Cook time: 2 hours 30 minutes | Serves 10

240 ml raw almonds
240 ml pumpkin seeds
240 ml raw walnuts
240 ml raw cashews
1 tablespoon coconut oil

60 ml unsweetened coconut chips
1 teaspoon sea salt
1 teaspoon cinnamon

1. In a large bowl, stir together the almonds, pumpkin seeds, walnuts, cashews and coconut oil. Make sure all the nuts are coated with the coconut oil. Place the nut mixture in the Ninja Foodi cooker and cover the pot with a paper towel. 2. Lock the lid. Select the Slow Cook mode and set the cooking time for 1 hour on More. When the timer goes off, stir the nuts. Set the timer for another hour. 3. Again, when the timer goes off, stir the nut mixture and add the coconut chips. Set the timer for another 30 minutes. The cashews should become a nice golden colour. 4. When the timer goes off, transfer the nut mixture to a baking pan to cool and sprinkle with the sea salt and cinnamon. Serve.

Tomato and Mozzarella Bruschetta

Prep time: 5 minutes | Cook time: 4 minutes | Serves 1

6 small loaf slices
120 ml tomatoes, finely chopped
85 g Mozzarella cheese, grated

1 tablespoon fresh basil, chopped
1 tablespoon olive oil

1. Preheat the Ninja Foodi cooker to 175ºC. 2. Put the loaf slices inside the Ninja Foodi cooker and air crisp for about 3 minutes. 3. Add the tomato, Mozzarella, basil, and olive oil on top. 4. Air crisp for an additional minute before serving.

Onion Omelette

Prep time: 10 minutes | Cook time: 12 minutes | Serves 2

3 eggs
Salt and ground black pepper, to taste
½ teaspoons soy sauce

1 large onion, chopped
2 tablespoons grated Cheddar cheese
Cooking spray

1. Preheat the Ninja Foodi cooker to 180ºC. 2. In a bowl, whisk together the eggs, salt, pepper, and soy sauce. 3. Spritz a small pan with cooking spray. Spread the chopped onion across the bottom of the pan, then transfer the pan to the Ninja Foodi cooker. 4. Bake in the preheated Ninja Foodi cooker for 6 minutes or until the onion is translucent. 5. Add the egg mixture on top of the onions to coat well. Add the cheese on top, then continue baking for another 6 minutes. 6. Allow to cool before serving.

Homemade Toaster Pastries

Prep time: 10 minutes | Cook time: 11 minutes | Makes 6 pastries

Oil, for spraying
1 (425 g) package refrigerated piecrust
6 tablespoons jam or preserves of choice

475 ml icing sugar
3 tablespoons milk
1 to 2 tablespoons sprinkles of choice

1. Preheat the Ninja Foodi cooker to 175ºC. Line the cook & crisp basket with parchment and spray lightly with oil. 2. Cut the piecrust into 12 rectangles, about 3 by 4 inches each. You will need to reroll the dough scraps to get 12 rectangles. 3. Spread 1 tablespoon of jam in the center of 6 rectangles, leaving ¼ inch around the edges. 4. Pour some water into a small bowl. Use your finger to moisten the edge of each rectangle. 5. Top each rectangle with another and use your fingers to press around the edges. Using the tines of a fork, seal the edges of the dough and poke a few holes in the top of each one. Place the pastries in the prepared basket. 6. Air crisp for 11 minutes. Let cool completely. 7. In a medium bowl, whisk together the icing sugar and milk. Spread the icing over the tops of the pastries and add sprinkles. Serve immediately.

Quick and Easy Blueberry Muffins

Prep time: 10 minutes | Cook time: 12 minutes | Makes 8 muffins

315 ml flour
120 ml sugar
2 teaspoons baking powder
¼ teaspoon salt
80 ml rapeseed oil

1 egg
120 ml milk
160 ml blueberries, fresh or frozen and thawed

1. Preheat the Ninja Foodi cooker to 165°C. 2. In a medium bowl, stir together flour, sugar, baking powder, and salt. 3. In a separate bowl, combine oil, egg, and milk and mix well. 4. Add egg mixture to dry ingredients and stir just until moistened. 5. Gently stir in the blueberries. 6. Spoon batter evenly into parchment paper-lined muffin cups. 7. Put 4 muffin cups in cook & crisp basket and bake for 12 minutes or until tops spring back when touched lightly. 8. Repeat previous step to bake remaining muffins. 9. Serve immediately.

Avocado Green Power Bowl

Prep time: 10 minutes | Cook time: 10 minutes | Serves 1

240 ml water
2 eggs
1 tablespoon coconut oil
1 tablespoon butter
30 g sliced almonds
240 ml fresh spinach, sliced into strips

120 ml kale, sliced into strips
½ clove garlic, minced
½ teaspoon salt
⅛ teaspoon pepper
½ avocado, sliced
⅛ teaspoon red pepper flakes

1. Pour water into Ninja Foodi cooker and place steam rack on bottom. Place eggs on steam rack. Click lid closed. Adjust time for 6 minutes. When timer beeps, quick-release the pressure. Set eggs aside. 2. Pour water out, clean pot, and replace. Press the Sauté button and add coconut oil, butter, and almonds. Sauté for 2 to 3 minutes until butter begins to turn golden and almonds soften. Add spinach, kale, garlic, salt, and pepper to Ninja Foodi cooker. Sauté for 4 to 6 minutes until greens begin to wilt. Press the Start/Stop button. Place greens in bowl for serving. Peel eggs, cut in half, and add to bowl. Slice avocado and place in bowl. Sprinkle red pepper flakes over all. Serve warm.

Quesadillas

Prep time: 10 minutes | Cook time: 15 minutes | Serves 4

4 eggs
2 tablespoons skimmed milk
Salt and pepper, to taste
Oil for misting or cooking spray
4 flour tortillas

4 tablespoons salsa
60 g Cheddar cheese, grated
½ small avocado, peeled and thinly sliced

1. Preheat the Ninja Foodi cooker to 130°C. 2. Beat together eggs, milk, salt, and pepper. 3. Spray a baking pan lightly with cooking spray and add egg mixture. 4. Bake for 8 to 9 minutes, stirring every 1 to 2 minutes, until eggs are scrambled to your liking. Remove and set aside. 5. Spray one side of each tortilla with oil or cooking spray. Flip over. 6. Divide eggs, salsa, cheese, and avocado among the tortillas, covering only half of each tortilla. 7. Fold each tortilla in half and press down lightly. 8. Place 2 tortillas in cook & crisp basket and air crisp at 200°C for 3 minutes or until cheese melts and outside feels slightly crispy. Repeat with remaining two tortillas. 9. Cut each cooked tortilla into halves or thirds.

Apple Cider Doughnut Holes

Prep time: 10 minutes | Cook time: 6 minutes | Makes 10 mini doughnuts

Doughnut Holes:
350 ml plain flour
2 tablespoons granulated sugar
2 teaspoons baking powder
1 teaspoon baking soda
½ teaspoon coarse or flaky salt
Pinch of freshly grated nutmeg
60 ml plus 2 tablespoons buttermilk, chilled
2 tablespoons apple cider or

apple juice, chilled
1 large egg, lightly beaten
Vegetable oil, for brushing
Glaze:
120 ml icing sugar
2 tablespoons unsweetened applesauce
¼ teaspoon vanilla extract
Pinch of coarse or flaky salt

1. Make the doughnut holes: In a bowl, whisk together the flour, granulated sugar, baking powder, baking soda, salt, and nutmeg until smooth. Add the buttermilk, cider, and egg and stir with a small rubber spatula or spoon until the dough just comes together. 2. Using a 28 g ice cream scoop or 2 tablespoons, scoop and drop 10 balls of dough into the cook & crisp basket, spaced evenly apart, and brush the tops lightly with oil. Air crisp at 175°C until the doughnut holes are golden brown and fluffy, about 6 minutes. Transfer the doughnut holes to a wire rack to cool completely. 3. Make the glaze: In a small bowl, stir together the powdered sugar, applesauce, vanilla, and salt until smooth. 4. Dip the tops of the doughnuts holes in the glaze, then let stand until the glaze sets before serving. If you're impatient and want warm doughnuts, have the glaze ready to go while the doughnuts cook, then use the glaze as a dipping sauce for the warm doughnuts, fresh out of the Ninja Foodi cooker.

Keto Cabbage Hash Browns

Prep time: 5 minutes | Cook time: 8 minutes | Serves 3

240 ml shredded white cabbage
3 eggs, beaten
½ teaspoon ground nutmeg
½ teaspoon salt

½ teaspoon onion powder
½ courgette, grated
1 tablespoon coconut oil

1. In a bowl, stir together all the ingredients, except for the coconut oil. Form the cabbage mixture into medium hash browns. 2. Press the Sauté button on the Ninja Foodi cooker and heat the coconut oil. 3. Place the hash browns in the hot coconut oil. Cook for 4 minutes on each side, or until lightly browned. 4. Transfer the hash browns to a plate and serve warm.

Ninja Foodi cooker Hard-Boiled Eggs

Prep time: 10 minutes | Cook time: 5 minutes | Serves 7

240 ml water

6–8 eggs

1. Pour the water into the inner pot. Place the eggs in a steamer basket or rack that came with pot. 2. Close the lid and secure to the locking position. Be sure the vent is turned to sealing. Set for 5 minutes at high pressure. (It takes about 5 minutes for pressure to build and then 5 minutes to cook.) 3. Let pressure naturally release for 5 minutes, then do quick pressure release. 4. Place hot eggs into cool water to halt cooking process. You can peel cooled eggs immediately or refrigerate unpeeled.

Poached Eggs

Prep time: 5 minutes | Cook time: 5 minutes | Serves 4

Nonstick cooking spray

4 large eggs

1. Lightly spray 1 L of a 7-count silicone egg bite mold with nonstick cooking spray. Crack each egg into a sprayed cup. 2. Pour 240 ml of water into the electric pressure cooker. Place the egg bite mold on the wire rack and carefully lower it into the pot. 3. Close and lock the lid of the pressure cooker. Set the valve to sealing. 4. Cook on high pressure for 5 minutes. 5. When the cooking is complete, hit Start/Stop and quick release the pressure. 6. Once the pin drops, unlock and remove the lid. 7. Run a small rubber spatula or spoon around each egg and carefully remove it from the mold. The white should be cooked, but the yolk should be runny. 8. Serve immediately.

Honey-Apricot Granola with Greek Yoghurt

Prep time: 10 minutes | Cook time: 30 minutes | Serves 6

235 ml rolled oats
60 ml dried apricots, diced
60 ml almond slivers
60 ml walnuts, chopped
60 ml pumpkin seeds
60 to 80 ml honey, plus more for drizzling
1 tablespoon olive oil

1 teaspoon ground cinnamon
¼ teaspoon ground nutmeg
¼ teaspoon salt
2 tablespoons sugar-free dark chocolate chips (optional)
700 ml fat-free plain Greek yoghurt

1. Preheat the Ninja Foodi cooker to 130°C. Line the cook & crisp basket with parchment paper. 2. In a large bowl, combine the oats, apricots, almonds, walnuts, pumpkin seeds, honey, olive oil, cinnamon, nutmeg, and salt, mixing so that the honey, oil, and spices are well distributed. 3. Pour the mixture onto the parchment paper and spread it into an even layer. 4. Bake for 10 minutes, then shake or stir and spread back out into an even layer. Continue baking for 10 minutes more, then repeat the process of shaking or stirring the mixture. Bake for an additional 10 minutes before removing from the Ninja Foodi cooker. 5. Allow the granola to cool completely before stirring in the chocolate chips (if using) and pouring into an airtight container for storage. 6. For each serving, top 120 ml Greek yoghurt with 80 ml granola and a drizzle of honey, if needed.

Nutty Granola

Prep time: 5 minutes | Cook time: 1 hour | Serves 4

120 ml pecans, coarsely chopped
120 ml walnuts or almonds, coarsely chopped
60 ml desiccated coconut
60 ml almond flour
60 ml ground flaxseed or chia seeds

2 tablespoons sunflower seeds
2 tablespoons melted butter
60 ml granulated sweetener
½ teaspoon ground cinnamon
½ teaspoon vanilla extract
¼ teaspoon ground nutmeg
¼ teaspoon salt
2 tablespoons water

1. Preheat the Ninja Foodi cooker to 120°C. Cut a piece of parchment paper to fit inside the cook & crisp basket. 2. In a large bowl, toss the nuts, coconut, almond flour, ground flaxseed or chia seeds, sunflower seeds, butter, sweetener, cinnamon, vanilla, nutmeg, salt, and water until thoroughly combined. 3. Spread the granola on the parchment paper and flatten to an even thickness. 4. Air crisp for about an hour, or until golden throughout. Remove from the Ninja Foodi cooker and allow to fully cool. Break the granola into bite-size pieces and store in a covered container for up to a week.

Potato-Bacon Gratin

Prep time: 20 minutes | Cook time: 40 minutes | Serves 8

1 tablespoon olive oil
170 g fresh spinach
1 clove garlic, minced
4 large potatoes, peeled or unpeeled, divided

170 g Canadian bacon slices, divided
140 g grated Swiss cheddar, divided
240 ml chicken broth

1. Set the Ninja Foodi cooker to Sauté and pour in the olive oil. Cook the spinach and garlic in olive oil just until spinach is wilted (5 minutes or less). Turn off the Ninja Foodi cooker. 2. Cut potatoes into thin slices about ¼" thick. 3. In a springform pan that will fit into the inner pot of your Ninja Foodi cooker, spray it with nonstick spray then layer ⅓ the potatoes, half the bacon, ⅓ the cheese, and half the wilted spinach. 4. Repeat layers ending with potatoes. Reserve ⅓ cheese for later. 5. Pour chicken broth over all. 6. Wipe the bottom of your Ninja Foodi cooker to soak up any remaining oil, then add in 480 ml of water and the steaming rack. Place the springform pan on top. 7. Close the lid and secure to the locking position. Be sure the vent is turned to sealing. Set for 35 minutes at high pressure. 8. Perform a quick release. 9. Top with the remaining cheese, then allow to stand 10 minutes before removing from the Ninja Foodi cooker, cutting and serving.

Blueberry Cobbler

Prep time: 5 minutes | Cook time: 15 minutes | Serves 4

80 ml wholemeal pastry flour
¾ teaspoon baking powder
Dash sea salt
120 ml semi-skimmed milk
2 tablespoons pure maple syrup

½ teaspoon vanilla extract
Cooking oil spray
120 ml fresh blueberries
60 ml granola

1. In a medium bowl, whisk the flour, baking powder, and salt. Add the milk, maple syrup, and vanilla and gently whisk, just until thoroughly combined. 2. Preheat the unit by selecting BAKE, setting the temperature to 175ºC, and setting the time to 3 minutes. Press START/STOP to begin. 3. Spray a 6-by-2-inch round baking pan with cooking oil and pour the batter into the pan. Top evenly with the blueberries and granola. 4. Once the unit is preheated, place the pan into the basket. 5. Select BAKE, set the temperature to 175ºC, and set the time to 15 minutes. Press START/STOP to begin. 6. When the cooking is complete, the cobbler should be nicely browned and a knife inserted into the middle should come out clean. Enjoy plain or topped with a little vanilla yoghurt.

Mexican Breakfast Pepper Rings

Prep time: 5 minutes | Cook time: 10 minutes | Serves 4

Olive oil
1 large red, yellow, or orange pepper, cut into four ¾-inch rings

4 eggs
Salt and freshly ground black pepper, to taste
2 teaspoons salsa

1. Preheat the Ninja Foodi cooker to 175ºC. Lightly spray a baking pan with olive oil. 2. Place 2 bell pepper rings on the pan. Crack one egg into each bell pepper ring. Season with salt and black pepper. 3. Spoon ½ teaspoon of salsa on top of each egg. 4. Place the pan in the cook & crisp basket. Air crisp until the yolk is slightly runny, 5 to 6 minutes or until the yolk is fully cooked, 8 to 10 minutes. 5. Repeat with the remaining 2 pepper rings. Serve hot.

Smoked Salmon and Asparagus Quiche Cups

Prep time: 15 minutes | Cook time: 15 minutes | Serves 2

Nonstick cooking spray
4 asparagus spears, cut into ½-inch pieces
2 tablespoons finely chopped onion
85 g smoked salmon (skinless

and boneless), chopped
3 large eggs
2 tablespoons semi-skimmed milk
¼ teaspoon dried dill
Pinch ground white pepper

1. Pour 360 ml of water into the electric pressure cooker and insert a wire rack or reversible rack. 2. Lightly spray the bottom and sides of the ramekins with nonstick cooking spray. Divide the asparagus, onion, and salmon between the ramekins. 3. In a measuring cup with a spout, whisk together the eggs, milk, dill, and white pepper. Pour half of the egg mixture into each ramekin. Loosely cover the ramekins with aluminium foil. 4. Carefully place the ramekins inside the pot on the rack. 5. Close and lock the lid of the pressure cooker. Set the valve to sealing. 6. Cook on high pressure for 15 minutes. 7. When the cooking is complete, hit Start/Stop and quick release the pressure. 8. Once the pin drops, unlock and remove the lid. 9. Carefully remove the ramekins from the pot. Cool, covered, for 5 minutes. 10. Run a small silicone spatula or a knife around the edge of each ramekin. Invert each quiche onto a small plate and serve.

Spinach and Cheese Frittata

Prep time: 5 minutes | Cook time: 20 minutes | Serves 4 to 5

6 eggs
240 ml chopped spinach
240 ml shredded full-fat Cheddar cheese
240 ml shredded full-fat Monterey Jack cheese (optional)
2 tablespoons coconut oil

240 ml chopped bell peppers
½ teaspoon dried parsley
½ teaspoon dried basil
½ teaspoon ground turmeric
½ teaspoon freshly ground black pepper
½ teaspoon rock salt

1. Pour 240 ml of filtered water into the inner pot of the Ninja Foodi cooker, then insert the reversible rack. 2. In a large bowl, combine the eggs, spinach, Cheddar cheese, Monterey Jack cheese, coconut oil, bell peppers, parsley, basil, turmeric, black pepper, and salt, and stir thoroughly. Transfer this mixture into a well-greased Ninja Foodi cooker-friendly dish. 3. Using a sling if desired, place the dish onto the reversible rack, and cover loosely with aluminium foil. Close the lid, set the pressure release to Sealing. Set the Ninja Foodi cooker to 20 minutes on High Pressure, and let cook. 4. Once cooked, let the pressure naturally disperse from the Ninja Foodi cooker for about 10 minutes, then carefully switch the pressure release to Venting. 5. Open the Ninja Foodi cooker, serve, and enjoy!

Bourbon Vanilla French Toast

Prep time: 15 minutes | Cook time: 6 minutes | Serves 4

2 large eggs
2 tablespoons water
160 ml whole or semi-skimmed milk
1 tablespoon butter, melted

2 tablespoons bourbon
1 teaspoon vanilla extract
8 (1-inch-thick) French bread slices
Cooking spray

1. Preheat the Ninja Foodi cooker to 160ºC. Line the cook & crisp basket with parchment paper and spray it with cooking spray. 2. Beat the eggs with the water in a shallow bowl until combined. Add the milk, melted butter, bourbon, and vanilla and stir to mix well. 3. Dredge 4 slices of bread in the batter, turning to coat both sides evenly. Transfer the bread slices onto the parchment paper. 4. Bake for 6 minutes until nicely browned. Flip the slices halfway through the cooking time. 5. Remove from the basket to a plate and repeat with the remaining 4 slices of bread. 6. Serve warm.

Soft-Scrambled Eggs

Prep time: 5 minutes | Cook time: 7 minutes | Serves 4

6 eggs	¼ teaspoon pepper
2 tablespoons double cream	2 tablespoons butter
1 teaspoon salt	60 g cream cheese, softened

1. In large bowl, whisk eggs, double cream, salt, and pepper. Press the Sauté button and then press the Adjust button to set heat to Less. 2. Gently push eggs around pot with rubber spatula. When they begin to firm up, add butter and softened cream cheese. Continue stirring slowly in a figure-8 pattern until eggs are fully cooked, approximately 7 minutes total.

Lemon-Blueberry Muffins

Prep time: 5 minutes | Cook time: 20 to 25 minutes | Makes 6

muffins	2 large eggs
300 ml almond flour	3 tablespoons melted butter
3 tablespoons granulated	1 tablespoon almond milk
sweetener	1 tablespoon fresh lemon juice
1 teaspoon baking powder	120 ml fresh blueberries

1. Preheat the Ninja Foodi cooker to 175°C. Lightly coat 6 silicone muffin cups with vegetable oil. Set aside. 2. In a large mixing bowl, combine the almond flour, sweetener, and baking soda. Set aside. 3. In a separate small bowl, whisk together the eggs, butter, milk, and lemon juice. Add the egg mixture to the flour mixture and stir until just combined. Fold in the blueberries and let the batter sit for 5 minutes. 4. Spoon the muffin batter into the muffin cups, about two-thirds full. Air crisp for 20 to 25 minutes, or until a toothpick inserted into the center of a muffin comes out clean. 5. Remove the basket from the Ninja Foodi cooker and let the muffins cool for about 5 minutes before transferring them to a wire rack to cool completely.

Classic Coffee Cake

Prep time: 5 minutes | Cook time: 40 minutes | Serves 5 to 6

Base:	½ teaspoon ground cinnamon
2 eggs	½ teaspoon ground nutmeg
2 tablespoons salted grass-fed	¼ teaspoon bicarbonate of soda
butter, softened	Topping:
240 ml blanched almond flour	240 ml sugar-free chocolate
240 ml chopped pecans	chips
60 ml sour cream, at room	240 ml chopped pecans
temperature	120 ml granulated sweetener, or
60 ml full-fat cream cheese,	more to taste
softened	120 ml heavy whipping cream
½ teaspoon salt	

1. Pour 240 ml of filtered water into the inner pot of the Ninja Foodi cooker, then insert the reversible rack. Using an electric mixer, combine the eggs, butter, flour, pecans, sour cream, cream cheese, salt, cinnamon, nutmeg, and bicarbonate of soda. Mix thoroughly. Transfer this mixture into a well-greased, Ninja Foodi cooker-friendly pan (or dish). 2. Using a sling if desired, place the pan onto the reversible rack, and cover loosely with aluminium foil. Close the lid, set the pressure release to Sealing. Set the Ninja Foodi cooker to 40 minutes on High Pressure and let cook. 3. While cooking, in a large bowl, mix the chocolate chips, pecans, granulated sweetener, and whipping cream thoroughly. Set aside. 4. Once cooked, let the pressure naturally disperse from the Ninja Foodi cooker for about 10 minutes, then carefully switch the pressure release to Venting. 5. Open the Ninja Foodi cooker and remove the pan. Evenly sprinkle the topping mixture over the cake. Let cool, serve, and enjoy!

Spinach and Swiss Frittata with Mushrooms

Prep time: 10 minutes | Cook time: 20 minutes | Serves 4

Olive oil cooking spray	110 g baby mushrooms, sliced
8 large eggs	1 shallot, diced
½ teaspoon salt	120 ml shredded Swiss cheese,
½ teaspoon black pepper	divided
1 garlic clove, minced	Hot sauce, for serving (optional)
475 ml fresh baby spinach	

1. Preheat the Ninja Foodi cooker to 180°C. Lightly coat the inside of a 6-inch round cake pan with olive oil cooking spray. 2. In a large bowl, beat the eggs, salt, pepper, and garlic for 1 to 2 minutes, or until well combined. 3. Fold in the spinach, mushrooms, shallot, and 60 ml the Swiss cheese. 4. Pour the egg mixture into the prepared cake pan, and sprinkle the remaining 60 ml Swiss over the top. 5. Place into the Ninja Foodi cooker and bake for 18 to 20 minutes, or until the eggs are set in the center. 6. Remove from the Ninja Foodi cooker and allow to cool for 5 minutes. Drizzle with hot sauce (if using) before serving.

Mexican Breakfast Beef Chili

Prep time: 5 minutes | Cook time: 45 minutes | Serves 4

2 tablespoons coconut oil	½ teaspoon chili powder
450 g ground grass-fed beef	½ teaspoon crushed red pepper
1 (400 g) can sugar-free or low-sugar diced tomatoes	½ teaspoon ground cumin
120 ml shredded full-fat	½ teaspoon rock salt
Cheddar cheese (optional)	½ teaspoon freshly ground black
1 teaspoon hot sauce	pepper

1. Set the Ninja Foodi cooker to Sauté and melt the oil. 2. Pour in 120 ml of filtered water, then add the beef, tomatoes, cheese, hot sauce, chili powder, red pepper, cumin, salt, and black pepper to the Ninja Foodi cooker, stirring thoroughly. 3. Close the lid, set the pressure release to Sealing, and hit Start/Stop to stop the current program. Set the Ninja Foodi cooker to 45 minutes on High Pressure and let cook. 4. Once cooked, let the pressure naturally disperse from the Ninja Foodi cooker for about 10 minutes, then carefully switch the pressure release to Venting. 5. Open the Ninja Foodi cooker, serve, and enjoy!

Simple Scotch Eggs

Prep time: 5 minutes | Cook time: 25 minutes | Serves 4

4 large hard boiled eggs
1 (340 g) package pork sausage meat

8 slices thick-cut bacon
4 wooden toothpicks, soaked in water for at least 30 minutes

1. Slice the sausage meat into four parts and place each part into a large circle. 2. Put an egg into each circle and wrap it in the sausage. Put in the refrigerator for 1 hour. 3. Preheat the Ninja Foodi cooker to 235°C. 4. Make a cross with two pieces of thick-cut bacon. Put a wrapped egg in the center, fold the bacon over top of the egg, and secure with a toothpick. 5. Air crisp in the preheated Ninja Foodi cooker for 25 minutes. 6. Serve immediately.

Ham and Cheese Crescents

Prep time: 5 minutes | Cook time: 7 minutes | Makes 8 rolls

Oil, for spraying
1 (230 g) can ready-to-bake croissants
4 slices wafer-thin ham

8 cheese slices
2 tablespoons unsalted butter, melted

1. Line the cook & crisp basket with parchment and spray lightly with oil. 2. Separate the dough into 8 pieces. 3. Tear the ham slices in half and place 1 piece on each piece of dough. Top each with 1 slice of cheese. 4. Roll up each piece of dough, starting on the wider side. 5. Place the rolls in the prepared basket. Brush with the melted butter. 6. Air crisp at 160°C for 6 to 7 minutes, or until puffed and golden brown and the cheese is melted.

Sausage and Cauliflower Breakfast Casserole

Prep time: 5 minutes | Cook time: 10 minutes | Serves 6

240 ml water
½ head cauliflower, chopped into bite-sized pieces
4 slices bacon
450 g breakfast sausage
4 tablespoons melted butter
10 eggs

80 ml double cream
2 teaspoons salt
1 teaspoon pepper
2 tablespoons hot sauce
2 stalks spring onion
240 ml shredded sharp Cheddar cheese

1. Pour water into Ninja Foodi cooker and place steamer basket in bottom. Add cauliflower. Click lid closed. 2. Press the Steam button and adjust time for 1 minute. When timer beeps, quick-release the pressure and place cauliflower to the side in medium bowl. 3. Drain water from Ninja Foodi cooker, clean, and replace. Press the Sauté button. Press the Adjust button to set heat to Less. Cook bacon until crispy. Once fully cooked, set aside on paper towels. Add breakfast sausage to pot and brown (still using the Sauté function). 4. While sausage is cooking, whisk butter, eggs, double cream, salt, pepper, and hot sauce. 5. When sausage is fully cooked, pour egg mixture into Ninja Foodi cooker. Gently stir using silicone spatula until eggs are completely cooked and fluffy. Press the Start/Stop button. Slice spring onions. Sprinkle spring onions, bacon, and cheese over mixture and let melt. Serve warm.

Golden Avocado Tempura

Prep time: 5 minutes | Cook time: 10 minutes | Serves 4

120 ml bread crumbs
½ teaspoons salt
1 Haas avocado, pitted, peeled

and sliced
Liquid from 1 can white beans

1. Preheat the Ninja Foodi cooker to 175°C. 2. Mix the bread crumbs and salt in a shallow bowl until well-incorporated. 3. Dip the avocado slices in the bean liquid, then into the bread crumbs. 4. Put the avocados in the Ninja Foodi cooker, taking care not to overlap any slices, and air crisp for 10 minutes, giving the basket a good shake at the halfway point. 5. Serve immediately.

Cheesy Bell Pepper Eggs

Prep time: 10 minutes | Cook time: 15 minutes | Serves 4

4 medium green peppers
85 g cooked ham, chopped
¼ medium onion, peeled and

chopped
8 large eggs
235 ml mild Cheddar cheese

1. Cut the tops off each pepper. Remove the seeds and the white membranes with a small knife. Place ham and onion into each pepper. 2. Crack 2 eggs into each pepper. Top with 60 ml cheese per pepper. Place into the cook & crisp basket. 3. Adjust the temperature to 200°C and air crisp for 15 minutes. 4. When fully cooked, peppers will be tender and eggs will be firm. Serve immediately.

Blueberry Almond Cereal

Prep time: 5 minutes | Cook time: 2 minutes | Serves 4

80 ml crushed roasted almonds
60 ml almond flour
60 ml unsalted butter, softened
60 ml vanilla-flavored egg white protein powder

2 tablespoons granulated sweetener
1 teaspoon blueberry extract
1 teaspoon ground cinnamon

1. Add all the ingredients to the Ninja Foodi cooker and stir to combine. 2. Lock the lid, Set the cooking time for 2 minutes on High Pressure. When the timer goes off, do a natural pressure release for 10 minutes, then release any remaining pressure. Open the lid. 3. Stir well and pour the mixture onto a sheet lined with baking paper to cool. It will be crispy when completely cool. 4. Serve the cereal in bowls.

Vegetable and Cheese Bake

Prep time: 7 minutes | Cook time: 9 minutes | Serves 3

3 eggs, beaten
60 ml coconut cream
¼ teaspoon salt
85 g Brussel sprouts, chopped

60 g tomato, chopped
85 g provolone cheese, shredded
1 teaspoon butter
1 teaspoon smoked paprika

1. Grease the Ninja Foodi cooker pan with the butter. 2. Put eggs in the bowl, add salt, and smoked paprika. Whisk the eggs well. 3. After this, add chopped Brussel sprouts and tomato. 4. Pour the mixture into the Ninja Foodi cooker pan and sprinkle over with the shredded cheese. 5. Pour 240 ml of the water in the Ninja Foodi cooker. Then place the pan with the egg mixture and close the lid. 6. Cook the meal on High Pressure for 4 minutes. Then make naturally release for 5 minutes.

Herbed Buttery Breakfast Steak

Prep time: 5 minutes | Cook time: 1 minute | Serves 2

120 ml water
450 g boneless beef sirloin steak
½ teaspoon salt
½ teaspoon black pepper
1 clove garlic, minced

2 tablespoons butter, softened
¼ teaspoon dried rosemary
¼ teaspoon dried parsley
Pinch of dried thyme

1. Pour the water into the Ninja Foodi cooker and put the reversible rack in the pot. 2. Rub the steak all over with salt and black pepper. Place the steak on the reversible rack. 3. In a small bowl, stir together the remaining ingredients. Spread half of the butter mixture over the steak. 4. Set the lid in place. Set the cooking time for 1 minute on Low Pressure. When the timer goes off, perform a quick pressure release. Carefully open the lid. 5. Remove the steak from the pot. Top with the remaining half of the butter mixture. Serve hot.

Keto Quiche

Prep time: 10 minutes | Cook time: 1 hour | Makes 1 (6-inch) quiche

Crust:
300 ml blanched almond flour
300 ml grated Parmesan or Gouda cheese
¼ teaspoon fine sea salt
1 large egg, beaten
Filling:
120 ml chicken or beef stock (or vegetable stock for vegetarian)
235 ml shredded Swiss cheese (about 110 g)

110 g cream cheese (120 ml)
1 tablespoon unsalted butter, melted
4 large eggs, beaten
80 ml minced leeks or sliced spring onions
¾ teaspoon fine sea salt
⅛ teaspoon cayenne pepper
Chopped spring onions, for garnish

1. Preheat the Ninja Foodi cooker to 165°C. Grease a pie pan. Spray two large pieces of parchment paper with avocado oil and set them on the countertop. 2. Make the crust: In a medium-sized bowl, combine the flour, cheese, and salt and mix well. Add the egg and mix until the dough is well combined and stiff. 3. Place the dough in the center of one of the greased pieces of parchment. Top with the other piece of parchment. Using a rolling pin, roll out the dough into a circle about 1/16 inch thick. 4. Press the pie crust into the prepared pie pan. Place it in the Ninja Foodi cooker and bake for 12 minutes, or until it starts to lightly brown. 5. While the crust bakes, make the filling: In a large bowl, combine the stock, Swiss cheese, cream cheese, and butter. Stir in the eggs, leeks, salt, and cayenne pepper. When the crust is ready, pour the mixture into the crust. 6. Place the quiche in the Ninja Foodi cooker and bake for 15 minutes. Turn the heat down to 150°C and bake for an additional 30 minutes, or until a knife inserted 1 inch from the edge comes out clean. You may have to cover the edges of the crust with foil to prevent burning. 7. Allow the quiche to cool for 10 minutes before garnishing it with chopped spring onions and cutting it into wedges. 8. Store leftovers in an airtight container in the refrigerator for up to 4 days or in the freezer for up to a month. Reheat in a preheated 175°C Ninja Foodi cooker for a few minutes, until warmed through.

Gold Avocado

Prep time: 5 minutes | Cook time: 6 minutes | Serves 4

2 large avocados, sliced
¼ teaspoon paprika
Salt and ground black pepper, to taste

120 ml flour
2 eggs, beaten
235 ml bread crumbs

1. Preheat the Ninja Foodi cooker to 205°C. 2. Sprinkle paprika, salt and pepper on the slices of avocado. 3. Lightly coat the avocados with flour. Dredge them in the eggs, before covering with bread crumbs. 4. Transfer to the Ninja Foodi cooker and air crisp for 6 minutes. 5. Serve warm.

Almond Pancakes

Prep time: 10 minutes | Cook time: 15 minutes per batch | Serves 6

4 eggs, beaten
480 ml almond flour
120 ml butter, melted
2 tablespoons granulated sweetener

1 tablespoon avocado oil
1 teaspoon baking powder
1 teaspoon vanilla extract
Pinch of salt
180 ml water, divided

1. In a blender, combine all the ingredients, except for the 120 ml of the water. Pulse until fully combined and smooth. Let the batter rest for 5 minutes before cooking. 2. Fill each cup with 2 tablespoons of the batter, about two-thirds of the way full. Cover the cups with aluminium foil. 3. Pour the remaining 120 ml of the water and insert the reversible rack in the Ninja Foodi cooker. Place the cups on the reversible rack. 4. Set the lid in place. Set the cooking time for 15 minutes on High Pressure. When the timer goes off, do a quick pressure release. Carefully open the lid. 5. Repeat with the remaining batter, until all the batter is used. Add more water to the pot before cooking each batch, if needed. 6. Serve warm.

Nutty "Oatmeal"

Prep time: 5 minutes | Cook time: 4 minutes | Serves 4

2 tablespoons coconut oil
240 ml full-fat coconut milk
240 ml heavy whipping cream
120 ml macadamia nuts
120 ml chopped pecans
80 ml granulated sweetener, or

more to taste
60 ml unsweetened coconut flakes
2 tablespoons chopped hazelnuts
2 tablespoons chia seeds
½ teaspoon ground cinnamon

1. Before you get started, soak the chia seeds for about 5 to 10 minutes (can be up to 20, if desired) in 240 ml of filtered water. After soaking, set the Ninja Foodi cooker to Sauté and add the coconut oil. Once melted, pour in the milk, whipping cream, and 240 ml of filtered water. Then add the macadamia nuts, pecans, granulated sweetener, coconut flakes, hazelnuts, chia seeds, and cinnamon. Mix thoroughly inside the Ninja Foodi cooker. 2. Close the lid, set the pressure release to Sealing, and hit Start/Stop to stop the current program. Set the Ninja Foodi cooker to 4 minutes on High Pressure, and let cook. 3. Once cooked, carefully switch the pressure release to Venting. 4. Open the Ninja Foodi cooker, serve, and enjoy!

Lettuce Wrapped Chicken Sandwich

Prep time: 10 minutes | Cook time: 15 minutes | Serves 4

1 tablespoon butter
85 g spring onions, chopped
480 ml minced chicken
½ teaspoon ground nutmeg

1 tablespoon coconut flour
1 teaspoon salt
240 ml lettuce

1. Press the Sauté button on the Ninja Foodi cooker and melt the butter. Add the chopped spring onions, minced chicken and ground nutmeg to the pot and sauté for 4 minutes. Add the coconut flour and salt and continue to sauté for 10 minutes. 2. Fill the lettuce with the minced chicken and transfer it on the plate. Serve immediately.

Gruyère Asparagus Frittata

Prep time: 10 minutes | Cook time: 22 minutes | Serves 6

6 eggs
6 tablespoons double cream
½ teaspoon salt
½ teaspoon black pepper
1 tablespoon butter
70 g asparagus, chopped

1 clove garlic, minced
160 ml shredded Gruyère cheese, divided
Cooking spray
85 g halved cherry tomatoes
120 ml water

1. In a large bowl, stir together the eggs, cream, salt, and pepper. 2. Set the Ninja Foodi cooker on the Sauté mode and melt the butter. Add the asparagus and garlic to the pot and sauté for 2 minutes, or until the garlic is fragrant. The asparagus should still be crisp. 3. Transfer the asparagus and garlic to the bowl with the egg mixture. Stir in 240 ml of the cheese. Clean the pot. 4. Spritz a baking pan with cooking spray. Spread the tomatoes in a single layer in the pan. Pour the egg mixture on top of the tomatoes and sprinkle with the remaining 60 ml of the cheese. Cover the pan tightly with aluminium foil. 5. Pour the water in the Ninja Foodi cooker and insert the reversible rack. Place the pan on the reversible rack. 6. Set the lid in place. Set the cooking time for 20 minutes on High Pressure. When the timer goes off, perform a quick pressure release. Carefully open the lid. 7. Remove the pan from the pot and remove the foil. Blot off any excess moisture with a paper towel. Let the frittata cool for 5 to 10 minutes before transferring onto a plate.

Kale and Potato Nuggets

Prep time: 10 minutes | Cook time: 18 minutes | Serves 4

1 teaspoon extra virgin olive oil
1 clove garlic, minced
1 L kale, rinsed and chopped
475 ml potatoes, boiled and mashed

30 ml milk
Salt and ground black pepper, to taste
Cooking spray

1. Preheat the Ninja Foodi cooker to 200°C. 2. In a skillet over medium heat, sauté the garlic in the olive oil, until it turns golden brown. Sauté with the kale for an additional 3 minutes and remove from the heat. 3. Mix the mashed potatoes, kale and garlic in a bowl. Pour in the milk and sprinkle with salt and pepper. 4. Shape the mixture into nuggets and spritz with cooking spray. 5. Put in the cook & crisp basket and air crisp for 15 minutes, flip the nuggets halfway through cooking to make sure the nuggets fry evenly. 6. Serve immediately.

Breakfast Cereal

Prep time: 5 minutes | Cook time: 5 minutes | Serves 4

2 tablespoons coconut oil
240 ml full-fat coconut milk
120 ml chopped cashews
120 ml heavy whipping cream
120 ml chopped pecans
80 ml granulated sweetener
60 ml unsweetened coconut flakes

2 tablespoons flax seeds
2 tablespoons chopped hazelnuts
2 tablespoons chopped macadamia nuts
½ teaspoon ground cinnamon
½ teaspoon ground nutmeg
½ teaspoon ground turmeric

1. Set the Ninja Foodi cooker to Sauté and melt the coconut oil. Pour in the coconut milk. 2. Add the cashews, whipping cream, pecans, granulated sweetener, coconut flakes, flax seeds, hazelnuts, macadamia nuts, cinnamon, nutmeg, and turmeric to the Ninja Foodi cooker. Stir thoroughly. 3. Close the lid, set the pressure release to Sealing, and hit Start/Stop to stop the current program. Set the Ninja Foodi cooker to 5 minutes on High Pressure, and let cook. 4. Once cooked, let the pressure naturally disperse from the Ninja Foodi cooker for about 10 minutes, then carefully switch the pressure release to Venting. 5. Open the Ninja Foodi cooker, serve, and enjoy!

Southwestern Egg Casserole

Prep time: 10 minutes | Cook time: 20 minutes | Serves 12

240 ml water
600 ml egg substitute
120 ml flour
1 teaspoon baking powder
⅛ teaspoon salt

⅛ teaspoon pepper
480 ml fat-free cottage cheese
360 ml shredded 75%-less-fat sharp cheddar cheese
60 ml no-trans-fat tub margarine, melted
2 (110 g each) cans chopped green chilies

1. Place the steaming rack into the bottom of the inner pot and pour in 240 ml of water. 2. Grease a round springform pan that will fit into the inner pot of the Ninja Foodi cooker. 3. Combine the egg substitute, flour, baking powder, salt and pepper in a mixing bowl. It will be lumpy. 4. Stir in the cheese, margarine, and green chilies then pour into the springform pan. 5. Place the springform pan onto the steaming rack, close the lid, and secure to the locking position. Be sure the vent is turned to sealing. Set for 20 minutes at high pressure. 6. Let the pressure release naturally. 7. Carefully remove the springform pan with the handles of the steaming rack and allow to stand 10 minutes before cutting and serving.

Parmesan Ranch Risotto

Prep time: 10 minutes | Cook time: 30 minutes | Serves 2

1 tablespoon olive oil
1 clove garlic, minced
1 tablespoon unsalted butter
1 onion, diced

180 ml Arborio rice
475 ml chicken stock, boiling
120 ml Parmesan cheese, grated

1. Preheat the Ninja Foodi cooker to 200°C. 2. Grease a round baking tin with olive oil and stir in the garlic, butter, and onion. 3. Transfer the tin to the Ninja Foodi cooker and bake for 4 minutes. Add the rice and bake for 4 more minutes. 4. Turn the Ninja Foodi cooker to 160°C and pour in the chicken stock. Cover and bake for 22 minutes. 5. Scatter with cheese and serve.

Chapter 3 Vegetables and Sides

Caesar Whole Cauliflower

Prep time: 20 minutes | Cook time: 30 minutes | Serves 2 to 4

3 tablespoons olive oil
2 tablespoons red wine vinegar
2 tablespoons Worcestershire sauce
2 tablespoons grated Parmesan cheese
1 tablespoon Dijon mustard
4 garlic cloves, minced
4 oil-packed anchovy fillets, drained and finely minced
coarse sea salt and freshly ground black pepper, to taste
1 small head cauliflower (about 450 g), green leaves trimmed and stem trimmed flush with the bottom of the head
1 tablespoon roughly chopped fresh flat-leaf parsley (optional)

1. In a liquid measuring jug, whisk together the olive oil, vinegar, Worcestershire, Parmesan, mustard, garlic, anchovies, and salt and pepper to taste. Place the cauliflower head upside down on a cutting board and use a paring knife to make an "x" through the full length of the core. Transfer the cauliflower head to a large bowl and pour half the dressing over it. Turn the cauliflower head to coat it in the dressing, then let it rest, stem-side up, in the dressing for at least 10 minutes and up to 30 minutes to allow the dressing to seep into all its nooks and crannies. 2. Transfer the cauliflower head, stem-side down, to the Ninja Foodi cooker and air crisp at 170°C or 25 minutes. Drizzle the remaining dressing over the cauliflower and air crisp at 200°C until the top of the cauliflower is golden brown and the core is tender, about 5 minutes more. 3. Remove the basket from the Ninja Foodi cooker and transfer the cauliflower to a large plate. Sprinkle with the parsley, if you like, and serve hot.

Parmesan Cauliflower Mash

Prep time: 7 minutes | Cook time: 5 minutes | Serves 4

1 head cauliflower, cored and cut into large florets
½ teaspoon rock salt
½ teaspoon garlic pepper
2 tablespoons plain Greek yoghurt
180 ml freshly grated Parmesan cheese
1 tablespoon unsalted butter or ghee (optional)
Chopped fresh chives

1. Pour 240 ml of water into the electric pressure cooker and insert a steamer basket or wire rack. 2. Place the cauliflower in the basket. 3. Close and lock the lid of the pressure cooker. Set the valve to sealing. 4. Cook on high pressure for 5 minutes. 5. When the cooking is complete, hit Start/Stop and quick release the pressure. 6. Once the pin drops, unlock and remove the lid. 7. Remove the cauliflower from the pot and pour out the water. Return the cauliflower to the pot and add the salt, garlic pepper, yoghurt, and cheese. Use an immersion blender or potato masher to purée or mash the cauliflower in the pot. 8. Spoon into a serving bowl, and garnish with butter (if using) and chives.

Buffalo Cauliflower with Blue Cheese

Prep time: 15 minutes | Cook time: 5 to 7 minutes per batch | Serves 6

1 large head cauliflower, rinsed and separated into small florets
1 tablespoon extra-virgin olive oil
½ teaspoon garlic powder
Cooking oil spray
80 ml hot wing sauce
190 g nonfat Greek yogurt
60 g buttermilk
½ teaspoon hot sauce
1 celery stalk, chopped
2 tablespoons crumbled blue cheese

1. Insert the crisper plate into the basket and the basket into the unit. Preheat the unit by selecting AIR CRISP, setting the temperature to190°C, and setting the time to 3 minutes. Press START/STOP to begin. 2. In a large bowl, toss together the cauliflower florets and olive oil. Sprinkle with the garlic powder and toss again to coat. 3. Once the unit is preheated, spray the crisper plate with cooking oil. Put half the cauliflower into the basket. 4. Select AIR CRISP, set the temperature to190°C, and set the time to 7 minutes. Press START/STOP to begin. 5. After 3 minutes, remove the basket and shake the cauliflower. Reinsert the basket to resume cooking. After 2 minutes, check the cauliflower. It is done when it is browned. If not, resume cooking. 6. When the cooking is complete, transfer the cauliflower to a serving bowl and toss with half the hot wing sauce. 7. Repeat steps 4, 5, and 6 with the remaining cauliflower and hot wing sauce. 8. In a small bowl, stir together the yogurt, buttermilk, hot sauce, celery, and blue cheese. Drizzle the sauce over the finished cauliflower and serve.

Southwestern Roasted Corn

Prep time: 10 minutes | Cook time: 10 minutes | Serves 4

Corn:
240 g thawed frozen corn kernels
50 g diced yellow onion
150 g mixed diced bell peppers
1 jalapeño, diced
1 tablespoon fresh lemon juice
1 teaspoon ground cumin
½ teaspoon ancho chili powder
½ teaspoon coarse sea salt
For Serving:
150 g queso fresco or feta cheese
10 g chopped fresh coriander
1 tablespoon fresh lemon juice

1. For the corn: In a large bowl, stir together the corn, onion, bell peppers, jalapeño, lemon juice, cumin, chili powder, and salt until well incorporated. 2. Pour the spiced vegetables into the cook & crisp basket. Set the Ninja Foodi cooker to 190°C for 10 minutes, stirring halfway through the cooking time. 3. Transfer the corn mixture to a serving bowl. Add the cheese, coriander, and lemon juice and stir well to combine. Serve immediately.

Rosemary-Roasted Red Potatoes

Prep time: 5 minutes | Cook time: 20 minutes | Serves 6

450 g red potatoes, quartered
65 ml olive oil
½ teaspoon coarse sea salt

¼ teaspoon black pepper
1 garlic clove, minced
4 rosemary sprigs

1. Preheat the Ninja Foodi cooker to 180ºC. 2. In a large bowl, toss the potatoes with the olive oil, salt, pepper, and garlic until well coated. 3. Pour the potatoes into the cook & crisp basket and top with the sprigs of rosemary. 4. Roast for 10 minutes, then stir or toss the potatoes and roast for 10 minutes more. 5. Remove the rosemary sprigs and serve the potatoes. Season with additional salt and pepper, if needed.

Almond Butter Courgette Noodles

Prep time: 10 minutes | Cook time: 4 minutes | Serves 4

2 tablespoons coconut oil
1 brown onion, chopped
2 courgette, julienned
240 ml shredded Chinese cabbage

2 garlic cloves, minced
2 tablespoons almond butter
Sea salt and freshly ground black pepper, to taste
1 teaspoon cayenne pepper

1. Press the Sauté button to heat up your Ninja Foodi cooker. Heat the coconut oil and sweat the onion for 2 minutes. 2. Add the other ingredients. 3. Secure the lid. Choose High Pressure; cook for 2 minutes. Once cooking is complete, use a quick pressure release; carefully remove the lid. Bon appétit!

Cauliflower Mac and Cheese

Prep time: 6 minutes | Cook time: 3 minutes | Serves 6

240 ml water
1 large cauliflower, chopped into bite-size florets
240 ml heavy whipping cream
120 ml sour cream
240 ml shredded Gruyère or Mozzarella cheese

600 ml shredded sharp Cheddar cheese
1 teaspoon ground mustard
1 teaspoon ground turmeric
Sea salt, to taste
Pinch of cayenne pepper (optional)

1. Pour the water into the Ninja Foodi cooker. Place a metal steaming basket inside. Put the cauliflower florets in the basket. Secure the lid and set the steam release valve to Sealing. Set the cook time to 3 minutes. When the Ninja Foodi cooker beeps, carefully switch the steam release valve to Venting to quick-release the pressure. When fully released, open the lid. 2. Meanwhile, prepare the cheese sauce. In a large skillet, gently bring the cream to a simmer over medium to medium-low heat. Whisk in the sour cream until smooth, then gradually whisk in the Gruyère and 480 ml of the Cheddar until melted. Stir in the ground mustard and turmeric. Taste and adjust the salt. 3. Remove the cauliflower from the pot and toss it in the cheese sauce to coat. Serve warm, topped with the remaining Cheddar and a sprinkling of cayenne (if using).

Lemony Brussels Sprouts with Poppy Seeds

Prep time: 10 minutes | Cook time: 2 minutes | Serves 4

450 g Brussels sprouts
2 tablespoons avocado oil, divided
240 ml vegetable broth or chicken bone broth
1 tablespoon minced garlic

½ teaspoon rock salt
Freshly ground black pepper, to taste
½ medium lemon
½ tablespoon poppy seeds

1. Trim the Brussels sprouts by cutting off the stem ends and removing any loose outer leaves. Cut each in half lengthwise (through the stem). 2. Set the electric pressure cooker to the Sauté/More setting. When the pot is hot, pour in 1 tablespoon of the avocado oil. 3. Add half of the Brussels sprouts to the pot, cut-side down, and let them brown for 3 to 5 minutes without disturbing. Transfer to a bowl and add the remaining tablespoon of avocado oil and the remaining Brussels sprouts to the pot. Hit Start/Stop and return all of the Brussels sprouts to the pot. 4. Add the broth, garlic, salt, and a few grinds of pepper. Stir to distribute the seasonings. 5. Close and lock the lid of the pressure cooker. Set the valve to sealing. 6. Cook on high pressure for 2 minutes. 7. While the Brussels sprouts are cooking, zest the lemon, then cut it into quarters. 8. When the cooking is complete, hit Start/Stop and quick release the pressure. 9. Once the pin drops, unlock and remove the lid. 10. Using a slotted spoon, transfer the Brussels sprouts to a serving bowl. Toss with the lemon zest, a squeeze of lemon juice, and the poppy seeds. Serve immediately.

Shishito Pepper Roast

Prep time: 4 minutes | Cook time: 9 minutes | Serves 4

Cooking oil spray (sunflower, safflower, or refined coconut)
450 g shishito, Anaheim, or bell peppers, rinsed

1 tablespoon soy sauce
2 teaspoons freshly squeezed lime juice
2 large garlic cloves, pressed

1. Insert the crisper plate into the basket and the basket into the unit. Preheat the unit by selecting AIR ROAST, setting the temperature to 200ºC, and setting the time to 3 minutes. Press START/STOP to begin. 2. Once the unit is preheated, spray the crisper plate and the basket with cooking oil. Place the peppers into the basket and spray them with oil. 3. Select AIR ROAST, set the temperature to 200ºC, and set the time to 9 minutes. Press START/STOP to begin. 4. After 3 minutes, remove the basket and shake the peppers. Spray the peppers with more oil. Reinsert the basket to resume cooking. Repeat this step again after 3 minutes. 5. While the peppers roast, in a medium bowl, whisk the soy sauce, lime juice, and garlic until combined. Set aside. 6. When the cooking is complete, several of the peppers should have lots of nice browned spots on them. If using Anaheim or bell peppers, cut a slit in the side of each pepper and remove the seeds, which can be bitter. 7. Place the roasted peppers in the bowl with the sauce. Toss to coat the peppers evenly and serve.

Ninja Foodi cooker Courgette Sticks

Prep time: 5 minutes | Cook time: 8 minutes | Serves 2

2 courgettes, trimmed and cut into sticks
2 teaspoons olive oil

½ teaspoon white pepper
½ teaspoon salt
240 ml water

1. Place the courgette sticks in the Ninja Foodi cooker pan and sprinkle with the olive oil, white pepper and salt. 2. Pour the water and put the reversible rack in the pot. Place the pan on the reversible rack. 3. Lock the lid. Set the cooking time for 8 minutes at High Pressure. Once the timer goes off, use a quick pressure release. Carefully open the lid. 4. Remove the courgettes from the pot and serve.

Citrus Sweet Potatoes and Carrots

Prep time: 5 minutes | Cook time: 20 to 25 minutes | Serves 4

2 large carrots, cut into 1-inch chunks
1 medium sweet potato, peeled and cut into 1-inch cubes
25 g chopped onion

2 garlic cloves, minced
2 tablespoons honey
1 tablespoon freshly squeezed orange juice
2 teaspoons butter, melted

1. Insert the crisper plate into the basket and the basket into the unit. Preheat the unit by selecting AIR ROAST, setting the temperature to 200°C, and setting the time to 3 minutes. Press START/STOP to begin. 2. In a 6-by-2-inch round pan, toss together the carrots, sweet potato, onion, garlic, honey, orange juice, and melted butter to coat. 3. Once the unit is preheated, place the pan into the basket. 4. Select AIR ROAST, set the temperature to 200°C, and set the time to 25 minutes. Press START/STOP to begin. 5. After 15 minutes, remove the basket and shake the vegetables. Reinsert the basket to resume cooking. After 5 minutes, if the vegetables are tender and glazed, they are done. If not, resume cooking. 6. When the cooking is complete, serve immediately.

Flatbread

Prep time: 5 minutes | Cook time: 7 minutes | Serves 2

225 g shredded Mozzarella cheese
25 g blanched finely ground

almond flour
30 g full-fat cream cheese, softened

1. In a large microwave-safe bowl, melt Mozzarella in the microwave for 30 seconds. Stir in almond flour until smooth and then add cream cheese. Continue mixing until dough forms, gently kneading it with wet hands if necessary. 2. Divide the dough into two pieces and roll out to ¼-inch thickness between two pieces of parchment. Cut another piece of parchment to fit your cook & crisp basket. 3. Place a piece of flatbread onto your parchment and into the Ninja Foodi cooker, working in two batches if needed. 4. Adjust the temperature to 160°C and air crisp for 7 minutes. 5. Halfway through the cooking time flip the flatbread. Serve warm.

Courgette Balls

Prep time: 5 minutes | Cook time: 10 minutes | Serves 4

4 courgettes
1 egg
45 g grated Parmesan cheese

1 tablespoon Italian herbs
75 g grated coconut

1. Thinly grate the courgettes and dry with a cheesecloth, ensuring to remove all the moisture. 2. In a bowl, combine the courgettes with the egg, Parmesan, Italian herbs, and grated coconut, mixing well to incorporate everything. Using the hands, mold the mixture into balls. 3. Preheat the Ninja Foodi cooker to 200°C. 4. Lay the courgette balls in the cook & crisp basket and air crisp for 10 minutes. 5. Serve hot.

Courgette Fritters

Prep time: 10 minutes | Cook time: 10 minutes | Serves 4

2 courgette, grated (about 450 g)
1 teaspoon salt
25 g almond flour
20 g grated Parmesan cheese
1 large egg
¼ teaspoon dried thyme

¼ teaspoon ground turmeric
¼ teaspoon freshly ground black pepper
1 tablespoon olive oil
½ lemon, sliced into wedges

1. Preheat the Ninja Foodi cooker to 200°C. Cut a piece of parchment paper to fit slightly smaller than the bottom of the Ninja Foodi cooker. 2. Place the courgette in a large colander and sprinkle with the salt. Let sit for 5 to 10 minutes. Squeeze as much liquid as you can from the courgette and place in a large mixing bowl. Add the almond flour, Parmesan, egg, thyme, turmeric, and black pepper. Stir gently until thoroughly combined. 3. Shape the mixture into 8 patties and arrange on the parchment paper. Brush lightly with the olive oil. Pausing halfway through the cooking time to turn the patties, air crisp for 10 minutes until golden brown. Serve warm with the lemon wedges.

Spaghetti Squash

Prep time: 5 minutes | Cook time: 7 minutes | Serves 4

1 spaghetti squash (about 900 g)

1. Cut the spaghetti squash in half crosswise and use a large spoon to remove the seeds. 2. Pour 240 ml of water into the electric pressure cooker and insert a wire rack or reversible rack. 3. Place the squash halves on the rack, cut-side up. 4. Close and lock the lid of the pressure cooker. Set the valve to sealing. 5. Cook on high pressure for 7 minutes. 6. When the cooking is complete, hit Start/Stop and quick release the pressure. 7. Once the pin drops, unlock and remove the lid. 8. With tongs, remove the squash from the pot and transfer it to a plate. When it is cool enough to handle, scrape the squash with the tines of a fork to remove the strands. Discard the skin.

Lemon Cabbage and Tempeh

Prep time: 8 minutes | Cook time: 10 minutes | Serves 3

2 tablespoons sesame oil
120 ml chopped spring onions
480 ml shredded cabbage
170 g tempeh, cubed
1 tablespoon coconut aminos
240 ml vegetable stock

2 garlic cloves, minced
1 tablespoon lemon juice
Salt and pepper, to taste
¼ teaspoon paprika
60 ml roughly chopped fresh coriander

1. Press the Sauté button to heat up your Ninja Foodi cooker. Heat the sesame oil and sauté the spring onions until tender and fragrant. 2. Then, add the cabbage, tempeh, coconut aminos, vegetable stock, garlic, lemon juice, salt, pepper, and paprika. 3. Secure the lid. Choose Low Pressure; cook for 3 minutes. Once cooking is complete, use a quick pressure release; carefully remove the lid. 4. Press the Sauté button to thicken the sauce if desired. Divide between serving bowls, garnish with fresh coriander, and serve warm. Bon appétit!

Falafel and Lettuce Salad

Prep time: 10 minutes | Cook time: 6 to 8 minutes | Serves 4

240 ml shredded cauliflower
80 ml coconut flour
1 teaspoon grated lemon zest
1 egg, beaten
2 tablespoons coconut oil

480 ml chopped lettuce
1 cucumber, chopped
1 tablespoon olive oil
1 teaspoon lemon juice
½ teaspoon cayenne pepper

1. In a bowl, combine the cauliflower, coconut flour, grated lemon zest and egg. Form the mixture into small balls. 2. Set the Ninja Foodi cooker to the Sauté mode and melt the coconut oil. Place the balls in the pot in a single layer. Cook for 3 to 4 minutes per side, or until they are golden brown. 3. In a separate bowl, stir together the remaining ingredients. 4. Place the cooked balls on top and serve.

Maple-Roasted Tomatoes

Prep time: 15 minutes | Cook time: 20 minutes | Serves 2

280 g cherry tomatoes, halved
coarse sea salt, to taste
2 tablespoons maple syrup
1 tablespoon vegetable oil

2 sprigs fresh thyme, stems removed
1 garlic clove, minced
Freshly ground black pepper

1. Place the tomatoes in a colander and sprinkle liberally with salt. Let stand for 10 minutes to drain. 2. Transfer the tomatoes cut-side up to a cake pan, then drizzle with the maple syrup, followed by the oil. Sprinkle with the thyme leaves and garlic and season with pepper. Place the pan in the Ninja Foodi cooker and roast at 160°C until the tomatoes are soft, collapsed, and lightly caramelized on top, about 20 minutes. 3. Serve straight from the pan or transfer the tomatoes to a plate and drizzle with the juices from the pan to serve.

Mediterranean Courgette Boats

Prep time: 5 minutes | Cook time: 10 minutes | Serves 4

1 large courgette, ends removed, halved lengthwise
6 grape tomatoes, quartered
¼ teaspoon salt

65 g feta cheese
1 tablespoon balsamic vinegar
1 tablespoon olive oil

1. Use a spoon to scoop out 2 tablespoons from centre of each courgette half, making just enough space to fill with tomatoes and feta. 2. Place tomatoes evenly in centres of courgette halves and sprinkle with salt. Place into ungreased cook & crisp basket. Adjust the temperature to 180°C and roast for 10 minutes. When done, courgette will be tender. 3. Transfer boats to a serving tray and sprinkle with feta, then drizzle with vinegar and olive oil. Serve warm.

Fried Courgette Salad

Prep time: 10 minutes | Cook time: 5 to 7 minutes | Serves 4

2 medium courgette, thinly sliced
5 tablespoons olive oil, divided
15 g chopped fresh parsley
2 tablespoons chopped fresh mint

Zest and juice of ½ lemon
1 clove garlic, minced
65 g crumbled feta cheese
Freshly ground black pepper, to taste

1. Preheat the Ninja Foodi cooker to 200°C. 2. In a large bowl, toss the courgette slices with 1 tablespoon of the olive oil. 3. Working in batches if necessary, arrange the courgette slices in an even layer in the cook & crisp basket. Pausing halfway through the cooking time to shake the basket, air crisp for 5 to 7 minutes until soft and lightly browned on each side. 4. Meanwhile, in a small bowl, combine the remaining 4 tablespoons olive oil, parsley, mint, lemon zest, lemon juice, and garlic. 5. Arrange the courgette on a plate and drizzle with the dressing. Sprinkle the feta and black pepper on top. Serve warm or at room temperature.

Marinara Pepperoni Mushroom Pizza

Prep time: 5 minutes | Cook time: 18 minutes | Serves 4

4 large portobello mushrooms, stems removed
4 teaspoons olive oil
225 g marinara sauce

225 g shredded Mozzarella cheese
10 slices sugar-free pepperoni

1. Preheat the Ninja Foodi cooker to 190°C. 2. Brush each mushroom cap with the olive oil, one teaspoon for each cap. 3. Put on a baking sheet and bake, stem-side down, for 8 minutes. 4. Take out of the Ninja Foodi cooker and divide the marinara sauce, Mozzarella cheese and pepperoni evenly among the caps. 5. Air crisp for another 10 minutes until browned. 6. Serve hot.

Buttery Green Beans

Prep time: 5 minutes | Cook time: 8 to 10 minutes | Serves 6

450 g green beans, trimmed
1 tablespoon avocado oil
1 teaspoon garlic powder
Sea salt and freshly ground black pepper, to taste
4 tablespoons unsalted butter, melted
20 g freshly grated Parmesan cheese

1. In a large bowl, toss together the green beans, avocado oil, and garlic powder and season with salt and pepper. 2. Set the Ninja Foodi cooker to 200ºC. Arrange the green beans in a single layer in the cook & crisp basket. Air crisp for 8 to 10 minutes, tossing halfway through. 3. Transfer the beans to a large bowl and toss with the melted butter. Top with the Parmesan cheese and serve warm.

Ricotta Potatoes

Prep time: 15 minutes | Cook time: 15 minutes | Serves 4

4 potatoes
2 tablespoons olive oil
110 g Ricotta cheese, at room temperature
2 tablespoons chopped spring onions
1 tablespoon roughly chopped
fresh parsley
1 tablespoon minced coriander
60 g Cheddar cheese, preferably freshly grated
1 teaspoon celery seeds
½ teaspoon salt
½ teaspoon garlic pepper

1. Preheat the Ninja Foodi cooker to 180ºC. 2. Pierce the skin of the potatoes with a knife. 3. Air crisp in the cook & crisp basket for 13 minutes. If they are not cooked through by this time, leave for 2 to 3 minutes longer. 4. In the meantime, make the stuffing by combining all the other ingredients. 5. Cut halfway into the cooked potatoes to open them. 6. Spoon equal amounts of the stuffing into each potato and serve hot.

Mushroom Stroganoff with Vodka

Prep time: 8 minutes | Cook time: 8 minutes | Serves 4

2 tablespoons olive oil
½ teaspoon crushed caraway seeds
120 ml chopped onion
2 garlic cloves, smashed
60 ml vodka
340 g button mushrooms,
chopped
1 celery stalk, chopped
1 ripe tomato, puréed
1 teaspoon mustard seeds
Sea salt and freshly ground pepper, to taste
480 ml vegetable broth

1. Press the Sauté button to heat up your Ninja Foodi cooker. Now, heat the oil and sauté caraway seeds until fragrant, about 40 seconds. 2. Then, add the onion and garlic, and continue sautéing for 1 to 2 minutes more, stirring frequently. 3. After that, add the remaining ingredients and stir to combine. 4. Secure the lid. Choose High Pressure; cook for 5 minutes. Once cooking is complete, use a quick pressure release; carefully remove the lid. 5. Ladle into individual bowls and serve warm. Bon appétit!

Lemon Broccoli

Prep time: 5 minutes | Cook time: 4 minutes | Serves 4

480 ml broccoli florets
1 tablespoon ground paprika
1 tablespoon lemon juice
1 teaspoon grated lemon zest
1 teaspoon olive oil
½ teaspoon chili powder
240 ml water

1. Pour the water in the Ninja Foodi cooker and insert the reversible rack. 2. In the Ninja Foodi cooker pan, stir together the remaining ingredients. 3. Place the pan on the reversible rack. 4. Set the lid in place. Set the cooking time for 4 minutes on High Pressure. When the timer goes off, do a quick pressure release. Carefully open the lid. 5. Serve immediately.

Perfect Sweet Potatoes

Prep time: 5 minutes | Cook time: 15 minutes | Serves 4 to 6

4–6 medium sweet potatoes   240 ml of water

1. Scrub skin of sweet potatoes with a brush until clean. Pour water into inner pot of the Ninja Foodi cooker. Place steamer basket in the bottom of the inner pot. Place sweet potatoes on top of steamer basket. 2. Secure the lid and turn valve to seal. 3. Set to pressure cook on high for 15 minutes. 4. Allow pressure to release naturally (about 10 minutes). 5. Once the pressure valve lowers, remove lid and serve immediately.

Gold Artichoke Hearts

Prep time: 15 minutes | Cook time: 8 minutes | Serves 4

12 whole artichoke hearts packed in water, drained
60 g plain flour
1 egg
40 g panko bread crumbs
1 teaspoon Italian seasoning
Cooking oil spray

1. Squeeze any excess water from the artichoke hearts and place them on paper towels to dry. 2. Place the flour in a small bowl. 3. In another small bowl, beat the egg. 4. In a third small bowl, stir together the panko and Italian seasoning. 5. Dip the artichoke hearts in the flour, in the egg, and into the panko mixture until coated. 6. Insert the crisper plate into the basket and the basket into the unit. Preheat the unit by selecting AIR CRISP, setting the temperature to 190ºC, and setting the time to 3 minutes. Press START/STOP to begin. 7. Once the unit is preheated, spray the crisper plate and the basket with cooking oil. Place the breaded artichoke hearts into the basket, stacking them if needed. 8. Select AIR CRISP, set the temperature to 190ºC, and set the time to 8 minutes. Press START/STOP to begin. 9. After 4 minutes, use tongs to flip the artichoke hearts. I recommend flipping instead of shaking because the hearts are small, and this will help keep the breading intact. Re-insert the basket to resume cooking. 10. When the cooking is complete, the artichoke hearts should be deep golden brown and crisp. Cool for 5 minutes before serving.

Braised Fennel with radicchio, Pear, and Pecorino

Prep time: 20 minutes | Cook time: 12 minutes | Serves 4

6 tablespoons extra-virgin olive oil, divided
2 fennel bulbs (340 g each), 2 tablespoons fronds chopped, stalks discarded, bulbs halved, each half cut into 1-inch-thick wedges
¾ teaspoon table salt, divided
½ teaspoon grated lemon zest plus 4 teaspoons juice

140 g baby rocket
1 small head radicchio (170 g), shredded
1 Bosc or Bartlett pear, quartered, cored, and sliced thin
60 ml whole almonds, toasted and chopped
Shaved Pecorino Romano cheese

1. Using highest sauté function, heat 2 tablespoons oil in Ninja Foodi cooker for 5 minutes (or until just smoking). Brown half of fennel, about 3 minutes per side; transfer to plate. Repeat with 1 tablespoon oil and remaining fennel; do not remove from pot. 2. Return first batch of fennel to pot along with 120 ml water and ½ teaspoon salt. Lock lid in place and close pressure release valve. Select high pressure and cook for 2 minutes. Turn off Ninja Foodi cooker and quick-release pressure. Carefully remove lid, allowing steam to escape away from you. Using slotted spoon, transfer fennel to plate; discard cooking liquid. 3. Whisk remaining 3 tablespoons oil, lemon zest and juice, and remaining ¼ teaspoon salt together in large bowl. Add rocket, radicchio, and pear and toss to coat. Transfer rocket mixture to serving dish and arrange fennel wedges on top. Sprinkle with almonds, fennel fronds, and Pecorino. Serve.

Green Beans with Potatoes and Basil

Prep time: 20 minutes | Cook time: 10 minutes | Serves 4

2 tablespoons extra-virgin olive oil, plus extra for drizzling
1 onion, chopped fine
2 tablespoons minced fresh oregano or 2 teaspoons dried
2 tablespoons tomato paste
4 garlic cloves, minced
1 (410 g) can whole peeled tomatoes, drained with juice reserved, chopped
240 ml water

1 teaspoon table salt
¼ teaspoon pepper
680 g green beans, trimmed and cut into 2-inch lengths
450 g Yukon Gold potatoes, peeled and cut into 1-inch pieces
3 tablespoons chopped fresh basil or parsley
2 tablespoons toasted pine nuts
Shaved Parmesan cheese

1. Using highest sauté function, heat oil in Ninja Foodi cooker until shimmering. Add onion and cook until softened, about 5 minutes. Stir in oregano, tomato paste, and garlic and cook until fragrant, about 30 seconds. Stir in tomatoes and their juice, water, salt, and pepper, then stir in green beans and potatoes. Lock lid in place and close pressure release valve. Select high pressure and cook for 5 minutes. 2. Turn off Ninja Foodi cooker and quick-release pressure. Carefully remove lid, allowing steam to escape away from you. Season with salt and pepper to taste. Sprinkle individual portions with basil, pine nuts, and Parmesan and drizzle with extra oil. Serve.

Lemony Asparagus with Gremolata

Prep time: 15 minutes | Cook time: 2 minutes | Serves 2 to 4

Gremolata:
240 ml finely chopped fresh Italian flat-leaf parsley leaves
3 garlic cloves, peeled and grated
Zest of 2 small lemons
Asparagus:
680 g asparagus, trimmed
240 ml water
Lemony Vinaigrette:

1½ tablespoons fresh lemon juice
1 teaspoon granulated sweetener
1 teaspoon Dijon mustard
2 tablespoons extra-virgin olive oil
rock salt and freshly ground black pepper, to taste
Garnish:
3 tablespoons slivered almonds

1. In a small bowl, stir together all the ingredients for the gremolata. 2. Pour the water into the Ninja Foodi cooker. Arrange the asparagus in a steamer basket. Lower the steamer basket into the pot. 3. Lock the lid. Select the Steam mode and set the cooking time for 2 minutes on Low Pressure. 4. Meanwhile, prepare the lemony vinaigrette: In a bowl, combine the lemon juice, granulated sweetener and mustard and whisk to combine. Slowly drizzle in the olive oil and continue to whisk. Season generously with salt and pepper. 5. When the timer goes off, perform a quick pressure release. Carefully open the lid. Remove the steamer basket from the Ninja Foodi cooker. 6. Transfer the asparagus to a serving platter. Drizzle with the vinaigrette and sprinkle with the gremolata. Serve the asparagus topped with the slivered almonds.

Bacon-Wrapped Asparagus

Prep time: 10 minutes | Cook time: 10 minutes | Serves 4

8 slices reduced-sodium bacon, cut in half

16 thick (about 450 g) asparagus spears, trimmed of woody ends

1. Preheat the Ninja Foodi cooker to 180ºC. 2. Wrap a half piece of bacon around the centre of each stalk of asparagus. 3. Working in batches, if necessary, arrange seam-side down in a single layer in the cook & crisp basket. Air crisp for 10 minutes until the bacon is crisp and the stalks are tender.

Fried Asparagus

Prep time: 5 minutes | Cook time: 12 minutes | Serves 4

1 tablespoon olive oil
450 g asparagus spears, ends trimmed
¼ teaspoon salt

¼ teaspoon ground black pepper
1 tablespoon salted butter, melted

1. In a large bowl, drizzle olive oil over asparagus spears and sprinkle with salt and pepper. 2. Place spears into ungreased cook & crisp basket. Adjust the temperature to 190ºC and set the timer for 12 minutes, shaking the basket halfway through cooking. Asparagus will be lightly browned and tender when done. 3. Transfer to a large dish and drizzle with butter. Serve warm.

Spaghetti Squash Noodles with Tomatoes

Prep time: 15 minutes | Cook time: 14 to 16 minutes | Serves 4

1 medium spaghetti squash
240 ml water
2 tablespoons olive oil
1 small brown onion, diced
6 garlic cloves, minced
2 teaspoons crushed red pepper flakes
2 teaspoons dried oregano
240 ml sliced cherry tomatoes
1 teaspoon rock salt
½ teaspoon freshly ground black pepper
1 (410 g) can sugar-free crushed tomatoes
60 ml capers
1 tablespoon caper brine
120 ml sliced olives

1. With a sharp knife, halve the spaghetti squash crosswise. Using a spoon, scoop out the seeds and sticky gunk in the middle of each half. 2. Pour the water into the Ninja Foodi cooker and place the reversible rack in the pot with the handles facing up. Arrange the squash halves, cut side facing up, on the reversible rack. 3. Lock the lid. Set the cooking time for 7 minutes on High Pressure. When the timer goes off, use a quick pressure release. Carefully open the lid. 4. Remove the reversible rack and pour out the water that has collected in the squash cavities. Using the tines of a fork, separate the cooked strands into spaghetti-like pieces and set aside in a bowl. 5. Pour the water out of the pot. Select the Sauté mode and heat the oil. 6. Add the onion to the pot and sauté for 3 minutes. Add the garlic, pepper flakes and oregano to the pot and sauté for 1 minute. 7. Stir in the cherry tomatoes, salt and black pepper and cook for 2 minutes, or until the tomatoes are tender. 8. Pour in the crushed tomatoes, capers, caper brine and olives and bring the mixture to a boil. Continue to cook for 2 to 3 minutes to allow the flavors to meld. 9. Stir in the spaghetti squash noodles and cook for 1 to 2 minutes to warm everything through. 10. Transfer the dish to a serving platter and serve.

Beetroot and Watercress Salad with Orange and Dill

Prep time: 20 minutes | Cook time: 8 minutes | Serves 4

900 g beetroots, scrubbed, trimmed, and cut into ¾-inch pieces
120 ml water
1 teaspoon caraway seeds
½ teaspoon table salt
240 ml plain Greek yoghurt
1 small garlic clove, minced to paste
140 g watercress, torn into bite-size pieces
1 tablespoon extra-virgin olive
oil, divided, plus extra for drizzling
1 tablespoon white wine vinegar, divided
1 teaspoon grated orange zest plus 2 tablespoons juice
60 ml hazelnuts, toasted, skinned, and chopped
60 ml coarsely chopped fresh dill
Coarse sea salt

1. Combine beetroots, water, caraway seeds, and table salt in Ninja Foodi cooker. Lock lid in place and close pressure release valve. Select high pressure and cook for 8 minutes. Turn off Ninja Foodi cooker and quick-release pressure. Carefully remove lid, allowing steam to escape away from you. 2. Using slotted spoon, transfer beetroots to plate; set aside to cool slightly. Combine yoghurt, garlic, and 3 tablespoons beetroot cooking liquid in bowl; discard remaining cooking liquid. In large bowl toss watercress with 2 teaspoons oil and 1 teaspoon vinegar. Season with table salt and pepper to taste. 3. Spread yoghurt mixture over surface of serving dish. Arrange watercress on top of yoghurt mixture, leaving 1-inch border of yoghurt mixture. Add beetroots to now-empty large bowl and toss with orange zest and juice, remaining 2 teaspoons vinegar, and remaining 1 teaspoon oil. Season with table salt and pepper to taste. Arrange beetroots on top of watercress mixture. Drizzle with extra oil and sprinkle with hazelnuts, dill, and sea salt. Serve.

Green Cabbage Turmeric Stew

Prep time: 5 minutes | Cook time: 4 minutes | Serves 4

2 tablespoons olive oil
120 ml sliced brown onion
1 teaspoon crushed garlic
Sea salt and freshly ground black pepper, to taste
1 teaspoon turmeric powder
1 serrano pepper, chopped
450 g green cabbage, shredded
1 celery stalk, chopped
2 tablespoons rice wine
240 ml roasted vegetable broth

1. Place all of the above ingredients in the Ninja Foodi cooker. 2. Secure the lid. Choose High Pressure; cook for 4 minutes. Once cooking is complete, use a quick pressure release; carefully remove the lid. 3. Divide between individual bowls and serve warm. Bon appétit!

Hasselback Potatoes with Chive Pesto

Prep time: 10 minutes | Cook time: 40 minutes | Serves 2

2 medium Maris Piper potatoes
5 tablespoons olive oil
coarse sea salt and freshly ground black pepper, to taste
10 g roughly chopped fresh chives
2 tablespoons packed fresh flat-
leaf parsley leaves
1 tablespoon chopped walnuts
1 tablespoon grated Parmesan cheese
1 teaspoon fresh lemon juice
1 small garlic clove, peeled
60 g sour cream

1. Place the potatoes on a cutting board and lay a chopstick or thin-handled wooden spoon to the side of each potato. Thinly slice the potatoes crosswise, letting the chopstick or spoon handle stop the blade of your knife, and stop ½ inch short of each end of the potato. Rub the potatoes with 1 tablespoon of the olive oil and season with salt and pepper. 2. Place the potatoes, cut-side up, in the Ninja Foodi cooker and air crisp at 190°C until golden brown and crisp on the outside and tender inside, about 40 minutes, drizzling the insides with 1 tablespoon more olive oil and seasoning with more salt and pepper halfway through. 3. Meanwhile, in a small blender or food processor, combine the remaining 3 tablespoons olive oil, the chives, parsley, walnuts, Parmesan, lemon juice, and garlic and purée until smooth. Season the chive pesto with salt and pepper. 4. Remove the potatoes from the Ninja Foodi cooker and transfer to plates. Drizzle the potatoes with the pesto, letting it drip down into the grooves, then dollop each with sour cream and serve hot.

Courgette and Daikon Fritters

Prep time: 10 minutes | Cook time: 8 minutes | Serves 4

2 large courgettes, grated	1 teaspoon ground flax meal
1 daikon, diced	1 teaspoon salt
1 egg, beaten	1 tablespoon coconut oil

1. In the mixing bowl, combine all the ingredients, except for the coconut oil. Form the courgette mixture into fritters. 2. Press the Sauté button on the Ninja Foodi cooker and melt the coconut oil. 3. Place the courgette fritters in the hot oil and cook for 4 minutes on each side, or until golden brown. 4. Transfer to a plate and serve.

Caramelized Aubergine with Harissa Yogurt

Prep time: 10 minutes | Cook time: 15 minutes | Serves 2

1 medium aubergine (about 340 g), cut crosswise into ½-inch-thick slices and quartered	ground black pepper, to taste
	120 g plain yogurt (not Greek)
2 tablespoons vegetable oil	2 tablespoons harissa paste
coarse sea salt and freshly	1 garlic clove, grated
	2 teaspoons honey

1. In a bowl, toss together the aubergine and oil, season with salt and pepper, and toss to coat evenly. Transfer to the Ninja Foodi cooker and air crisp at 200ºC, shaking the basket every 5 minutes, until the aubergine is caramelized and tender, about 15 minutes. 2. Meanwhile, in a small bowl, whisk together the yogurt, harissa, and garlic, then spread onto a serving plate. 3. Pile the warm aubergine over the yogurt and drizzle with the honey just before serving.

Wild Rice Salad with Cranberries and Almonds

Prep time: 10 minutes | Cook time: 25 minutes | Serves 18

For the rice	Juice of 1 medium orange (about 60 ml)
480 ml wild rice blend, rinsed	
1 teaspoon rock salt	1 teaspoon honey or pure maple syrup
600 ml Vegetable Broth or Chicken Bone Broth	
	For the salad
For the dressing	180 ml unsweetened dried cranberries
60 ml extra-virgin olive oil	
60 ml white wine vinegar	120 ml sliced almonds, toasted
1½ teaspoons grated orange zest	Freshly ground black pepper

Make the Rice 1. In the electric pressure cooker, combine the rice, salt, and broth. 2. Close and lock the lid. Set the valve to sealing. 3. Cook on high pressure for 25 minutes. 4. When the cooking is complete, hit Start/Stop and allow the pressure to release naturally for 15 minutes, then quick release any remaining pressure. 5. Once the pin drops, unlock and remove the lid. 6. Let the rice cool briefly, then fluff it with a fork. Make the Dressing 7. While the rice cooks, make the dressing: In a small jar with a screw-top lid, combine the olive oil, vinegar, zest, juice, and honey. (If you don't have a jar, whisk the ingredients together in a small bowl.) Shake to combine. Make the Salad 8. In a large bowl, combine the rice, cranberries, and almonds. 9. Add the dressing and season with pepper. 10. Serve warm or refrigerate.

Thyme Cabbage

Prep time: 10 minutes | Cook time: 5 minutes | Serves 4

450 g white cabbage	½ teaspoon salt
2 tablespoons butter	240 ml water
1 teaspoon dried thyme	

1. Cut the white cabbage on medium size petals and sprinkle with the butter, dried thyme and salt. Place the cabbage petals in the Ninja Foodi cooker pan. 2. Pour the water and insert the reversible rack in the Ninja Foodi cooker. Put the pan on the reversible rack. 3. Set the lid in place. Set the cooking time for 5 minutes on High Pressure. When the timer goes off, do a quick pressure release. Carefully open the lid. 4. Serve immediately.

Cheese-Walnut Stuffed Mushrooms

Prep time: 5 minutes | Cook time: 10 minutes | Serves 4

4 large portobello mushrooms	35 g minced walnuts
1 tablespoon rapeseed oil	2 tablespoons chopped fresh parsley
110 g shredded Mozzarella cheese	
	Cooking spray

1. Preheat the Ninja Foodi cooker to 180ºC. Spritz the cook & crisp basket with cooking spray. 2. On a clean work surface, remove the mushroom stems. Scoop out the gills with a spoon and discard. Coat the mushrooms with rapeseed oil. Top each mushroom evenly with the shredded Mozzarella cheese, followed by the minced walnuts. 3. Arrange the mushrooms in the Ninja Foodi cooker and roast for 10 minutes until golden brown. 4. Transfer the mushrooms to a plate and sprinkle the parsley on top for garnish before serving.

Simple Cauliflower Gnocchi

Prep time: 5 minutes | Cook time: 2 minutes | Serves 4

480 ml cauliflower, boiled	1 teaspoon salt
120 ml almond flour	240 ml water
1 tablespoon sesame oil	

1. In a bowl, mash the cauliflower until puréed. Mix it up with the almond flour, sesame oil and salt. 2. Make the log from the cauliflower dough and cut it into small pieces. 3. Pour the water in the Ninja Foodi cooker and add the gnocchi. 4. Lock the lid. Set the cooking time for 2 minutes on High Pressure. Once the timer goes off, perform a natural pressure release for 5 minutes, then release any remaining pressure. Carefully open the lid. 5. Remove the cooked gnocchi from the water and serve.

Stuffed Red Peppers with Herbed Ricotta and Tomatoes

Prep time: 10 minutes | Cook time: 20 minutes | Serves 4

2 red peppers
250 g cooked brown rice
2 plum tomatoes, diced
1 garlic clove, minced
¼ teaspoon salt
¼ teaspoon black pepper
115 g ricotta

3 tablespoons fresh basil, chopped
3 tablespoons fresh oregano, chopped
20 g shredded Parmesan, for topping

1. Preheat the Ninja Foodi cooker to 180ºC. 2. Cut the bell peppers in half and remove the seeds and stem. 3. In a medium bowl, combine the brown rice, tomatoes, garlic, salt, and pepper. 4. Distribute the rice filling evenly among the four bell pepper halves. 5. In a small bowl, combine the ricotta, basil, and oregano. Put the herbed cheese over the top of the rice mixture in each bell pepper. 6. Place the bell peppers into the Ninja Foodi cooker and roast for 20 minutes. 7. Remove and serve with shredded Parmesan on top.

Chinese-Style Pe-Tsai with Onion

Prep time: 5 minutes | Cook time: 8 minutes | Serves 4

2 tablespoons sesame oil
1 brown onion, chopped
450 g pe-tsai cabbage, shredded
60 ml rice wine vinegar

1 tablespoon coconut aminos
1 teaspoon finely minced garlic
½ teaspoon salt
¼ teaspoon Szechuan pepper

1. Set the Ninja Foodi cooker on the Sauté mode and heat the sesame oil. Add the onion to the pot and sauté for 5 minutes, or until tender. Stir in the remaining ingredients. 2. Lock the lid. Set the cooking time for 3 minutes on High Pressure. When the timer goes off, perform a quick pressure release. Carefully open the lid. 3. Transfer the cabbage mixture to a bowl and serve immediately.

Garlicky Broccoli with Roasted Almonds

Prep time: 10 minutes | Cook time: 4 minutes | Serves 4 to 6

1.5 L broccoli florets
240 ml water
1½ tablespoons olive oil
8 garlic cloves, thinly sliced
2 shallots, thinly sliced
½ teaspoon crushed red pepper flakes

Grated zest and juice of 1 medium lemon
½ teaspoon rock salt
Freshly ground black pepper, to taste
60 ml chopped roasted almonds
60 ml finely slivered fresh basil

1. Pour the water into the Ninja Foodi cooker. Place the broccoli florets in a steamer basket and lower into the pot. 2. Close and secure the lid. Select the Steam setting and set the cooking time for 2 minutes at Low Pressure. Once the timer goes off, use a quick pressure release. Carefully open the lid. 3. Transfer the broccoli to a large bowl filled with cold water and ice. Once cooled, drain the broccoli and pat dry. 4. Select the Sauté mode on the Ninja Foodi cooker and heat the olive oil. Add the garlic to the pot and sauté for 30 seconds, tossing constantly. Add the shallots and pepper flakes to the pot and sauté for 1 minute. 5. Stir in the cooked broccoli, lemon juice, salt and black pepper. Toss the ingredients together and cook for 1 minute. 6. Transfer the broccoli to a serving platter and sprinkle with the chopped almonds, lemon zest and basil. Serve immediately.

Roasted Grape Tomatoes and Asparagus

Prep time: 5 minutes | Cook time: 12 minutes | Serves 6

400 g grape tomatoes
1 bunch asparagus, trimmed
2 tablespoons olive oil

3 garlic cloves, minced
½ teaspoon coarse sea salt

1. Preheat the Ninja Foodi cooker to 190ºC. 2. In a large bowl, combine all of the ingredients, tossing until the vegetables are well coated with oil. 3. Pour the vegetable mixture into the cook & crisp basket and spread into a single layer, then roast for 12 minutes.

Five-Spice Roasted Sweet Potatoes

Prep time: 10 minutes | Cook time: 12 minutes | Serves 4

½ teaspoon ground cinnamon
¼ teaspoon ground cumin
¼ teaspoon paprika
1 teaspoon chili powder
⅛ teaspoon turmeric
½ teaspoon salt (optional)

Freshly ground black pepper, to taste
2 large sweet potatoes, peeled and cut into ¾-inch cubes
1 tablespoon olive oil

1. In a large bowl, mix together cinnamon, cumin, paprika, chili powder, turmeric, salt, and pepper to taste. 2. Add potatoes and stir well. 3. Drizzle the seasoned potatoes with the olive oil and stir until evenly coated. 4. Place seasoned potatoes in a baking pan or an ovenproof dish that fits inside your cook & crisp basket. 5. Cook for 6 minutes at 200ºC, stop, and stir well. 6. Cook for an additional 6 minutes.

Best Brown Rice

Prep time: 5 minutes | Cook time: 22 minutes | Serves 6 to 12

480 ml brown rice

600 ml water

1. Rinse brown rice in a fine-mesh strainer. 2. Add rice and water to the inner pot of the Ninja Foodi cooker. 3. Secure the lid and make sure vent is on sealing. 4. Select 22 minutes cooking time on high pressure. 5. When cooking time is done, let the pressure release naturally for 10 minutes, then press Start/Stop and manually release any remaining pressure.

Crispy Lemon Artichoke Hearts

Prep time: 10 minutes | Cook time: 15 minutes | Serves 2

1 (425 g) can artichoke hearts in water, drained
1 egg
1 tablespoon water
30 g whole wheat bread crumbs
¼ teaspoon salt
¼ teaspoon paprika
½ lemon

1. Preheat the Ninja Foodi cooker to 190ºC. 2. In a medium shallow bowl, beat together the egg and water until frothy. 3. In a separate medium shallow bowl, mix together the bread crumbs, salt, and paprika. 4. Dip each artichoke heart into the egg mixture, then into the bread crumb mixture, coating the outside with the crumbs. Place the artichokes hearts in a single layer of the cook & crisp basket. 5. Fry the artichoke hearts for 15 minutes. 6. Remove the artichokes from the Ninja Foodi cooker, and squeeze fresh lemon juice over the top before serving.

Mashed Sweet Potato Tots

Prep time: 10 minutes | Cook time: 12 to 13 minutes per batch | Makes 18 to 24 tots

210 g cooked mashed sweet potatoes
1 egg white, beaten
⅛ teaspoon ground cinnamon
1 dash nutmeg
2 tablespoons chopped pecans
1½ teaspoons honey
Salt, to taste
50 g panko bread crumbs
Oil for misting or cooking spray

1. Preheat the Ninja Foodi cooker to 200ºC. 2. In a large bowl, mix together the potatoes, egg white, cinnamon, nutmeg, pecans, honey, and salt to taste. 3. Place panko crumbs on a sheet of wax paper. 4. For each tot, use about 2 teaspoons of sweet potato mixture. To shape, drop the measure of potato mixture onto panko crumbs and push crumbs up and around potatoes to coat edges. Then turn tot over to coat other side with crumbs. 5. Mist tots with oil or cooking spray and place in cook & crisp basket in single layer. 6. Air crisp at 200ºC for 12 to 13 minutes, until browned and crispy. 7. Repeat steps 5 and 6 to cook remaining tots.

Sesame Courgette Noddles with Spring Onions

Prep time: 10 minutes | Cook time: 3 minutes | Serves 6

2 large courgettes, trimmed and spiralized
60 ml chicken broth
1 tablespoon chopped spring onions
1 tablespoon coconut aminos
1 teaspoon sesame oil
1 teaspoon sesame seeds
¼ teaspoon chili flakes

1. Set the Ninja Foodi cooker on the Sauté mode. Add the courgette spirals to the pot and pour in the chicken broth. Sauté for 3 minutes and transfer to the serving bowls. 2. Sprinkle with the spring onions, coconut aminos, sesame oil, sesame seeds and chili flakes. Gently stir the courgette noddles. 3. Serve immediately.

Tofu Bites

Prep time: 15 minutes | Cook time: 30 minutes | Serves 4

1 packaged firm tofu, cubed and pressed to remove excess water
1 tablespoon soy sauce
1 tablespoon ketchup
1 tablespoon maple syrup
½ teaspoon vinegar
1 teaspoon liquid smoke
1 teaspoon hot sauce
2 tablespoons sesame seeds
1 teaspoon garlic powder
Salt and ground black pepper, to taste
Cooking spray

1. Preheat the Ninja Foodi cooker to 190ºC. 2. Spritz a baking dish with cooking spray. 3. Combine all the ingredients to coat the tofu completely and allow the marinade to absorb for half an hour. 4. Transfer the tofu to the baking dish, then air crisp for 15 minutes. Flip the tofu over and air crisp for another 15 minutes on the other side. 5. Serve immediately.

Asparagus and Mushroom Soup

Prep time: 10 minutes | Cook time: 7 minutes | Serves 4

2 tablespoons coconut oil
120 ml chopped shallots
2 cloves garlic, minced
450 g asparagus, washed, trimmed, and chopped
110 g button mushrooms, sliced
1 L vegetable broth
2 tablespoons balsamic vinegar
Himalayan salt, to taste
¼ teaspoon ground black pepper
¼ teaspoon paprika
60 ml vegan sour cream

1. Press the Sauté button to heat up your Ninja Foodi cooker. Heat the oil and cook the shallots and garlic for 2 to 3 minutes. 2. Add the remaining ingredients, except for sour cream, to the Ninja Foodi cooker. 3. Secure the lid. Choose High Pressure; cook for 4 minutes. Once cooking is complete, use a quick pressure release; carefully remove the lid. 4. Spoon into four soup bowls; add a dollop of sour cream to each serving and serve immediately. Bon appétit!

Turnip Fries

Prep time: 10 minutes | Cook time: 20 to 30 minutes | Serves 4

900 g turnip, peeled and cut into ¼ to ½-inch fries
2 tablespoons olive oil
Salt and freshly ground black pepper, to taste

1. Preheat the Ninja Foodi cooker to 200ºC. 2. In a large bowl, combine the turnip and olive oil. Season to taste with salt and black pepper. Toss gently until thoroughly coated. 3. Working in batches if necessary, spread the turnip in a single layer in the cook & crisp basket. Pausing halfway through the cooking time to shake the basket, air crisp for 20 to 30 minutes until the fries are lightly browned and crunchy.

Satarash with Eggs

Prep time: 10 minutes | Cook time: 5 minutes | Serves 4

2 tablespoons olive oil
1 white onion, chopped
2 cloves garlic
2 ripe tomatoes, puréed
1 green bell pepper, deseeded and sliced
1 red bell pepper, deseeded and sliced

1 teaspoon paprika
½ teaspoon dried oregano
½ teaspoon turmeric
rock salt and ground black pepper, to taste
240 ml water
4 large eggs, lightly whisked

1. Press the Sauté button on the Ninja Foodi cooker and heat the olive oil. Add the onion and garlic to the pot and sauté for 2 minutes, or until fragrant. Stir in the remaining ingredients, except for the eggs. 2. Lock the lid. Set the cooking time for 3 minutes on High Pressure. When the timer goes off, perform a quick pressure release. Carefully open the lid. 3. Fold in the eggs and stir to combine. Lock the lid and let it sit in the residual heat for 5 minutes. Serve warm.

Masala Cauliflower

Prep time: 6 minutes | Cook time: 5 minutes | Serves 4

2 tablespoons olive oil
120 ml chopped spring onions
2 cloves garlic, pressed
1 tablespoon garam masala
1 teaspoon curry powder
1 red chili pepper, minced
½ teaspoon ground cumin
Sea salt and ground black

pepper, to taste
1 tablespoon chopped fresh coriander
2 tomatoes, puréed
450 g cauliflower, broken into florets
120 ml water
120 ml almond yoghurt

1. Press the Sauté button to heat up your Ninja Foodi cooker. Now, heat the oil and sauté the spring onions for 1 minute. 2. Add garlic and continue to cook an additional 30 seconds or until aromatic. 3. Add garam masala, curry powder, chili pepper, cumin, salt, black pepper, coriander, tomatoes, cauliflower, and water. 4. Secure the lid. Choose High Pressure; cook for 3 minutes. Once cooking is complete, use a quick pressure release; carefully remove the lid. 5. Pour in the almond yoghurt, stir well and serve warm. Bon appétit!

Parmesan-Topped Acorn Squash

Prep time: 10 minutes | Cook time: 20 minutes | Serves 4

1 acorn squash (about 450 g)
1 tablespoon extra-virgin olive oil
1 teaspoon dried sage leaves, crumbled
¼ teaspoon freshly grated

nutmeg
⅛ teaspoon rock salt
⅛ teaspoon freshly ground black pepper
2 tablespoons freshly grated Parmesan cheese

1. Cut the acorn squash in half lengthwise and remove the seeds. Cut each half in half for a total of 4 wedges. Snap off the stem if it's easy to do. 2. In a small bowl, combine the olive oil, sage, nutmeg, salt, and pepper. Brush the cut sides of the squash with the olive oil mixture. 3. Pour 240 ml of water into the electric pressure cooker and insert a wire rack or reversible rack. 4. Place the squash on the reversible rack in a single layer, skin-side down. 5. Close and lock the lid of the pressure cooker. Set the valve to sealing. 6. Cook on high pressure for 20 minutes. 7. When the cooking is complete, hit Start/Stop and quick release the pressure. 8. Once the pin drops, unlock and remove the lid. 9. Carefully remove the squash from the pot, sprinkle with the Parmesan, and serve.

Chermoula-Roasted Beetroots

Prep time: 15 minutes | Cook time: 25 minutes | Serves 4

Chermoula:
30 g packed fresh coriander leaves
15 g packed fresh parsley leaves
6 cloves garlic, peeled
2 teaspoons smoked paprika
2 teaspoons ground cumin
1 teaspoon ground coriander
½ to 1 teaspoon cayenne pepper
Pinch crushed saffron (optional)

115 ml extra-virgin olive oil
coarse sea salt, to taste
Beetroots:
3 medium beetroots, trimmed, peeled, and cut into 1-inch chunks
2 tablespoons chopped fresh coriander
2 tablespoons chopped fresh parsley

1. For the chermoula: In a food processor, combine the fresh coriander, parsley, garlic, paprika, cumin, ground coriander, and cayenne. Pulse until coarsely chopped. Add the saffron, if using, and process until combined. With the food processor running, slowly add the olive oil in a steady stream; process until the sauce is uniform. Season to taste with salt. 2. For the beetroots: In a large bowl, drizzle the beetroots with ½ cup of the chermoula, or enough to coat. Arrange the beetroots in the cook & crisp basket. Set the Ninja Foodi cooker to 190ºC for 25 to minutes, or until the beetroots are tender. 3. Transfer the beetroots to a serving platter. Sprinkle with chopped coriander and parsley and serve.

Broccoli Tots

Prep time: 15 minutes | Cook time: 10 minutes | Makes 24 tots

230 g broccoli florets
1 egg, beaten
⅛ teaspoon onion powder
¼ teaspoon salt
⅛ teaspoon pepper

2 tablespoons grated Parmesan cheese
25 g panko bread crumbs
Oil for misting

1. Steam broccoli for 2 minutes. Rinse in cold water, drain well, and chop finely. 2. In a large bowl, mix broccoli with all other ingredients except the oil. 3. Scoop out small portions of mixture and shape into 24 tots. Lay them on a cookie sheet or wax paper as you work. 4. Spray tots with oil and place in cook & crisp basket in single layer. 5. Air crisp at 200ºC for 5 minutes. Shake basket and spray with oil again. Cook 5 minutes longer or until browned and crispy.

Curried Cauliflower and Tomatoes

Prep time: 10 minutes | Cook time: 2 minutes | Serves 4 to 6

1 medium head cauliflower, cut into bite-size pieces
1 (400 g) can sugar-free diced tomatoes, undrained
1 bell pepper, thinly sliced
1 (400 g) can full-fat coconut milk
½ to 240 ml water
2 tablespoons red curry paste

1 teaspoon salt
1 teaspoon garlic powder
½ teaspoon onion powder
½ teaspoon ground ginger
¼ teaspoon chili powder
Freshly ground black pepper, to taste

1. Add all the ingredients, except for the black pepper, to the Ninja Foodi cooker and stir to combine. 2. Lock the lid. Set the cooking time for 2 minutes at High Pressure. Once the timer goes off, use a quick pressure release. Carefully open the lid. 3. Sprinkle the black pepper and stir well. Serve immediately.

Braised Cabbage with Ginger

Prep time: 10 minutes | Cook time: 8 minutes | Serves 6

1 tablespoon avocado oil
1 tablespoon butter or ghee (or more avocado oil)
½ medium onion, diced
1 medium bell pepper (any colour), diced
1 teaspoon sea salt

½ teaspoon ground black pepper
1 clove garlic, minced
1-inch piece fresh ginger, grated
450 g green or red cabbage, cored and leaves chopped
120 ml bone broth or vegetable broth

1. Set the Ninja Foodi cooker to Sauté and heat the oil and butter together. When the butter has stopped foaming, add the onion, bell pepper, salt, and black pepper. Sauté, stirring frequently, until just softened, about 3 minutes. Add the garlic and ginger and cook 1 minute longer. Add the cabbage and stir to combine. Pour in the broth. 2. Secure the lid and set the steam release valve to Sealing. Set the cook time to 2 minutes. 3. When the Ninja Foodi cooker beeps, carefully switch the steam release valve to Venting to quick-release the pressure. When fully released, open the lid. Stir the cabbage and transfer it to a serving dish. Serve warm.

Chapter 4 Snacks and Appetisers

Garlicky and Cheesy French Fries

Prep time: 5 minutes | Cook time: 20 to 25 minutes | Serves 4

3 medium russet or Maris Piper potatoes, rinsed, dried, and cut into thin wedges or classic fry shapes
2 tablespoons extra-virgin olive oil
1 tablespoon granulated garlic
80 ml grated Parmesan cheese
½ teaspoon salt
¼ teaspoon freshly ground black pepper
Cooking oil spray
2 tablespoons finely chopped fresh parsley (optional)

1. In a large bowl combine the potato wedges or fries and the olive oil. Toss to coat. 2. Sprinkle the potatoes with the granulated garlic, Parmesan cheese, salt, and pepper, and toss again. 3. Insert the crisper plate into the basket and the basket into the unit. Preheat the unit by selecting AIR CRISP, setting the temperature to 205ºC, and setting the time to 3 minutes. Press START/STOP to begin. 4. Once the unit is preheated, spray the crisper plate with cooking oil. Place the potatoes into the basket. 5. Select AIR CRISP, set the temperature to 205ºC, and set the time to 20 to 25 minutes. Press START/STOP to begin. 6. After about 10 minutes, remove the basket and shake it so the fries at the bottom come up to the top. Reinsert the basket to resume cooking. 7. When the cooking is complete, top the fries with the parsley (if using) and serve hot.

Hush Puppies

Prep time: 45 minutes | Cook time: 10 minutes | Serves 12

240 ml self-raising yellow cornmeal
120 ml plain flour
1 teaspoon sugar
1 teaspoon salt
1 teaspoon freshly ground black pepper
1 large egg
80 ml canned creamed corn
240 ml minced onion
2 teaspoons minced jalapeño pepper
2 tablespoons olive oil, divided

1. Thoroughly combine the cornmeal, flour, sugar, salt, and pepper in a large bowl. 2. Whisk together the egg and corn in a small bowl. Pour the egg mixture into the bowl of cornmeal mixture and stir to combine. Stir in the minced onion and jalapeño. Cover the bowl with plastic wrap and place in the refrigerator for 30 minutes. 3. Preheat the Ninja Foodi cooker to 190ºC. Line the cook & crisp basket with parchment paper and lightly brush it with 1 tablespoon of olive oil. 4. Scoop out the cornmeal mixture and form into 24 balls, about 1 inch. 5. Arrange the balls in the parchment paper-lined basket, leaving space between each ball. 6. Air crisp in batches for 5 minutes. Shake the basket and brush the balls with the remaining 1 tablespoon of olive oil. Continue cooking for 5 minutes until golden brown. 7. Remove the balls (hush puppies) from the basket and serve on a plate.

Courgette Feta Roulades

Prep time: 10 minutes | Cook time: 10 minutes | Serves 6

120 ml feta
1 garlic clove, minced
2 tablespoons fresh basil, minced
1 tablespoon capers, minced
⅛ teaspoon salt
⅛ teaspoon red pepper flakes
1 tablespoon lemon juice
2 medium courgette
12 toothpicks

1. Preheat the Ninja Foodi cooker to 180ºC. (If using a grill attachment, make sure it is inside the Ninja Foodi cooker during preheating.) 2. In a small bowl, combine the feta, garlic, basil, capers, salt, red pepper flakes, and lemon juice. 3. Slice the courgette into ⅛-inch strips lengthwise. (Each courgette should yield around 6 strips.) 4. Spread 1 tablespoon of the cheese filling onto each slice of courgette, then roll it up and secure it with a toothpick through the middle. 5. Place the courgette roulades into the cook & crisp basket in a single layer, making sure that they don't touch each other. 6. Bake or grill in the Ninja Foodi cooker for 10 minutes. 7. Remove the courgette roulades from the Ninja Foodi cooker and gently remove the toothpicks before serving.

Cheese Drops

Prep time: 15 minutes | Cook time: 10 minutes per batch | Serves 8

177 ml plain flour
½ teaspoon rock salt
¼ teaspoon cayenne pepper
¼ teaspoon smoked paprika
¼ teaspoon black pepper
Dash garlic powder (optional)
60 ml butter, softened
240 ml shredded extra mature Cheddar cheese, at room temperature
Olive oil spray

1. In a small bowl, combine the flour, salt, cayenne, paprika, pepper, and garlic powder, if using. 2. Using a food processor, cream the butter and cheese until smooth. Gently add the seasoned flour and process until the dough is well combined, smooth, and no longer sticky. (Or make the dough in a stand mixer fitted with the paddle attachment: Cream the butter and cheese on medium speed until smooth, then add the seasoned flour and beat at low speed until smooth.) 3. Divide the dough into 32 equal-size pieces. On a lightly floured surface, roll each piece into a small ball. 4. Spray the cook & crisp basket with oil spray. Arrange 16 cheese drops in the basket. Set the Ninja Foodi cooker to 165ºC for 10 minutes, or until drops are just starting to brown. Transfer to a wire rack. Repeat with remaining dough, checking for doneness at 8 minutes. 5. Cool the cheese drops completely on the wire rack. Store in an airtight container until ready to serve, or up to 1 or 2 days.

Chicken and Cabbage Salad

Prep time: 15 minutes | Cook time: 10 minutes | Serves 4

340 g chicken fillet, chopped
1 teaspoon Cajun seasoning
1 tablespoon coconut oil
240 ml chopped Chinese

cabbage
1 tablespoon avocado oil
1 teaspoon sesame seeds

1. Sprinkle the chopped chicken with the Cajun seasoning. 2. Set your Ninja Foodi cooker to Sauté and heat the coconut oil. Add the chicken and cook for 10 minutes, stirring occasionally. 3. When the chicken is cooked, transfer to a salad bowl. Add the cabbage, avocado oil, and sesame seeds and gently toss to combine. Serve immediately.

Cheddar Cauliflower Rice

Prep time: 3 minutes | Cook time: 1 minute | Serves 4

1 head fresh cauliflower, chopped into florets
240 ml water
3 tablespoons butter
1 tablespoon double cream

240 ml shredded sharp Cheddar cheese
½ teaspoon salt
¼ teaspoon pepper
¼ teaspoon garlic powder

1. Place cauliflower in steamer basket. Pour water into Ninja Foodi cooker and lower steamer rack into pot. Click lid closed. Press the Steam button and adjust time for 1 minute. When timer beeps, quick-release the pressure. 2. Remove steamer basket and place cauliflower in food processor. Pulse until cauliflower is broken into small pearls. Place cauliflower into large bowl, and add remaining ingredients. Gently fold until fully combined.

Herbed Mushrooms

Prep time: 5 minutes | Cook time: 10 minutes | Serves 4

2 tablespoons butter
2 cloves garlic, minced
570 g button mushrooms
1 tablespoon coconut aminos
1 teaspoon dried rosemary
1 teaspoon dried basil
1 teaspoon dried sage
1 bay leaf

Sea salt, to taste
½ teaspoon freshly ground black pepper
120 ml chicken broth
120 ml water
1 tablespoon roughly chopped fresh parsley leaves, for garnish

1. Set your Ninja Foodi cooker to Sauté and melt the butter. 2. Add the garlic and mushrooms and sauté for 3 to 4 minutes until the garlic is fragrant. 3. Add the remaining ingredients except the parsley to the Ninja Foodi cooker and stir well. 4. Lock the lid. Set the cooking time for 5 minutes at High Pressure. 5. When the timer beeps, perform a quick pressure release. Carefully open the lid. 6. Remove the mushrooms from the pot to a platter. Serve garnished with the fresh parsley leaves.

Crispy Brussels Sprouts with Bacon

Prep time: 5 minutes | Cook time: 10 minutes | Serves 4

230 g bacon
450 g Brussels sprouts
4 tablespoons butter

1 teaspoon salt
½ teaspoon pepper
120 ml water

1. Press the Sauté button and press the Adjust button to lower heat to Less. Add bacon to Ninja Foodi cooker and fry for 3 to 5 minutes or until fat begins to render. Press the Start/Stop button. 2. Press the Sauté button, with heat set to Normal, and continue frying bacon until crispy. While bacon is frying, wash Brussels sprouts and remove damaged outer leaves. Cut in half or quarters. 3. When bacon is done, remove and set aside. Add Brussels sprouts to hot bacon grease and add butter. Sprinkle with salt and pepper. Sauté for 8 to 10 minutes until caramelized and crispy, adding a few tablespoons of water at a time as needed to deglaze pan. Serve warm.

Air Fried Pot Stickers

Prep time: 10 minutes | Cook time: 18 to 20 minutes | Makes 30 pot stickers

120 ml finely chopped cabbage
60 ml finely chopped red pepper
2 spring onions, finely chopped
1 egg, beaten
2 tablespoons cocktail sauce

2 teaspoons low-salt soy sauce
30 wonton wrappers
1 tablespoon water, for brushing the wrappers

1. Preheat the Ninja Foodi cooker to 180°C. 2. In a small bowl, combine the cabbage, pepper, spring onions, egg, cocktail sauce, and soy sauce, and mix well. 3. Put about 1 teaspoon of the mixture in the centre of each wonton wrapper. Fold the wrapper in half, covering the filling; dampen the edges with water, and seal. You can crimp the edges of the wrapper with your fingers, so they look like the pot stickers you get in restaurants. Brush them with water. 4. Place the pot stickers in the cook & crisp basket and air crisp in 2 batches for 9 to 10 minutes, or until the pot stickers are hot and the bottoms are lightly browned. 5. Serve hot.

Broccoli Cheese Dip

Prep time: 5 minutes | Cook time: 10 minutes | Serves 6

4 tablespoons butter
½ medium onion, diced
360 ml chopped broccoli
230 g cream cheese

120 ml mayonnaise
120 ml chicken broth
240 ml shredded Cheddar cheese

1. Press the Sauté button and then press the Adjust button to set heat to Less. Add butter to Ninja Foodi cooker. Add onion and sauté until softened, about 5 minutes. Press the Start/Stop button. 2. Add broccoli, cream cheese, mayo, and broth to pot. Adjust time for 4 minutes. 3. When timer beeps, quick-release the pressure and stir in Cheddar. Serve warm.

Lemon-Cheese Cauliflower Bites

Prep time: 5 minutes | Cook time: 8 minutes | Serves 6

240 ml water
450 g cauliflower, broken into florets
Sea salt and ground black pepper, to taste
2 tablespoons extra-virgin olive oil
2 tablespoons lemon juice
240 ml grated Cheddar cheese

1. Pour the water into the Ninja Foodi cooker and insert a steamer basket. Place the cauliflower florets in the basket. 2. Lock the lid. Set the cooking time for 3 minutes at Low Pressure. 3. When the timer beeps, perform a quick pressure release. Carefully remove the lid. 4. Season the cauliflower with salt and pepper. Drizzle with olive oil and lemon juice. Sprinkle the grated cheese all over the cauliflower. 5. Press the Sauté button to heat the Ninja Foodi cooker. Allow to cook for about 5 minutes, or until the cheese melts. Serve warm.

Crunchy Basil White Beans

Prep time: 2 minutes | Cook time: 19 minutes | Serves 2

1 (425 g) can cooked white beans
2 tablespoons olive oil
1 teaspoon fresh sage, chopped
¼ teaspoon garlic powder
¼ teaspoon salt, divided
1 teaspoon chopped fresh basil

1. Preheat the Ninja Foodi cooker to 190°C. 2. In a medium bowl, mix together the beans, olive oil, sage, garlic, ⅛ teaspoon salt, and basil. 3. Pour the white beans into the Ninja Foodi cooker and spread them out in a single layer. 4. Bake for 10 minutes. Stir and continue cooking for an additional 5 to 9 minutes, or until they reach your preferred level of crispiness. 5. Toss with the remaining ⅛ teaspoon salt before serving.

Garlic Edamame

Prep time: 5 minutes | Cook time: 10 minutes | Serves 4

Olive oil
1 (454 g) bag frozen edamame in pods
½ teaspoon salt
½ teaspoon garlic salt
¼ teaspoon freshly ground black pepper
½ teaspoon red pepper flakes (optional)

1. Spray the cook & crisp basket lightly with olive oil. 2. In a medium bowl, add the frozen edamame and lightly spray with olive oil. Toss to coat. 3. In a small bowl, mix together the salt, garlic salt, black pepper, and red pepper flakes (if using). Add the mixture to the edamame and toss until evenly coated. 4. Place half the edamame in the cook & crisp basket. Do not overfill the basket. 5. Air crisp at 190°C for 5 minutes. Shake the basket and cook until the edamame is starting to brown and get crispy, 3 to 5 more minutes. 6. Repeat with the remaining edamame and serve immediately.

Southern Boiled Peanuts

Prep time: 5 minutes | Cook time: 1 hour 20 minutes | Makes 2 L

450 g raw jumbo peanuts in the shell
3 tablespoons fine sea salt

1. Remove the inner pot from the Ninja Foodi cooker and add the peanuts to it. Cover the peanuts with water and use your hands to agitate them, loosening any dirt. Drain the peanuts in a colander, rinse out the pot, and return the peanuts to it. Return the inner pot to the Ninja Foodi cooker housing. 2. Add the salt and 2.2 L water to the pot and stir to dissolve the salt. Select a salad plate just small enough to fit inside the pot and set it on top of the peanuts to weight them down, submerging them all in the water. 3. Secure the lid and set the Pressure Release to Sealing. Select the Steam setting and set the cooking time for 1 hour at low pressure. (The pot will take about 20 minutes to come up to pressure before the cooking program begins.) 4. When the cooking program ends, let the pressure release naturally (this will take about 1 hour). Open the pot and, wearing heat-resistant mitts, remove the inner pot from the housing. Let the peanuts cool to room temperature in the brine (this will take about 1½ hours). 5. Serve at room temperature or chilled. Transfer the peanuts with their brine to an airtight container and refrigerate for up to 1 week.

Red Wine Mushrooms

Prep time: 5 minutes | Cook time: 15 minutes | Serves 2

230 g sliced mushrooms
60 ml dry red wine
2 tablespoons beef broth
½ teaspoon garlic powder
¼ teaspoon Worcestershire
sauce
Pinch of salt
Pinch of black pepper
¼ teaspoon xanthan gum

1. Add the mushrooms, wine, broth, garlic powder, Worcestershire sauce, salt, and pepper to the pot. 2. Close the lid and seal the vent. Cook on High Pressure for 13 minutes. Quick release the steam. Press Start/Stop. 3. Turn the pot to Sauté mode. Add the xanthan gum and whisk until the juices have thickened, 1 to 2 minutes.

Crispy Chilli Chickpeas

Prep time: 5 minutes | Cook time: 15 minutes | Serves 4

1 (425 g) can cooked chickpeas, drained and rinsed
1 tablespoon olive oil
¼ teaspoon salt
⅛ teaspoon chilli powder
⅛ teaspoon garlic powder
⅛ teaspoon paprika

1. Preheat the Ninja Foodi cooker to 190°C. 2. In a medium bowl, toss all of the ingredients together until the chickpeas are well coated. 3. Pour the chickpeas into the Ninja Foodi cooker and spread them out in a single layer. 4. Roast for 15 minutes, stirring once halfway through the cook time.

Bruschetta with Basil Pesto

Prep time: 10 minutes | Cook time: 5 to 11 minutes | Serves 4

8 slices French bread, ½ inch thick
2 tablespoons softened butter
240 ml shredded Mozzarella
cheese
120 ml basil pesto
240 ml chopped grape tomatoes
2 spring onions, thinly sliced

1. Preheat the Ninja Foodi cooker to 175°C. 2. Spread the bread with the butter and place butter-side up in the cook & crisp basket. Bake for 3 to 5 minutes, or until the bread is light golden brown. 3. Remove the bread from the basket and top each piece with some of the cheese. Return to the basket in 2 batches and bake for 1 to 3 minutes, or until the cheese melts. 4. Meanwhile, combine the pesto, tomatoes, and spring onions in a small bowl. 5. When the cheese has melted, remove the bread from the Ninja Foodi cooker and place on a serving plate. Top each slice with some of the pesto mixture and serve.

Cheese Stuffed Bell Peppers

Prep time: 10 minutes | Cook time: 5 minutes | Serves 5

240 ml water
10 baby bell peppers, seeded and sliced lengthwise
110 g Monterey Jack cheese, shredded
110 g cream cheese
2 tablespoons chopped spring
onions
1 tablespoon olive oil
1 teaspoon minced garlic
½ teaspoon cayenne pepper
¼ teaspoon ground black pepper, or more to taste

1. Pour the water into the Ninja Foodi cooker and insert a steamer basket. 2. Stir together the remaining ingredients except the bell peppers in a mixing bowl until combined. Stuff the peppers evenly with the mixture. Arrange the stuffed peppers in the basket. 3. Lock the lid. Set the cooking time for 5 minutes at High Pressure. 4. When the timer beeps, perform a quick pressure release. Carefully remove the lid. 5. Cool for 5 minutes and serve.

Cayenne Beef Bites

Prep time: 5 minutes | Cook time: 23 minutes | Serves 6

2 tablespoons olive oil
450 g beef steak, cut into cubes
240 ml beef bone broth
60 ml dry white wine
1 teaspoon cayenne pepper
½ teaspoon dried marjoram
Sea salt and ground black pepper, to taste

1. Set your Ninja Foodi cooker to Sauté and heat the olive oil. 2. Add the beef and sauté for 2 to 3 minutes, stirring occasionally. 3. Add the remaining ingredients to the Ninja Foodi cooker and combine well. 4. Lock the lid. Set the cooking time for 20 minutes at High Pressure. 5. When the timer beeps, perform a natural pressure release for 10 minutes, then release any remaining pressure. Carefully remove the lid. 6. Remove the beef from the Ninja Foodi cooker to a platter and serve warm.

Browned Ricotta with Capers and Lemon

Prep time: 10 minutes | Cook time: 8 to 10 minutes | Serves 4 to 6

355 ml whole milk ricotta cheese
2 tablespoons extra-virgin olive oil
2 tablespoons capers, rinsed
Zest of 1 lemon, plus more for garnish
1 teaspoon finely chopped fresh rosemary
Pinch crushed red pepper flakes
Salt and freshly ground black pepper, to taste
1 tablespoon grated Parmesan cheese

1. Preheat the Ninja Foodi cooker to 190°C. 2. In a mixing bowl, stir together the ricotta cheese, olive oil, capers, lemon zest, rosemary, red pepper flakes, salt, and pepper until well combined. 3. Spread the mixture evenly in a baking dish and place it in the cook & crisp basket. 4. Air crisp for 8 to 10 minutes until the top is nicely browned. 5. Remove from the basket and top with a sprinkle of grated Parmesan cheese. 6. Garnish with the lemon zest and serve warm.

Kale Chips with Sesame

Prep time: 15 minutes | Cook time: 8 minutes | Serves 5

2 L deribbed kale leaves, torn into 2-inch pieces
1½ tablespoons olive oil
¾ teaspoon chilli powder
¼ teaspoon garlic powder
½ teaspoon paprika
2 teaspoons sesame seeds

1. Preheat Ninja Foodi cooker to 175°C. 2. In a large bowl, toss the kale with the olive oil, chilli powder, garlic powder, paprika, and sesame seeds until well coated. 3. Put the kale in the cook & crisp basket and air crisp for 8 minutes, flipping the kale twice during cooking, or until the kale is crispy. 4. Serve warm.

Easy Spiced Nuts

Prep time: 5 minutes | Cook time: 25 minutes | Makes 3 L

1 egg white, lightly beaten
60 ml sugar
1 teaspoon salt
½ teaspoon ground cinnamon
¼ teaspoon ground cloves
¼ teaspoon ground allspice
Pinch ground cayenne pepper
240 ml pecan halves
240 ml cashews
240 ml almonds

1. Combine the egg white with the sugar and spices in a bowl. 2. Preheat the Ninja Foodi cooker to 150°C. 3. Spray or brush the cook & crisp basket with vegetable oil. Toss the nuts together in the spiced egg white and transfer the nuts to the cook & crisp basket. 4. Air crisp for 25 minutes, stirring the nuts in the basket a few times during the cooking process. Taste the nuts (carefully because they will be very hot) to see if they are crunchy and nicely toasted. Air crisp for a few more minutes if necessary. 5. Serve warm or cool to room temperature and store in an airtight container for up to two weeks.

Bok Choy Salad Boats with Prawn

Prep time: 8 minutes | Cook time: 2 minutes | Serves 8

26 prawn, cleaned and deveined
2 tablespoons fresh lemon juice
240 ml water
Sea salt and ground black pepper, to taste
110 g feta cheese, crumbled
2 tomatoes, diced
80 ml olives, pitted and sliced
4 tablespoons olive oil
2 tablespoons apple cider vinegar
8 Bok choy leaves
2 tablespoons fresh basil leaves, snipped
2 tablespoons chopped fresh mint leaves

1. Toss the prawn and lemon juice in the Ninja Foodi cooker until well coated. Pour in the water. 2. Lock the lid. Set the cooking time for 2 minutes at Low Pressure. 3. When the timer beeps, perform a quick pressure release. Carefully remove the lid. 4. Season the prawn with salt and pepper to taste, then let them cool completely. 5. Toss the prawn with the feta cheese, tomatoes, olives, olive oil, and vinegar until well incorporated. 6. Divide the salad evenly onto each Bok choy leaf and place them on a serving plate. Scatter the basil and mint leaves on top and serve immediately.

Cinnamon-Apple Crisps

Prep time: 10 minutes | Cook time: 32 minutes | Serves 4

Oil, for spraying
2 Red Delicious or Honeycrisp apples
¼ teaspoon ground cinnamon, divided

1. Line the cook & crisp basket with parchment and spray lightly with oil. 2. Trim the uneven ends off the apples. Using a mandoline slicer on the thinnest setting or a sharp knife, cut the apples into very thin slices. Discard the cores. 3. Place half of the apple slices in a single layer in the prepared basket and sprinkle with half of the cinnamon. 4. Place a metal Ninja Foodi cooker trivet on top of the apples to keep them from flying around while they are cooking. 5. Air crisp at 150°C for 16 minutes, flipping every 5 minutes to ensure even cooking. Repeat with the remaining apple slices and cinnamon. 6. Let cool to room temperature before serving. The crisps will firm up as they cool.

Spiced Roasted Cashews

Prep time: 5 minutes | Cook time: 10 minutes | Serves 4

475 ml raw cashews
2 tablespoons olive oil
¼ teaspoon salt
¼ teaspoon chilli powder
⅛ teaspoon garlic powder
⅛ teaspoon smoked paprika

1. Preheat the Ninja Foodi cooker to 180°C. 2. In a large bowl, toss all of the ingredients together. 3. Pour the cashews into the cook & crisp basket and roast them for 5 minutes. Shake the basket, then cook for 5 minutes more. 4. Serve immediately.

Pickle Chips

Prep time: 30 minutes | Cook time: 12 minutes | Serves 4

Oil, for spraying
475 ml sliced dill or sweet pickles, drained
240 ml buttermilk
475 ml plain flour
2 large eggs, beaten
475 ml panko breadcrumbs
¼ teaspoon salt

1. Line the cook & crisp basket with parchment and spray lightly with oil. 2. In a shallow bowl, combine the pickles and buttermilk and let soak for at least 1 hour, then drain. 3. Place the flour, beaten eggs, and breadcrumbs in separate bowls. 4. Coat each pickle chip lightly in the flour, dip in the eggs, and dredge in the breadcrumbs. Be sure each one is evenly coated. 5. Place the pickle chips in the prepared basket, sprinkle with the salt, and spray lightly with oil. You may need to work in batches, depending on the size of your Ninja Foodi cooker. 6. Air crisp at 200°C for 5 minutes, flip, and cook for another 5 to 7 minutes, or until crispy. Serve hot.

Ranch Oyster Snack Crackers

Prep time: 3 minutes | Cook time: 12 minutes | Serves 6

Oil, for spraying
60 ml olive oil
2 teaspoons dry ranch seasoning
1 teaspoon chilli powder
½ teaspoon dried dill
½ teaspoon granulated garlic
½ teaspoon salt
1 (255 g) bag oyster crackers or low-salt crackers

1. Preheat the Ninja Foodi cooker to 165°C. Line the cook & crisp basket with parchment and spray lightly with oil. 2. In a large bowl, mix together the olive oil, ranch seasoning, chilli powder, dill, garlic, and salt. Add the crackers and toss until evenly coated. 3. Place the mixture in the prepared basket. 4. Cook for 10 to 12 minutes, shaking or stirring every 3 to 4 minutes, or until crisp and golden brown.

Sweet Bacon Potato Crunchies

Prep time: 5 minutes | Cook time: 7 minutes | Serves 4

24 frozen potato crunchies
6 slices cooked bacon
2 tablespoons maple syrup
240 ml shredded Cheddar cheese

1. Preheat the Ninja Foodi cooker to 205°C. 2. Put the potato crunchies in the cook & crisp basket. Air crisp for 10 minutes, shaking the basket halfway through the cooking time. 3. Meanwhile, cut the bacon into 1-inch pieces. 4. Remove the potato crunchies from the cook & crisp basket and put into a baking pan. Top with the bacon and drizzle with the maple syrup. Air crisp for 5 minutes, or until the crunchies and bacon are crisp. 5. Top with the cheese and air crisp for 2 minutes, or until the cheese is melted. 6. Serve hot.

Curried Broccoli Skewers

Prep time: 15 minutes | Cook time: 1 minute | Serves 2

240 ml broccoli florets	2 tablespoons coconut cream
½ teaspoon curry paste	240 ml water, for cooking

1. In the shallow bowl mix up curry paste and coconut cream. 2. Then sprinkle the broccoli florets with curry paste mixture and string on the skewers. 3. Pour water and insert the steamer rack in the Ninja Foodi cooker. 4. Place the broccoli skewers on the rack. Close and seal the lid. 5. Cook the meal on High Pressure for 1 minute. 6. Make a quick pressure release.

Egg Roll Pizza Sticks

Prep time: 10 minutes | Cook time: 5 minutes | Serves 4

Olive oil	24 slices turkey pepperoni or
8 pieces low-fat string cheese	salami
8 egg roll wrappers or spring roll pastry	Marinara sauce, for dipping (optional)

1. Spray the cook & crisp basket lightly with olive oil. Fill a small bowl with water. 2. Place each egg roll wrapper diagonally on a work surface. It should look like a diamond. 3. Place 3 slices of turkey pepperoni in a vertical line down the centre of the wrapper. 4. Place 1 Mozzarella cheese stick on top of the turkey pepperoni. 5. Fold the top and bottom corners of the egg roll wrapper over the cheese stick. 6. Fold the left corner over the cheese stick and roll the cheese stick up to resemble a spring roll. Dip a finger in the water and seal the edge of the roll 7. Repeat with the rest of the pizza sticks. 8. Place them in the cook & crisp basket in a single layer, making sure to leave a little space between each one. Lightly spray the pizza sticks with oil. You may need to cook these in batches. 9. Air crisp at 190ºC until the pizza sticks are lightly browned and crispy, about 5 minutes. 10. These are best served hot while the cheese is melted. Accompany with a small bowl of marinara sauce, if desired.

Baked Spanakopita Dip

Prep time: 10 minutes | Cook time: 15 minutes | Serves 2

Olive oil cooking spray	113 g feta cheese, divided
3 tablespoons olive oil, divided	Zest of 1 lemon
2 tablespoons minced white onion	¼ teaspoon ground nutmeg
2 garlic cloves, minced	1 teaspoon dried dill
1 L fresh spinach	½ teaspoon salt
113 g soft white cheese, softened	Pitta chips, carrot sticks, or sliced bread for serving (optional)

1. Preheat the Ninja Foodi cooker to 180ºC. Coat the inside of a 6-inch ramekin or baking dish with olive oil cooking spray. 2. In a large skillet over medium heat, heat 1 tablespoon of the olive oil. Add the onion, then cook for 1 minute. 3. Add in the garlic and cook, stirring for 1 minute more. 4. Reduce the heat to low and mix in the spinach and water. Let this cook for 2 to 3 minutes, or until the spinach has wilted. Remove the skillet from the heat. 5. In a medium bowl, combine the soft white cheese, 57 g of the feta, and the remaining 2 tablespoons of olive oil, along with the lemon zest, nutmeg, dill, and salt. Mix until just combined. 6. Add the vegetables to the cheese base and stir until combined. 7. Pour the dip mixture into the prepared ramekin and top with the remaining 57 g of feta cheese. 8. Place the dip into the cook & crisp basket and cook for 10 minutes, or until heated through and bubbling. 9. Serve with pitta chips, carrot sticks, or sliced bread.

Fast Spring Kale Appetizer

Prep time: 5 minutes | Cook time: 2 minutes | Serves 6

3 teaspoons butter	Himalayan salt and ground
240 ml chopped spring onions	black pepper, to taste
450 g kale, torn into pieces	120 ml shredded Colby cheese,
240 ml water	for serving
½ teaspoon cayenne pepper	

1. Set your Ninja Foodi cooker to Sauté and melt the butter. 2. Add the spring onions and sauté for 1 minute until wilted. 3. Add the remaining ingredients except the cheese to the Ninja Foodi cooker and mix well. 4. Lock the lid. Set the cooking time for 1 minute at High Pressure. 5. When the timer beeps, perform a quick pressure release. Carefully remove the lid. 6. Transfer the kale mixture to a bowl and serve topped with the cheese.

Sweet Potato Fries with Mayonnaise

Prep time: 5 minutes | Cook time: 20 minutes | Serves 2 to 3

1 large sweet potato (about 450 g), scrubbed	60 ml light mayonnaise
1 teaspoon vegetable or rapeseed oil	½ teaspoon sriracha sauce
Salt, to taste	1 tablespoon spicy brown mustard
Dipping Sauce:	1 tablespoon sweet Thai chilli sauce

1. Preheat the Ninja Foodi cooker to 90ºC. 2. On a flat work surface, cut the sweet potato into fry-shaped strips about ¼ inch wide and ¼ inch thick. You can use a mandoline to slice the sweet potato quickly and uniformly. 3. In a medium bowl, drizzle the sweet potato strips with the oil and toss well. 4. Transfer to the cook & crisp basket and air crisp for 10 minutes, shaking the basket twice during cooking. 5. Remove the cook & crisp basket and sprinkle with the salt and toss to coat. 6. Increase the Ninja Foodi cooker temperature to 205ºC and air crisp for an additional 10 minutes, or until the fries are crispy and tender. Shake the basket a few times during cooking. 7. Meanwhile, whisk together all the ingredients for the sauce in a small bowl. 8. Remove the sweet potato fries from the basket to a plate and serve warm alongside the dipping sauce.

Deviled Eggs with Tuna

Prep time: 10 minutes | Cook time: 8 minutes | Serves 3

240 ml water
6 eggs
1 (140 g) can tuna, drained
4 tablespoons mayonnaise
1 teaspoon lemon juice

1 celery stalk, diced finely
¼ teaspoon Dijon mustard
¼ teaspoon chopped fresh dill
¼ teaspoon salt
⅛ teaspoon garlic powder

1. Add water to Ninja Foodi cooker. Place steam rack or steamer basket inside pot. Carefully put eggs into steamer basket. Click lid closed. Adjust time for 8 minutes. 2. Add remaining ingredients to medium bowl and mix. 3. When timer beeps, quick-release the steam and remove eggs. Place in bowl of cool water for 10 minutes, then remove shells. 4. Cut eggs in half and remove hard-boiled yolks, setting whites aside. Place yolks in food processor and pulse until smooth, or mash with fork. Add yolks to bowl with tuna and mayo, mixing until smooth. 5. Spoon mixture into egg-white halves. Serve chilled.

Roasted Garlic Bulbs

Prep time: 2 minutes | Cook time: 25 minutes | Serves 4

4 bulbs garlic
1 tablespoon avocado oil
1 teaspoon salt

Pinch of black pepper
240 ml water

1. Slice the pointy tops off the bulbs of garlic to expose the cloves. 2. Drizzle the avocado oil on top of the garlic and sprinkle with the salt and pepper. 3. Place the bulbs in the steamer basket, cut-side up. Alternatively, you may place them on a piece of aluminium foil with the sides pulled up and resting on top of the reversible rack. Place the steamer basket in the pot. 4. Close the lid and seal the vent. Cook on High Pressure for 25 minutes. Quick release the steam. 5. Let the garlic cool completely before removing the bulbs from the pot. 6. Hold the stem end (bottom) of the bulb and squeeze out all the garlic. Mash the cloves with a fork to make a paste.

Brussels Sprouts with Aioli Sauce

Prep time: 5 minutes | Cook time: 7 mInutes | Serves 4

1 tablespoon butter
120 ml chopped spring onions
340 g Brussels sprouts
Aioli Sauce:

60 ml mayonnaise
1 tablespoon fresh lemon juice
1 garlic clove, minced
½ teaspoon Dijon mustard

1. Set your Ninja Foodi cooker to Sauté and melt the butter. 2. Add the spring onions and sauté for 2 minutes until softened. Add the Brussels sprouts and cook for another 1 minute. 3. Lock the lid. Set the cooking time for 4 minutes at High Pressure. 4. Meanwhile, whisk together all the ingredients for the Aioli sauce in a small bowl until well incorporated. 5. When the timer beeps, perform a quick pressure release. Carefully remove the lid. 6. Serve the Brussels sprouts with the Aioli sauce on the side.

Lemony Endive in Curried Yoghurt

Prep time: 5 minutes | Cook time: 10 minutes | Serves 6

6 heads endive
120 ml plain and fat-free yoghurt
3 tablespoons lemon juice

1 teaspoon garlic powder
½ teaspoon curry powder
Salt and ground black pepper, to taste

1. Wash the endives and slice them in half lengthwise. 2. In a bowl, mix together the yoghurt, lemon juice, garlic powder, curry powder, salt and pepper. 3. Brush the endive halves with the marinade, coating them completely. Allow to sit for at least 30 minutes or up to 24 hours. 4. Preheat the Ninja Foodi cooker to 160ºC. 5. Put the endives in the cook & crisp basket and air crisp for 10 minutes. 6. Serve hot.

Mozzarella Arancini

Prep time: 5 minutes | Cook time: 8 to 11 minutes | Makes 16 arancini

475 ml cooked rice, cooled
2 eggs, beaten
355 ml panko breadcrumbs, divided
120 ml grated Parmesan cheese

2 tablespoons minced fresh basil
16 ¾-inch cubes Mozzarella cheese
2 tablespoons olive oil

1. Preheat the Ninja Foodi cooker to 205ºC. 2. In a medium bowl, combine the rice, eggs, 120 ml of the breadcrumbs, Parmesan cheese, and basil. Form this mixture into 16 1½-inch balls. 3. Poke a hole in each of the balls with your finger and insert a Mozzarella cube. Form the rice mixture firmly around the cheese. 4. On a shallow plate, combine the remaining 240 ml of the breadcrumbs with the olive oil and mix well. Roll the rice balls in the breadcrumbs to coat. 5. Air crisp the arancini in batches for 8 to 11 minutes or until golden brown. 6. Serve hot.

Goat Cheese and Garlic Crostini

Prep time: 3 minutes | Cook time: 5 minutes | Serves 4

1 wholemeal baguette
60 ml olive oil
2 garlic cloves, minced

113 g goat cheese
2 tablespoons fresh basil, minced

1. Preheat the Ninja Foodi cooker to 190ºC. 2. Cut the baguette into ½-inch-thick slices. 3. In a small bowl, mix together the olive oil and garlic, then brush it over one side of each slice of bread. 4. Place the olive-oil-coated bread in a single layer in the cook & crisp basket and bake for 5 minutes. 5. Meanwhile, in a small bowl, mix together the goat cheese and basil. 6. Remove the toast from the Ninja Foodi cooker, then spread a thin layer of the goat cheese mixture over the top of each piece and serve.

Creamed Onion Spinach

Prep time: 3 minutes | Cook time: 5 minutes | Serves 6

4 tablespoons butter
60 ml diced onion
230 g cream cheese
1 (340 g) bag frozen spinach

120 ml chicken broth
240 ml shredded whole-milk Mozzarella cheese

1. Press the Sauté button and add butter. Once butter is melted, add onion to Ninja Foodi cooker and sauté for 2 minutes or until onion begins to turn translucent. 2. Break cream cheese into pieces and add to Ninja Foodi cooker. Press the Start/Stop button. Add frozen spinach and broth. Click lid closed. Adjust time for 5 minutes. When timer beeps, quick-release the pressure and stir in shredded Mozzarella. If mixture is too watery, press the Sauté button and reduce for additional 5 minutes, stirring constantly.

Sesame Mushrooms

Prep time: 2 minutes | Cook time: 10 minutes | Serves 6

3 tablespoons sesame oil
340 g small button mushrooms
1 teaspoon minced garlic
½ teaspoon smoked paprika

½ teaspoon cayenne pepper
Salt and ground black pepper, to taste

1. Set your Ninja Foodi cooker to Sauté and heat the sesame oil. 2. Add the mushrooms and sauté for 4 minutes until just tender, stirring occasionally. 3. Add the remaining ingredients to the Ninja Foodi cooker and stir to mix well. 4. Lock the lid. Set the cooking time for 5 minutes at High Pressure. 5. When the timer beeps, perform a quick pressure release. Carefully remove the lid. 6. Serve warm.

Lemony Pear Chips

Prep time: 15 minutes | Cook time: 9 to 13 minutes | Serves 4

2 firm Bosc or Anjou pears, cut crosswise into ⅛-inch-thick slices
1 tablespoon freshly squeezed

lemon juice
½ teaspoon ground cinnamon
⅛ teaspoon ground cardamom

1. Preheat the Ninja Foodi cooker to 190ºC. 2. Separate the smaller stem-end pear rounds from the larger rounds with seeds. Remove the core and seeds from the larger slices. Sprinkle all slices with lemon juice, cinnamon, and cardamom. 3. Put the smaller chips into the cook & crisp basket. Air crisp for 3 to 5 minutes, or until light golden brown, shaking the basket once during cooking. Remove from the Ninja Foodi cooker. 4. Repeat with the larger slices, AIR CRISPing for 6 to 8 minutes, or until light golden brown, shaking the basket once during cooking. 5. Remove the chips from the Ninja Foodi cooker. Cool and serve or store in an airtight container at room temperature up for to 2 days.

Herbed Courgette Slices

Prep time: 5 minutes | Cook time: 5 minutes | Serves 4

2 tablespoons olive oil
2 garlic cloves, chopped
450 g courgette, sliced
120 ml water

120 ml sugar-free tomato purée
1 teaspoon dried thyme
½ teaspoon dried rosemary
½ teaspoon dried oregano

1. Set your Ninja Foodi cooker to Sauté and heat the olive oil. 2. Add the garlic and sauté for 2 minutes until fragrant. 3. Add the remaining ingredients to the Ninja Foodi cooker and stir well. 4. Lock the lid. Set the cooking time for 3 minutes at Low Pressure. 5. When the timer beeps, perform a quick pressure release. Carefully remove the lid. 6. Serve warm.

Crispy Cajun Dill Pickle Chips

Prep time: 5 minutes | Cook time: 10 minutes | Makes 16 slices

60 ml plain flour
120 ml panko breadcrumbs
1 large egg, beaten
2 teaspoons Cajun seasoning

2 large dill pickles, sliced into 8 rounds each
Cooking spray

1. Preheat the Ninja Foodi cooker to 200ºC. 2. Place the plain flour, panko breadcrumbs, and egg into 3 separate shallow bowls, then stir the Cajun seasoning into the flour. 3. Dredge each pickle chip in the flour mixture, then the egg, and finally the breadcrumbs. Shake off any excess, then place each coated pickle chip on a plate. 4. Spritz the cook & crisp basket with cooking spray, then place 8 pickle chips in the basket and air crisp for 5 minutes, or until crispy and golden brown. Repeat this process with the remaining pickle chips. 5. Remove the chips and allow to slightly cool on a wire rack before serving.

Red Pepper Tapenade

Prep time: 5 minutes | Cook time: 5 minutes | Serves 4

1 large red pepper
2 tablespoons plus 1 teaspoon olive oil, divided
120 ml Kalamata olives, pitted

and roughly chopped
1 garlic clove, minced
½ teaspoon dried oregano
1 tablespoon lemon juice

1. Preheat the Ninja Foodi cooker to 190ºC. 2. Brush the outside of a whole red pepper with 1 teaspoon olive oil and place it inside the cook & crisp basket. Roast for 5 minutes. 3. Meanwhile, in a medium bowl combine the remaining 2 tablespoons of olive oil with the olives, garlic, oregano, and lemon juice. 4. Remove the red pepper from the Ninja Foodi cooker, then gently slice off the stem and remove the seeds. Roughly chop the roasted pepper into small pieces. 5. Add the red pepper to the olive mixture and stir all together until combined. 6. Serve with pitta chips, crackers, or crusty bread.

Creamy Spring Onion Dip

Prep time: 10 minutes | Cook time: 11 minutes | Serves 4

140 g spring onions, diced
4 tablespoons cream cheese
1 tablespoon chopped fresh parsley
1 teaspoon garlic powder
2 tablespoons coconut cream
½ teaspoon salt
1 teaspoon coconut oil

1. Heat up the Ninja Foodi cooker on Sauté mode. 2. Then add coconut oil and melt it. 3. Add diced spring onions and sauté it for 6 to 7 minutes or until it is light brown. 4. Add cream cheese, parsley, garlic powder, salt, and coconut cream. 5. Close the Ninja Foodi cooker lid and cook the spring onions dip for 5 minutes on High Pressure. 6. Make a quick pressure release. Blend the dip will it is smooth if desired.

Oregano Sausage Balls

Prep time: 10 minutes | Cook time: 16 minutes | Serves 10

425 g minced pork sausage
1 teaspoon dried oregano
110 g Mozzarella, shredded
240 ml coconut flour
1 garlic clove, grated
1 teaspoon coconut oil, melted

1. In the bowl mix up minced pork sausages, dried oregano, shredded Mozzarella, coconut flour, and garlic clove. 2. When the mixture is homogenous, make the balls. 3. After this, pour coconut oil in the Ninja Foodi cooker. 4. Arrange the balls in the Ninja Foodi cooker and cook them on Sauté mode for 8 minutes from each side.

Thyme Sautéed Radishes

Prep time: 5 minutes | Cook time: 15 minutes | Serves 4

450 g radishes, quartered (remove leaves and ends)
2 tablespoons butter
¼ teaspoon dried thyme
¼ teaspoon minced garlic
⅛ teaspoon salt
⅛ teaspoon garlic powder
⅛ teaspoon dried rosemary

1. Press the Sauté button and then press the Adjust button to lower heat to Less. 2. Place radishes into Ninja Foodi cooker with butter and seasoning. 3. Sauté, stirring occasionally until tender, about 10 to 15 minutes. Add a couple of teaspoons of water if radishes begin to stick.

Italian Tomatillos

Prep time: 10 minutes | Cook time: 10 minutes | Serves 4

1 tablespoon Italian seasoning
4 tomatillos, sliced
4 teaspoons olive oil
4 tablespoons water

1. Sprinkle the tomatillos with Italian seasoning. 2. Then pour the olive oil in the Ninja Foodi cooker and heat it up on Sauté mode for 1 minute. 3. Put the tomatillos in the Ninja Foodi cooker in one layer and cook them for 2 minutes from each side. 4. Then add water and close the lid. 5. Sauté the vegetables for 3 minutes more.

Garlic Meatballs

Prep time: 20 minutes | Cook time: 15 minutes | Serves 6

200 g minced beef
200 g minced pork
1 teaspoon minced garlic
3 tablespoons water
1 teaspoon chili flakes
1 teaspoon dried parsley
1 tablespoon coconut oil
60 ml beef broth

1. In the mixing bowl, mix up minced beef, minced pork, minced garlic, water, chili flakes, and dried parsley. 2. Make the medium size meatballs from the mixture. 3. After this, heat up coconut oil in the Ninja Foodi cooker on Sauté mode. 4. Put the meatballs in the hot coconut oil in one layer and cook them for 2 minutes from each side. 5. Then add beef broth and close the lid. 6. Cook the meatballs for 10 minutes on High Pressure. 7. Then make a quick pressure release and transfer the meatballs on the plate.

Easy Roasted Chickpeas

Prep time: 5 minutes | Cook time: 15 minutes | Makes about 240 ml

1 (425 g) can chickpeas, drained
2 teaspoons curry powder
¼ teaspoon salt
1 tablespoon olive oil

1. Drain chickpeas thoroughly and spread in a single layer on paper towels. Cover with another paper towel and press gently to remove extra moisture. Don't press too hard or you'll crush the chickpeas. 2. Mix curry powder and salt together. 3. Place chickpeas in a medium bowl and sprinkle with seasonings. Stir well to coat. 4. Add olive oil and stir again to distribute oil. 5. Air crisp at 200°C for 15 minutes, stopping to shake basket about halfway through cooking time. 6. Cool completely and store in airtight container.

Spicy Baked Feta in Foil

Prep time: 10 minutes | Cook time: 6 minutes | Serves 6

340 g feta cheese
½ tomato, sliced
30 g bell pepper, sliced
1 teaspoon ground paprika
1 tablespoon olive oil
240 ml water, for cooking

1. Sprinkle the cheese with olive oil and ground paprika and place it on the foil. 2. Then top feta cheese with sliced tomato and bell pepper. Wrap it in the foil well. 3. After this, pour water and insert the steamer rack in the Ninja Foodi cooker. 4. Put the wrapped cheese on the rack. Close and seal the lid. 5. Cook the cheese on High Pressure for 6 minutes. Then make a quick pressure release. 6. Discard the foil and transfer the cheese on the serving plates.

Cheesy Hash Brown Bruschetta

Prep time: 5 minutes | Cook time: 6 to 8 minutes | Serves 4

4 frozen hash brown patties
1 tablespoon olive oil
80 ml chopped cherry tomatoes
3 tablespoons diced fresh Mozzarella

2 tablespoons grated Parmesan cheese
1 tablespoon balsamic vinegar
1 tablespoon minced fresh basil

4 frozen hash brown patties 1 tablespoon olive oil 80 ml chopped cherry tomatoes 3 tablespoons diced fresh Mozzarella 2 tablespoons grated Parmesan cheese 1 tablespoon balsamic vinegar 1 tablespoon minced fresh basil

Courgette and Cheese Tots

Prep time: 15 minutes | Cook time: 10 minutes | Serves 6

110 g Parmesan, grated
110 g Cheddar cheese, grated
1 courgette, grated

1 egg, beaten
1 teaspoon dried oregano
1 tablespoon coconut oil

1. In the mixing bowl, mix up Parmesan, Cheddar cheese, courgette, egg, and dried oregano. 2. Make the small tots with the help of the fingertips. 3. Then melt the coconut oil in the Ninja Foodi cooker on Sauté mode. 4. Put the prepared courgette tots in the hot coconut oil and cook them for 3 minutes from each side or until they are light brown. Cool the courgette tots for 5 minutes.

Garlic Herb Butter

Prep time: 10 minutes | Cook time: 8 minutes | Serves 4

80 ml butter
1 teaspoon dried parsley
1 tablespoon dried dill

½ teaspoon minced garlic
¼ teaspoon dried thyme

1. Preheat the Ninja Foodi cooker on Sauté mode. 2. Then add butter and melt it. 3. Add dried parsley, dill, minced garlic, and thyme. Stir the butter mixture well. 4. Transfer it in the butter mold and refrigerate until it is solid.

Veggie Salmon Nachos

Prep time: 10 minutes | Cook time: 9 to 12 minutes | Serves 6

57 g baked no-salt corn tortilla chips
1 (142 g) baked salmon fillet, flaked
120 ml canned low-salt black beans, rinsed and drained
1 red pepper, chopped

120 ml grated carrot
1 jalapeño pepper, minced
80 ml shredded low-salt low-fat Swiss cheese
1 tomato, chopped

1. Preheat the Ninja Foodi cooker to 180°C. 2. In a baking pan, layer the tortilla chips. Top with the salmon, black beans, red pepper, carrot, jalapeño, and Swiss cheese. 3. Bake in the Ninja Foodi cooker for 9 to 12 minutes, or until the cheese is melted and starts to brown. 4. Top with the tomato and serve.

Chapter 5 Fish and Seafood

Browned Prawns Patties

Prep time: 15 minutes | Cook time: 10 to 12 minutes | Serves 4

230 g raw prawns, peeled, deveined and chopped finely
500 g cooked sushi rice
35 g chopped red bell pepper
35 g chopped celery
35 g chopped spring onion
2 teaspoons Worcestershire sauce
½ teaspoon salt
½ teaspoon garlic powder
½ teaspoon Old Bay seasoning
75 g plain bread crumbs
Cooking spray

1. Preheat the Ninja Foodi cooker to 200°C. 2. Put all the ingredients except the bread crumbs and oil in a large bowl and stir to incorporate. 3. Scoop out the prawn mixture and shape into 8 equal-sized patties with your hands, no more than ½-inch thick. Roll the patties in the bread crumbs on a plate and spray both sides with cooking spray. 4. Place the patties in the cook & crisp basket. You may need to work in batches to avoid overcrowding. 5. Air crisp for 10 to 12 minutes, flipping the patties halfway through, or until the outside is crispy brown. 6. Divide the patties among four plates and serve warm.

Cajun Cod Fillet

Prep time: 10 minutes | Cook time: 4 minutes | Serves 2

280 g cod fillet
1 tablespoon olive oil
1 teaspoon Cajun seasoning
2 tablespoons coconut aminos

1. Sprinkle the cod fillet with coconut aminos and Cajun seasoning. 2. Then heat up olive oil in the Ninja Foodi cooker on Sauté mode. 3. Add the spiced cod fillet and cook it for 4 minutes from each side. 4. Then cut it into halves and sprinkle with the oily liquid from the Ninja Foodi cooker.

Savory Prawns

Prep time: 5 minutes | Cook time: 8 to 10 minutes | Serves 4

455 g fresh large prawns, peeled and deveined
1 tablespoon avocado oil
2 teaspoons minced garlic, divided
½ teaspoon red pepper flakes
Sea salt and freshly ground black pepper, to taste
2 tablespoons unsalted butter, melted
2 tablespoons chopped fresh parsley

1. Place the prawns in a large bowl and toss with the avocado oil, 1 teaspoon of minced garlic, and red pepper flakes. Season with salt and pepper. 2. Set the Ninja Foodi cooker to 175°C. Arrange the prawns in a single layer in the cook & crisp basket, working in batches if necessary. Cook for 6 minutes. Flip the prawns and cook for 2 to 4 minutes more, until the internal temperature of the prawns reaches 50°C. (The time it takes to cook will depend on the size of the prawns.) 3. While the prawns are cooking, melt the butter in a small saucepan over medium heat and stir in the remaining 1 teaspoon of garlic. 4. Transfer the cooked prawns to a large bowl, add the garlic butter, and toss well. Top with the parsley and serve warm.

Cucumber and Salmon Salad

Prep time: 10 minutes | Cook time: 8 to 10 minutes | Serves 2

455 g salmon fillet
1½ tablespoons olive oil, divided
1 tablespoon sherry vinegar
1 tablespoon capers, rinsed and drained
1 seedless cucumber, thinly sliced
¼ white onion, thinly sliced
2 tablespoons chopped fresh parsley
Salt and freshly ground black pepper, to taste

1. Preheat the Ninja Foodi cooker to 205°C. 2. Lightly coat the salmon with ½ tablespoon of the olive oil. Place skin-side down in the cook & crisp basket and air crisp for 8 to 10 minutes until the fish is opaque and flakes easily with a fork. Transfer the salmon to a plate and let cool to room temperature. Remove the skin and carefully flake the fish into bite-size chunks. 3. In a small bowl, whisk the remaining 1 tablespoon olive oil and the vinegar until thoroughly combined. Add the flaked fish, capers, cucumber, onion, and parsley. Season to taste with salt and freshly ground black pepper. Toss gently to coat. Serve immediately or cover and refrigerate for up to 4 hours.

Tuna-Stuffed Tomatoes

Prep time: 5 minutes | Cook time: 5 minutes | Serves 2

2 medium beefsteak tomatoes, tops removed, seeded, membranes removed
2 (75 g) g tuna fillets packed in water, drained
1 medium stalk celery, trimmed and chopped
2 tablespoons mayonnaise
¼ teaspoon salt
¼ teaspoon ground black pepper
2 teaspoons coconut oil
25 g shredded mild Cheddar cheese

1. Scoop pulp out of each tomato, leaving ½-inch shell. 2. In a medium bowl, mix tuna, celery, mayonnaise, salt, and pepper. Drizzle with coconut oil. Spoon ½ mixture into each tomato and top each with 2 tablespoons Cheddar. 3. Place tomatoes into ungreased cook & crisp basket. Adjust the temperature to 160°C and air crisp for 5 minutes. Cheese will be melted when done. Serve warm.

Braised Striped Bass with Courgette and Tomatoes

Prep time: 20 minutes | Cook time: 16 minutes | Serves 4

2 tablespoons extra-virgin olive oil, divided, plus extra for drizzling
3 courgette (230 g each), halved lengthwise and sliced ¼ inch thick
1 onion, chopped
¾ teaspoon table salt, divided
3 garlic cloves, minced
1 teaspoon minced fresh oregano or ¼ teaspoon dried
¼ teaspoon red pepper flakes

1 (800 g) can whole peeled tomatoes, drained with juice reserved, halved
680 g skinless striped bass, 1½ inches thick, cut into 2-inch pieces
¼ teaspoon pepper
2 tablespoons chopped pitted kalamata olives
2 tablespoons shredded fresh mint

1. Using highest sauté function, heat 1 tablespoon oil in Ninja Foodi cooker for 5 minutes (or until just smoking). Add courgette and cook until tender, about 5 minutes; transfer to bowl and set aside. 2. Add remaining 1 tablespoon oil, onion, and ¼ teaspoon salt to now-empty pot and cook, using highest sauté function, until onion is softened, about 5 minutes. Stir in garlic, oregano, and pepper flakes and cook until fragrant, about 30 seconds. Stir in tomatoes and reserved juice. 3. Sprinkle bass with remaining ½ teaspoon salt and pepper. Nestle bass into tomato mixture and spoon some of cooking liquid on top of pieces. Lock lid in place and close pressure release valve. Select high pressure and set cook time for 0 minutes. Once Ninja Foodi cooker has reached pressure, immediately turn off pot and quick-release pressure. Carefully remove lid, allowing steam to escape away from you. 4. Transfer bass to plate, tent with aluminium foil, and let rest while finishing vegetables. Stir courgette into pot and let sit until heated through, about 5 minutes. Stir in olives and season with salt and pepper to taste. Serve bass with vegetables, sprinkling individual portions with mint and drizzling with extra oil.

Poached Salmon

Prep time: 10 minutes | Cook time: 5 minutes | Serves 4

1 lemon, sliced ¼ inch thick
4 (170 g) skinless salmon fillets, 1½ inches thick
½ teaspoon table salt
¼ teaspoon pepper

1. Add 120 ml water to Ninja Foodi cooker. Fold sheet of aluminium foil into 16 by 6-inch sling. Arrange lemon slices widthwise in 2 rows across center of sling. Sprinkle flesh side of salmon with salt and pepper, then arrange skinned side down on top of lemon slices. 2. Using sling, lower salmon into Ninja Foodi cooker; allow narrow edges of sling to rest along sides of insert. Lock lid in place and close pressure release valve. Select high pressure and cook for 3 minutes. 3. Turn off Ninja Foodi cooker and quick-release pressure. Carefully remove lid, allowing steam to escape away from you. Using sling, transfer salmon to large plate. Gently lift and tilt fillets with spatula to remove lemon slices. Serve.

South Indian Fried Fish

Prep time: 20 minutes | Cook time: 8 minutes | Serves 4

2 tablespoons olive oil
2 tablespoons fresh lime or lemon juice
1 teaspoon minced fresh ginger
1 clove garlic, minced
1 teaspoon ground turmeric
½ teaspoon kosher or coarse sea

salt
¼ to ½ teaspoon cayenne pepper
455 g tilapia fillets (2 to 3 fillets)
Olive oil spray
Lime or lemon wedges (optional)

1. In a large bowl, combine the oil, lime juice, ginger, garlic, turmeric, salt, and cayenne. Stir until well combined; set aside. 2. Cut each tilapia fillet into three or four equal-size pieces. Add the fish to the bowl and gently mix until all of the fish is coated in the marinade. Marinate for 10 to 15 minutes at room temperature. (Don't marinate any longer or the acid in the lime juice will "cook" the fish.) 3. Spray the cook & crisp basket with olive oil spray. Place the fish in the basket and spray the fish. Set the Ninja Foodi cooker to 165°C for 3 minutes to partially cook the fish. Set the Ninja Foodi cooker to 205°C for 5 minutes to finish cooking and crisp up the fish. (Thinner pieces of fish will cook faster so you may want to check at the 3-minute mark of the second cooking time and remove those that are cooked through, and then add them back toward the end of the second cooking time to crisp.) 4. Carefully remove the fish from the basket. Serve hot, with lemon wedges if desired.

Sesame-Crusted Tuna Steak

Prep time: 5 minutes | Cook time: 8 minutes | Serves 2

2 tuna steaks, 170 g each
1 tablespoon coconut oil, melted
½ teaspoon garlic powder

2 teaspoons white sesame seeds
2 teaspoons black sesame seeds

1. Brush each tuna steak with coconut oil and sprinkle with garlic powder. 2. In a large bowl, mix sesame seeds and then press each tuna steak into them, covering the steak as completely as possible. Place tuna steaks into the cook & crisp basket. 3. Adjust the temperature to 205°C and air crisp for 8 minutes. 4. Flip the steaks halfway through the cooking time. Steaks will be well-done at 65°C internal temperature. Serve warm.

Louisiana Prawn Gumbo

Prep time: 10 minutes | Cook time: 4 minutes | Serves 6

450 g prawn
60 ml chopped celery stalk
1 chili pepper, chopped
60 ml chopped okra

1 tablespoon coconut oil
480 ml chicken broth
1 teaspoon sugar-free tomato paste

1. Put all ingredients in the Ninja Foodi cooker and stir until you get a light red colour. 2. Then close and seal the lid. 3. Cook the meal on High Pressure for 4 minutes. 4. When the time is finished, allow the natural pressure release for 10 minutes.

Chunky Fish Soup with Tomatoes

Prep time: 10 minutes | Cook time: 8 minutes | Serves 4

2 teaspoons olive oil
1 brown onion, chopped
1 bell pepper, sliced
1 celery, diced
2 garlic cloves, minced
720 ml fish stock
2 ripe tomatoes, crushed

340 g haddock fillets
240 ml prawn
1 tablespoon sweet Hungarian paprika
1 teaspoon hot Hungarian paprika
½ teaspoon caraway seeds

1. Set the Ninja Foodi cooker to Sauté. Add and heat the oil. Once hot, add the onions and sauté until soft and fragrant. 2. Add the pepper, celery, and garlic and continue to sauté until soft. 3. Stir in the remaining ingredients. 4. Lock the lid. Set the cooking time for 5 minutes at High Pressure. 5. When the timer beeps, perform a quick pressure release. Carefully remove the lid. 6. Divide into serving bowls and serve hot.

Salmon Fritters with Courgette

Prep time: 15 minutes | Cook time: 12 minutes | Serves 4

2 tablespoons almond flour
1 courgette, grated
1 egg, beaten

170 g salmon fillet, diced
1 teaspoon avocado oil
½ teaspoon ground black pepper

1. Mix almond flour with courgette, egg, salmon, and ground black pepper. 2. Then make the fritters from the salmon mixture. 3. Sprinkle the cook & crisp basket with avocado oil and put the fritters inside. 4. Cook the fritters at 190ºC for 6 minutes per side.

Coconut Prawns with Pineapple-Lemon Sauce

Prep time: 10 minutes | Cook time: 18 minutes | Serves 4

100 g light brown sugar
2 teaspoons cornflour
⅛ teaspoon plus ½ teaspoon salt, divided
110 g crushed pineapple with syrup
2 tablespoons freshly squeezed lemon juice
1 tablespoon yellow mustard

680 g raw large prawns, peeled and deveined
2 eggs
60 g plain flour
95 g desiccated, unsweetened coconut
¼ teaspoon garlic granules
Olive oil spray

1. In a medium saucepan over medium heat, combine the brown sugar, cornflour, and ⅛ teaspoon of salt. 2. As the brown sugar mixture melts into a sauce, stir in the crushed pineapple with syrup, lemon juice, and mustard. Cook for about 4 minutes until the mixture thickens and begins to boil. Boil for 1 minute. Remove the pan from the heat, set aside, and let cool while you make the prawns. 3. Put the prawns on a plate and pat them dry with paper towels. 4. In a small bowl, whisk the eggs. 5. In a medium bowl,

stir together the flour, desiccated coconut, remaining ½ teaspoon of salt, and garlic granules. 6. Insert the crisper plate into the basket and the basket into the unit. Preheat the unit to 205ºC. 7. Dip the prawns into the egg and into the coconut mixture to coat. 8. Once the unit is preheated, place a baking paper liner into the basket. Place the coated prawns on the liner in a single layer and spray them with olive oil. 9. After 6 minutes, remove the basket, flip the prawns, and spray them with more olive oil. Reinsert the basket to resume cooking. Check the prawns after 3 minutes more. If browned, they are done; if not, resume cooking. 10. When the cooking is complete, serve with the prepared pineapple sauce.

Mackerel with Spinach

Prep time: 15 minutes | Cook time: 20 minutes | Serves 5

455 g mackerel, trimmed
1 bell pepper, chopped
15 g spinach, chopped

1 tablespoon avocado oil
1 teaspoon ground black pepper
1 teaspoon tomato paste

1. In the mixing bowl, mix bell pepper with spinach, ground black pepper, and tomato paste. 2. Fill the mackerel with spinach mixture. 3. Then brush the fish with avocado oil and put it in the Ninja Foodi cooker. 4. Cook the fish at 185ºC for 20 minutes.

Clam Chowder with Bacon and Celery

Prep time: 10 minutes | Cook time: 4 minutes | Serves 2

140 g clams
30 g bacon, chopped
85 g celery, chopped

120 ml water
120 ml double cream

1. Cook the bacon on Sauté mode for 1 minute. 2. Then add clams, celery, water, and double cream. 3. Close and seal the lid. 4. Cook the seafood on steam mode (High Pressure) for 3 minutes. Make a quick pressure release. 5. Ladle the clams with the double cream mixture in the bowls.

Italian Baked Cod

Prep time: 5 minutes | Cook time: 12 minutes | Serves 4

4 cod fillets, 170 g each
2 tablespoons salted butter, melted
1 teaspoon Italian seasoning

¼ teaspoon salt
120 ml tomato-based pasta sauce

1. Place cod into an ungreased round nonstick baking dish. Pour butter over cod and sprinkle with Italian seasoning and salt. Top with pasta sauce. 2. Place dish into cook & crisp basket. Adjust the temperature to 175ºC and bake for 12 minutes. Fillets will be lightly browned, easily flake, and have an internal temperature of at least 65ºC when done. Serve warm.

Baked Tilapia with Garlic Aioli

Prep time: 5 minutes | Cook time: 15 minutes | Serves 4

Tilapia:
4 tilapia fillets
1 tablespoon extra-virgin olive oil
1 teaspoon garlic powder
1 teaspoon paprika
1 teaspoon dried basil
A pinch of lemon-pepper

seasoning
Garlic Aioli:
2 garlic cloves, minced
1 tablespoon mayonnaise
Juice of ½ lemon
1 teaspoon extra-virgin olive oil
Salt and pepper, to taste

1. Preheat the Ninja Foodi cooker to 205ºC. 2. On a clean work surface, brush both sides of each fillet with the olive oil. Sprinkle with the garlic powder, paprika, basil, and lemon-pepper seasoning. 3. Place the fillets in the cook & crisp basket and bake for 15 minutes, flipping the fillets halfway through, or until the fish flakes easily and is no longer translucent in the center. 4. Meanwhile, make the garlic aioli: Whisk together the garlic, mayo, lemon juice, olive oil, salt, and pepper in a small bowl until smooth. 5. Remove the fish from the basket and serve with the garlic aioli on the side.

Rosemary Baked Haddock

Prep time: 7 minutes | Cook time: 10 minutes | Serves 2

2 eggs, beaten
340 g haddock fillet, chopped
1 tablespoon cream cheese

¾ teaspoon dried rosemary
60 g Parmesan, grated
1 teaspoon butter

1. Whisk the beaten eggs until homogenous. Add the cream cheese, dried rosemary, and dill. 2. Grease the springform with the butter and place the haddock inside. 3. Pour the egg mixture over the fish and add sprinkle with Parmesan. 4. Set the High Pressure and cook for 5 minutes. Then make a natural release pressure for 5 minutes.

Garlic Tuna Casserole

Prep time: 7 minutes | Cook time: 9 minutes | Serves 4

240 ml grated Parmesan or shredded Cheddar cheese, plus more for topping
1 (230 g) package cream cheese (240 ml), softened
120 ml chicken broth
1 tablespoon unsalted butter
½ small head cauliflower, cut into 1-inch pieces
240 ml diced onions

2 cloves garlic, minced, or more to taste
2 (110 g) cans chunk tuna packed in water, drained
360 ml cold water
For Garnish:
Chopped fresh flat-leaf parsley
Sliced spring onions
Cherry tomatoes, halved
Ground black pepper

1. In a blender, add the Parmesan cheese, cream cheese, and broth and blitz until smooth. Set aside. 2. Set your Ninja Foodi cooker to Sauté. Add and melt the butter. Add the cauliflower and onions and sauté for 4 minutes, or until the onions are softened. Fold in the garlic and sauté for an additional 1 minute. 3. Place the cheese sauce and tuna in a large bowl. Mix in the veggies and stir well. Transfer the mixture to a casserole dish. 4. Place a reversible rack in the bottom of your Ninja Foodi cooker and add the cold water. Use a foil sling, lower the casserole dish onto the reversible rack. Tuck in the sides of the sling. 5. Lock the lid. Set the cooking time for 5 minutes for al dente cauliflower or 8 minutes for softer cauliflower at High Pressure. 6. Once cooking is complete, do a quick pressure release. Carefully open the lid. 7. Serve topped with the cheese and garnished with the parsley, spring onions, cherry tomatoes, and freshly ground pepper.

Trout Casserole

Prep time: 5 minutes | Cook time: 10 minutes | Serves 3

360 ml water
1½ tablespoons olive oil
3 plum tomatoes, sliced
½ teaspoon dried oregano
1 teaspoon dried basil
3 trout fillets
½ teaspoon cayenne pepper, or

more to taste
⅓ teaspoon black pepper
Salt, to taste
1 bay leaf
240 ml shredded Monterey Jack cheese

1. Pour the water into your Ninja Foodi cooker and insert a reversible rack. 2. Grease a baking dish with the olive oil. Add the tomatoes slices to the baking dish and sprinkle with the oregano and basil. 3. Add the fish fillets and season with the cayenne pepper, black pepper, and salt. Add the bay leaf. Lower the baking dish onto the reversible rack. 4. Lock the lid. Set the cooking time for 10 minutes at High Pressure. 5. When the timer beeps, perform a quick pressure release. Carefully remove the lid. 6. Scatter the Monterey Jack cheese on top, lock the lid, and allow the cheese to melt. 7. Serve warm.

Aromatic Monkfish Stew

Prep time: 5 minutes | Cook time: 6 minutes | Serves 6

Juice of 1 lemon
1 tablespoon fresh basil
1 tablespoon fresh parsley
1 tablespoon olive oil
1 teaspoon garlic, minced
680 g monkfish
1 tablespoon butter
1 bell pepper, chopped
1 onion, sliced
½ teaspoon cayenne pepper

½ teaspoon mixed peppercorns
¼ teaspoon turmeric powder
¼ teaspoon ground cumin
Sea salt and ground black pepper, to taste
480 ml fish stock
120 ml water
60 ml dry white wine
2 bay leaves
1 ripe tomato, crushed

1. Stir together the lemon juice, basil, parsley, olive oil, and garlic in a ceramic dish. Add the monkfish and marinate for 30 minutes. 2. Set your Ninja Foodi cooker to Sauté. Add and melt the butter. Once hot, cook the bell pepper and onion until fragrant. 3. Stir in the remaining ingredients. 4. Lock the lid. Set the cooking time for 6 minutes at High Pressure. 5. When the timer beeps, perform a quick pressure release. Carefully remove the lid. 6. Discard the bay leaves and divide your stew into serving bowls. Serve hot.

Scallops with Asparagus and Peas

Prep time: 10 minutes | Cook time: 7 to 10 minutes | Serves 4

Cooking oil spray
455 g asparagus, ends trimmed, cut into 2-inch pieces
100 g sugar snap peas
455 g sea scallops
1 tablespoon freshly squeezed
lemon juice
2 teaspoons extra-virgin olive oil
½ teaspoon dried thyme
Salt and freshly ground black pepper, to taste

1. Insert the crisper plate into the basket and the basket into the unit. Preheat the unit to 205ºC. 2. Once the unit is preheated, spray the crisper plate with cooking oil. Place the asparagus and sugar snap peas into the basket. 3. Cook for 10 minutes. 4. Meanwhile, check the scallops for a small muscle attached to the side. Pull it off and discard. In a medium bowl, toss together the scallops, lemon juice, olive oil, and thyme. Season with salt and pepper. 5. After 3 minutes, the vegetables should be just starting to get tender. Place the scallops on top of the vegetables. Reinsert the basket to resume cooking. After 3 minutes more, remove the basket and shake it. Again reinsert the basket to resume cooking. 6. When the cooking is complete, the scallops should be firm when tested with your finger and opaque in the center, and the vegetables tender. Serve immediately.

Fish Tagine

Prep time: 25 minutes | Cook time: 12 minutes | Serves 4

2 tablespoons extra-virgin olive oil, plus extra for drizzling
1 large onion, halved and sliced ¼ inch thick
450 g carrots, peeled, halved lengthwise, and sliced ¼ inch thick
2 (2-inch) strips orange zest, plus 1 teaspoon grated zest
¾ teaspoon table salt, divided
2 tablespoons tomato paste
4 garlic cloves, minced, divided
1¼ teaspoons paprika
1 teaspoon ground cumin
¼ teaspoon red pepper flakes
¼ teaspoon saffron threads, crumbled
1 (230 g) bottle clam juice
680 g skinless halibut fillets, 1½ inches thick, cut into 2-inch pieces
60 ml pitted oil-cured black olives, quartered
2 tablespoons chopped fresh parsley
1 teaspoon sherry vinegar

1. Using highest sauté function, heat oil in Ninja Foodi cooker until shimmering. Add onion, carrots, orange zest strips, and ¼ teaspoon salt, and cook until vegetables are softened and lightly browned, 10 to 12 minutes. Stir in tomato paste, three-quarters of garlic, paprika, cumin, pepper flakes, and saffron and cook until fragrant, about 30 seconds. Stir in clam juice, scraping up any browned bits. 2. Sprinkle halibut with remaining ½ teaspoon salt. Nestle halibut into onion mixture and spoon some of cooking liquid on top of pieces. Lock lid in place and close pressure release valve. Select high pressure and set cook time for 0 minutes. Once Ninja Foodi cooker has reached pressure, immediately turn off pot and quick-release pressure. 3. Discard orange zest. Gently stir in olives, parsley, vinegar, grated orange zest, and remaining garlic. Season with salt and pepper to taste. Drizzle extra oil over individual portions before serving.

Steamed Cod with Garlic and Swiss Chard

Prep time: 5 minutes | Cook time: 12 minutes | Serves 4

1 teaspoon salt
½ teaspoon dried oregano
½ teaspoon dried thyme
½ teaspoon garlic powder
4 cod fillets
½ white onion, thinly sliced
135 g Swiss chard, washed, stemmed, and torn into pieces
60 ml olive oil
1 lemon, quartered

1. Preheat the Ninja Foodi cooker to 190ºC. 2. In a small bowl, whisk together the salt, oregano, thyme, and garlic powder. 3. Tear off four pieces of aluminum foil, with each sheet being large enough to envelop one cod fillet and a quarter of the vegetables. 4. Place a cod fillet in the middle of each sheet of foil, then sprinkle on all sides with the spice mixture. 5. In each foil packet, place a quarter of the onion slices and 30 g Swiss chard, then drizzle 1 tablespoon olive oil and squeeze ¼ lemon over the contents of each foil packet. 6. Fold and seal the sides of the foil packets and then place them into the cook & crisp basket. Steam for 12 minutes. 7. Remove from the basket, and carefully open each packet to avoid a steam burn.

Fish Taco Bowl

Prep time: 10 minutes | Cook time: 12 minutes | Serves 4

½ teaspoon salt
¼ teaspoon garlic powder
¼ teaspoon ground cumin
4 cod fillets, 110 g each
360 g finely shredded green
cabbage
735 g mayonnaise
¼ teaspoon ground black pepper
20 g chopped pickled jalapeños

1. Sprinkle salt, garlic powder, and cumin over cod and place into ungreased cook & crisp basket. Adjust the temperature to 175ºC and air crisp for 12 minutes, turning fillets halfway through cooking. Cod will flake easily and have an internal temperature of at least 65ºC when done. 2. In a large bowl, toss cabbage with mayonnaise, pepper, and jalapeños until fully coated. Serve cod warm over cabbage slaw on four medium plates.

Flounder Meuniere

Prep time: 15 minutes | Cook time: 10 minutes | Serves 4

450 g flounder fillet
½ teaspoon ground black pepper
½ teaspoon salt
120 ml almond flour
2 tablespoons olive oil
1 tablespoon lemon juice
1 teaspoon chopped fresh parsley

1. Cut the fish fillets into 4 servings and sprinkle with salt, ground black pepper, and lemon juice. 2. Heat up the Ninja Foodi cooker on Sauté mode for 2 minutes and add olive oil. 3. Coat the flounder fillets in the almond flour and put them in the hot olive oil. 4. Sauté the fish fillets for 4 minutes and then flip on another side. 5. Cook the meal for 3 minutes more or until it is golden brown. 6. Sprinkle the cooked flounder with the fresh parsley.

Prawn Courgette Noodle Alfredo

Prep time: 10 minutes | Cook time: 10 minutes | Serves 4

280 g salmon fillet (2 fillets)
110 g Mozzarella, sliced
4 cherry tomatoes, sliced
1 teaspoon sweetener
1 teaspoon dried basil

½ teaspoon ground black pepper
1 tablespoon apple cider vinegar
1 tablespoon butter
240 ml water, for cooking

1. Melt the butter on Sauté mode and add prawn. 2. Sprinkle them with seafood seasoning and sauté then for 2 minutes. 3. After this, spiralizer the courgette with the help of the spiralizer and add in the prawn. 4. Add coconut cream and close the lid. Cook the meal on Sauté mode for 8 minutes.

Tuna Nuggets in Hoisin Sauce

Prep time: 15 minutes | Cook time: 5 to 7 minutes | Serves 4

120 ml hoisin sauce
2 tablespoons rice wine vinegar
2 teaspoons sesame oil
1 teaspoon garlic powder
2 teaspoons dried lemongrass
¼ teaspoon red pepper flakes

½ small onion, quartered and thinly sliced
230 g fresh tuna, cut into 1-inch cubes
Cooking spray
560 g cooked jasmine rice

1. Mix the hoisin sauce, vinegar, sesame oil, and seasonings together. 2. Stir in the onions and tuna nuggets. 3. Spray a baking pan with nonstick spray and pour in tuna mixture. 4. Roast at 200ºC for 3 minutes. Stir gently. 5. Cook 2 minutes and stir again, checking for doneness. Tuna should be barely cooked through, just beginning to flake and still very moist. If necessary, continue cooking and stirring in 1-minute intervals until done. 6. Serve warm over hot jasmine rice.

Cod Fillets with Cherry Tomatoes

Prep time: 2 minutes | Cook time: 15 minutes | Serves 4

2 tablespoons butter
60 ml diced onion
1 clove garlic, minced
240 ml cherry tomatoes, halved
60 ml chicken broth
¼ teaspoon dried thyme

¼ teaspoon salt
⅛ teaspoon pepper
4 (110 g) cod fillets
240 ml water
60 ml fresh chopped Italian parsley

1. Set your Ninja Foodi cooker to Sauté. Add and melt the butter. Once hot, add the onions and cook until softened. Add the garlic and cook for another 30 seconds. 2. Add the tomatoes, chicken broth, thyme, salt, and pepper. Continue to cook for 5 to 7 minutes, or until the tomatoes start to soften. 3. Pour the sauce into a glass bowl. Add the fish fillets. Cover with foil. 4. Pour the water into the Ninja Foodi cooker and insert a reversible rack. Place the bowl on top. 5. Lock the lid. Set the cooking time for 3 minutes at Low Pressure. 6. Once cooking is complete, do a quick pressure release. Carefully open the lid. 7. Sprinkle with the fresh parsley and serve.

Fish Cakes

Prep time: 30 minutes | Cook time: 10 to 12 minutes | Serves 4

1 large russet potato, mashed
340 g cod or other white fish
Salt and pepper, to taste
Olive or vegetable oil for misting or cooking spray
1 large egg

50 g potato starch
60 g panko breadcrumbs
1 tablespoon fresh chopped chives
2 tablespoons minced onion

1. Peel potatoes, cut into cubes, and cook on stovetop till soft. 2. Salt and pepper raw fish to taste. Mist with oil or cooking spray, and air crisp at 180ºC for 6 to 8 minutes, until fish flakes easily. If fish is crowded, rearrange halfway through cooking to ensure all pieces cook evenly. 3. Transfer fish to a plate and break apart to cool. 4. Beat egg in a shallow dish. 5. Place potato starch in another shallow dish, and panko crumbs in a third dish. 6. When potatoes are done, drain in colander and rinse with cold water. 7. In a large bowl, mash the potatoes and stir in the chives and onion. Add salt and pepper to taste, then stir in the fish. 8. If needed, stir in a tablespoon of the beaten egg to help bind the mixture. 9. Shape into 8 small, fat patties. Dust lightly with potato starch, dip in egg, and roll in panko crumbs. Spray both sides with oil or cooking spray. 10. Air crisp for 10 to 12 minutes, until golden brown and crispy.

One-Pot Prawn Fried Rice

Prep time: 10 minutes | Cook time: 25 minutes | Serves 4

Prawns:
1 teaspoon cornflour
½ teaspoon kosher or coarse sea salt
¼ teaspoon black pepper
455 g jumbo raw prawns (21 to 25 count), peeled and deveined
Rice:
200 g cold cooked rice
140 g frozen peas and carrots, thawed
235 g chopped spring onions

(white and green parts)
3 tablespoons toasted sesame oil
1 tablespoon soy sauce
½ teaspoon kosher or coarse sea salt
1 teaspoon black pepper
Eggs:
2 large eggs, beaten
¼ teaspoon kosher or coarse sea salt
¼ teaspoon black pepper

1. For the prawns: In a small bowl, whisk together the cornflour, salt, and pepper until well combined. Place the prawns in a large bowl and sprinkle the seasoned cornflour over. Toss until well coated; set aside. 2. For the rice: In a baking pan, combine the rice, peas and carrots, spring onions, sesame oil, soy sauce, salt, and pepper. Toss and stir until well combined. 3. Place the pan in the cook & crisp basket. Set the Ninja Foodi cooker to 175ºC for 15 minutes, stirring and tossing the rice halfway through the cooking time. 4. Place the prawns on top of the rice. Cook for 5 minutes. 5. Meanwhile, for the eggs: In a medium bowl, beat the eggs with the salt and pepper. 6. Open the Ninja Foodi cooker and pour the eggs over the prawns and rice mixture. Cook for 5 minutes. 7. Remove the pan from the Ninja Foodi cooker. Stir to break up the rice and mix in the eggs and prawns.

Turmeric Salmon

Prep time: 10 minutes | Cook time: 4 minutes | Serves 3

450 g salmon fillet
1 teaspoon ground black pepper
½ teaspoon salt
1 teaspoon ground turmeric
1 teaspoon lemon juice
240 ml water

1. In the shallow bowl, mix up salt, ground black pepper, and ground turmeric. 2. Sprinkle the salmon fillet with lemon juice and rub with the spice mixture. 3. Then pour water in the Ninja Foodi cooker and insert the steamer rack. 4. Wrap the salmon fillet in the foil and place it on the rack. 5. Close and seal the lid. 6. Cook the fish on High Pressure for 4 minutes. 7. Make a quick pressure release and cut the fish on servings.

Fried Catfish Fillets

Prep time: 10 minutes | Cook time: 20 minutes | Serves 4

1 egg
100 g finely ground cornmeal
30 g plain flour
¾ teaspoon salt
1 teaspoon paprika
1 teaspoon Old Bay seasoning
¼ teaspoon garlic powder
¼ teaspoon freshly ground black pepper
4 140 g catfish fillets, halved crosswise
Olive oil spray

1. In a shallow bowl, beat the egg with 2 tablespoons water. 2. On a plate, stir together the cornmeal, flour, salt, paprika, Old Bay, garlic powder, and pepper. 3. Dip the fish into the egg mixture and into the cornmeal mixture to coat. Press the cornmeal mixture into the fish and gently shake off any excess. 4. Insert the crisper plate into the basket and the basket into the unit to 205°C. 5. Once the unit is preheated, place a baking paper liner into the basket. Place the coated fish on the liner and spray it with olive oil.. 6. Cook for 10 minutes, remove the basket and spray the fish with olive oil. Flip the fish and spray the other side with olive oil. Reinsert the basket to resume cooking. Check the fish after 7 minutes more. If the fish is golden and crispy and registers at least 65°C on a food thermometer, it is ready. If not, resume cooking. 8. When the cooking is complete, serve.

Sea Bass with Avocado Cream

Prep time: 30 minutes | Cook time: 9 minutes | Serves 4

Fish Fillets:
1½ tablespoons balsamic vinegar
120 ml vegetable broth
⅓ teaspoon shallot powder
1 tablespoon coconut aminos, or tamari
4 Sea Bass fillets
1 teaspoon ground black pepper
1½ tablespoons olive oil
Fine sea salt, to taste
⅓ teaspoon garlic powder
Avocado Cream:
2 tablespoons Greek-style yogurt
1 clove garlic, peeled and minced
1 teaspoon ground black pepper
½ tablespoon olive oil
80 ml vegetable broth
1 avocado
½ teaspoon lime juice

⅓ teaspoon fine sea salt

1. In a bowl, wash and pat the fillets dry using some paper towels. Add all the seasonings. In another bowl, stir in the remaining ingredients for the fish fillets. 2. Add the seasoned fish fillets; cover and let the fillets marinate in your refrigerator at least 3 hours. 3. Then, set the Ninja Foodi cooker to 165°C. Cook marinated sea bass fillets in the Ninja Foodi cooker grill basket for 9 minutes. 4. In the meantime, prepare the avocado sauce by mixing all the ingredients with an immersion blender or regular blender. Serve the sea bass fillets topped with the avocado sauce. Enjoy!

Crispy Herbed Salmon

Prep time: 5 minutes | Cook time: 9 to 12 minutes | Serves 4

4 skinless salmon fillets, 170 g each
3 tablespoons honey mustard
½ teaspoon dried thyme
½ teaspoon dried basil
15 g panko bread crumbs
30 g crushed ready salted crisps
2 tablespoons olive oil

1. Place the salmon on a plate. In a small bowl, combine the mustard, thyme, and basil, and spread evenly over the salmon. 2. In another small bowl, combine the bread crumbs and crisps and mix well. Drizzle in the olive oil and mix until combined. 3. Place the salmon in the cook & crisp basket and gently but firmly press the bread crumb mixture onto the top of each fillet. 4. Bake at 160°C for 9 to 12 minutes or until the salmon reaches at least 65°C on a meat thermometer and the topping is browned and crisp.

Salmon Burgers with Creamy Broccoli Slaw

Prep time: 15 minutes | Cook time: 10 minutes | Serves 4

For the salmon burgers
455 g salmon fillets, bones and skin removed
1 egg
10 g fresh dill, chopped
60 g fresh whole wheat bread crumbs
½ teaspoon salt
½ teaspoon cayenne pepper
2 garlic cloves, minced
4 whole wheat buns

For the broccoli slaw
270 g chopped or shredded broccoli
25 g shredded carrots
30 g sunflower seeds
2 garlic cloves, minced
½ teaspoon salt
2 tablespoons apple cider vinegar
285 g nonfat plain Greek yogurt

Make the salmon burgers 1. Preheat the Ninja Foodi cooker to 180°C. 2. In a food processor, pulse the salmon fillets until they are finely chopped. 3. In a large bowl, combine the chopped salmon, egg, dill, bread crumbs, salt, cayenne, and garlic until it comes together. 4. Form the salmon into 4 patties. Place them into the cook & crisp basket, making sure that they don't touch each other. 5. Bake for 5 minutes. Flip the salmon patties and bake for 5 minutes more. Make the broccoli slaw 6. In a large bowl, combine all of the ingredients for the broccoli slaw. Mix well. 7. Serve the salmon burgers on toasted whole wheat buns, and top with a generous portion of broccoli slaw.

Crispy Fish Sticks

Prep time: 15 minutes | Cook time: 10 minutes | Serves 4

30 g crushed panko breadcrumbs
25 g blanched finely ground almond flour
½ teaspoon Old Bay seasoning
1 tablespoon coconut oil
1 large egg
455 g cod fillet, cut into ¾-inch strips

1. Place panko, almond flour, Old Bay seasoning, and coconut oil into a large bowl and mix together. In a medium bowl, whisk egg. 2. Dip each fish stick into the egg and then gently press into the flour mixture, coating as fully and evenly as possible. Place fish sticks into the cook & crisp basket. 3. Adjust the temperature to 205°C and air crisp for 10 minutes or until golden. 4. Serve immediately.

Snapper in Spicy Tomato Sauce

Prep time: 5 minutes | Cook time: 5 minutes | Serves 6

2 teaspoons coconut oil, melted
1 teaspoon celery seeds
½ teaspoon fresh grated ginger
½ teaspoon cumin seeds
1 brown onion, chopped
2 cloves garlic, minced
680 g snapper fillets
180 ml vegetable broth
1 (110 g) can fire-roasted diced tomatoes
1 bell pepper, sliced
1 jalapeño pepper, minced
Sea salt and ground black pepper, to taste
¼ teaspoon chili flakes
½ teaspoon turmeric powder

1. Set the Ninja Foodi cooker to Sauté. Add and heat the sesame oil until hot. Sauté the celery seeds, fresh ginger, and cumin seeds. 2. Add the onion and continue to sauté until softened and fragrant. 3. Mix in the minced garlic and continue to cook for 30 seconds. Add the remaining ingredients and stir well. 4. Lock the lid. Set the cooking time for 3 minutes at Low Pressure. 5. When the timer beeps, perform a quick pressure release. Carefully remove the lid. 6. Serve warm

Fish Bake with Veggies

Prep time: 10 minutes | Cook time: 5 minutes | Serves 4

360 ml water
Cooking spray
2 ripe tomatoes, sliced
2 cloves garlic, minced
1 teaspoon dried oregano
1 teaspoon dried basil
½ teaspoon dried rosemary
1 red onion, sliced
1 head cauliflower, cut into florets
450 g tilapia fillets, sliced
Sea salt, to taste
1 tablespoon olive oil
240 ml crumbled feta cheese
80 ml Kalamata olives, pitted and halved

1. Pour the water into your Ninja Foodi cooker and insert a reversible rack. 2. Spritz a casserole dish with cooking spray. Add the tomato slices to the dish. Scatter the top with the garlic, oregano, basil, and rosemary. 3. Mix in the onion and cauliflower. Arrange the fish fillets on top. Sprinkle with the salt and drizzle with the olive oil. 4. Place the feta cheese and Kalamata olives on top. Lower the dish onto the reversible rack. 5. Lock the lid. Set the cooking time for 5 minutes at High Pressure. 6. When the timer beeps, perform a quick pressure release. Carefully remove the lid. 7. Allow to cool for 5 minutes before serving.

Fried Prawns

Prep time: 15 minutes | Cook time: 5 minutes | Serves 4

70 g self-raising flour
1 teaspoon paprika
1 teaspoon salt
½ teaspoon freshly ground black pepper
1 large egg, beaten
120 g finely crushed panko bread crumbs
20 frozen large prawns (about 900 g), peeled and deveined
Cooking spray

1. In a shallow bowl, whisk the flour, paprika, salt, and pepper until blended. Add the beaten egg to a second shallow bowl and the bread crumbs to a third. 2. One at a time, dip the prawns into the flour, the egg, and the bread crumbs, coating thoroughly. 3. Preheat the Ninja Foodi cooker to 205°C. Line the cook & crisp basket with baking paper. 4. Place the prawns on the baking paper and spritz with oil. 5. Air crisp for 2 minutes. Shake the basket, spritz the prawns with oil, and air crisp for 3 minutes more until lightly browned and crispy. Serve hot.

Prawn and Asparagus Risotto

Prep time: 15 minutes | Cook time: 20 minutes | Serves 4

60 ml extra-virgin olive oil, divided
230 g asparagus, trimmed and cut on bias into 1-inch lengths
½ onion, chopped fine
¼ teaspoon table salt
360 ml Arborio rice
3 garlic cloves, minced
120 ml dry white wine
720 ml chicken or vegetable broth, plus extra as needed
450 g large prawn, peeled and deveined
60 g Parmesan cheese, grated (240 ml)
1 tablespoon lemon juice
1 tablespoon minced fresh chives

1. Using highest sauté function, heat 1 tablespoon oil in Ninja Foodi cooker until shimmering. Add asparagus, partially cover, and cook until just crisp-tender, about 4 minutes. Using slotted spoon, transfer asparagus to bowl; set aside. 2. Add onion, 2 tablespoons oil, and salt to now-empty pot and cook, using highest sauté function, until onion is softened, about 5 minutes. Stir in rice and garlic and cook until grains are translucent around edges, about 3 minutes. Stir in wine and cook until nearly evaporated, about 1 minute. 3. Stir in broth, scraping up any rice that sticks to bottom of pot. Lock lid in place and close pressure release valve. Select high pressure and cook for 7 minutes. 4. Turn off Ninja Foodi cooker and quick-release pressure. Carefully remove lid, allowing steam to escape away from you. Stir prawn and asparagus into risotto, cover, and let sit until prawn are opaque throughout, 5 to 7 minutes. Add Parmesan and remaining 1 tablespoon oil, and stir vigorously until risotto becomes creamy. Adjust consistency with extra hot broth as needed. Stir in lemon juice and season with salt and pepper to taste. Sprinkle individual portions with chives before serving.

Foil-Packet Salmon

Prep time: 2 minutes | Cook time: 7 minutes | Serves 2

2 (85 g) salmon fillets
¼ teaspoon garlic powder
1 teaspoon salt
¼ teaspoon pepper
¼ teaspoon dried dill
½ lemon
240 ml water

1. Place each filet of salmon on a square of foil, skin-side down. 2. Season with garlic powder, salt, and pepper and squeeze the lemon juice over the fish. 3. Cut the lemon into four slices and place two on each filet. Close the foil packets by folding over edges. 4. Add the water to the Ninja Foodi cooker and insert a reversible rack. Place the foil packets on the reversible rack. 5. Secure the lid. Select the Steam mode and set the cooking time for 7 minutes at Low Pressure. 6. Once cooking is complete, do a quick pressure release. Carefully open the lid. 7. Check the internal temperature with a meat thermometer to ensure the thickest part of the filets reached at least 63°C. Salmon should easily flake when fully cooked. Serve immediately.

Dill Lemon Salmon

Prep time: 10 minutes | Cook time: 4 minutes | Serves 4

450 g salmon fillet
1 tablespoon butter, melted
2 tablespoons lemon juice
1 teaspoon dried dill
240 ml water

1. Cut the salmon fillet on 4 servings. 2. Line the Ninja Foodi cooker baking pan with foil and put the salmon fillets inside in one layer. 3. Then sprinkle the fish with dried dill, lemon juice, and butter. 4. Pour water in the Ninja Foodi cooker and insert the rack. 5. Place the baking pan with salmon on the rack and close the lid. 6. Cook the meal on High Pressure for 4 minutes. Allow the natural pressure release for 5 minutes and remove the fish from the Ninja Foodi cooker.

Basil Cod Fillets

Prep time: 5 minutes | Cook time: 12 minutes | Serves 4

120 ml water
4 frozen cod fillets (about 170 g each)
1 teaspoon dried basil
Pinch of salt
Pinch of black pepper
4 lemon slices
60 ml double cream
2 tablespoons butter, softened
30 g cream cheese, softened
2 teaspoons lemon juice
1½ teaspoons chopped fresh basil, plus more for garnish (optional)
Lemon wedges, for garnish (optional)

1. Place the reversible rack inside the pot and add the water. Lay a piece of aluminium foil on top of the reversible rack and place the cod on top. 2. Sprinkle the fish with the dried basil, salt, and pepper. Set a lemon slice on top of each fillet. 3. Close the lid and seal the vent. Cook on High Pressure for 9 minutes. Quick release the steam. Press Start/Stop. 4. Remove the reversible rack and fish from the pot. Rinse the pot if needed and turn to Sauté mode. 5. Add the cream and butter and whisk as the butter melts and the cream warms up. Add the cream cheese and whisk until thickened, 2 to 3 minutes. Add the lemon juice and another pinch of salt and pepper. Once the sauce is thickened and well combined, 1 to 2 minutes, press Start/Stop and add the fresh basil. 6. Pour the sauce over the fish. Garnish with fresh basil or a lemon wedge, if desired.

Tilapia Fillets with Rocket

Prep time: 5 minutes | Cook time: 4 minutes | Serves 4

1 lemon, juiced
240 ml water
450 g tilapia fillets
½ teaspoon cayenne pepper, or more to taste
2 teaspoons butter, melted
Sea salt and ground black pepper, to taste
½ teaspoon dried basil
480 ml rocket

1. Pour the fresh lemon juice and water into your Ninja Foodi cooker and insert a steamer basket. 2. Brush the fish fillets with the melted butter. 3. Sprinkle with the cayenne pepper, salt, and black pepper. Place the tilapia fillets in the basket. Sprinkle the dried basil on top. 4. Lock the lid. Set the cooking time for 4 minutes at Low Pressure. 5. When the timer beeps, perform a quick pressure release. Carefully remove the lid. 6. Serve with the fresh rocket.

Parmesan Salmon Loaf

Prep time: 15 minutes | Cook time: 25 minutes | Serves 6

340 g salmon, boiled and shredded
3 eggs, beaten
120 ml almond flour
1 teaspoon garlic powder
60 ml grated Parmesan
1 teaspoon butter, softened
240 ml water, for cooking

1. Pour water in the Ninja Foodi cooker. 2. Mix up the rest of the ingredients in the mixing bowl and stir until smooth. 3. After this, transfer the salmon mixture in the loaf pan and flatten; insert the pan in the Ninja Foodi cooker. Close and seal the lid. 4. Cook the meal on High Pressure for 25 minutes. 5. When the cooking time is finished, make a quick pressure release and cool the loaf well before serving.

Mascarpone Tilapia with Nutmeg

Prep time: 10 minutes | Cook time: 20 minutes | Serves 2

280 g tilapia
120 ml mascarpone
1 garlic clove, diced
1 teaspoon ground nutmeg
1 tablespoon olive oil
½ teaspoon salt

1. Pour olive oil in the Ninja Foodi cooker. 2. Add diced garlic and sauté it for 4 minutes. 3. Add tilapia and sprinkle it with ground nutmeg. Sauté the fish for 3 minutes per side. 4. Add mascarpone and close the lid. 5. Sauté tilapia for 10 minutes.

Tandoori Prawns

Prep time: 25 minutes | Cook time: 6 minutes | Serves 4

455 g jumbo raw prawns (21 to 25 count), peeled and deveined
1 tablespoon minced fresh ginger
3 cloves garlic, minced
5 g chopped fresh coriander or parsley, plus more for garnish
1 teaspoon ground turmeric
1 teaspoon garam masala
1 teaspoon smoked paprika
1 teaspoon kosher or coarse sea salt
½ to 1 teaspoon cayenne pepper
2 tablespoons olive oil (for Paleo) or melted ghee
2 teaspoons fresh lemon juice

1. In a large bowl, combine the prawns, ginger, garlic, coriander, turmeric, garam masala, paprika, salt, and cayenne. Toss well to coat. Add the oil or ghee and toss again. Marinate at room temperature for 15 minutes, or cover and refrigerate for up to 8 hours. 2. Place the prawns in a single layer in the cook & crisp basket. Set the Ninja Foodi cooker to 165°C for 6 minutes. Transfer the prawns to a serving platter. Cover and let the prawns finish cooking in the residual heat, about 5 minutes. 3. Sprinkle the prawns with the lemon juice and toss to coat. Garnish with additional cilantro and serve.

Sea Bass with Roasted Root Vegetables

Prep time: 10 minutes | Cook time: 15 minutes | Serves 4

1 carrot, diced small
1 parsnip, diced small
1 swede, diced small
60 ml olive oil
1 teaspoon salt, divided
4 sea bass fillets
½ teaspoon onion powder
2 garlic cloves, minced
1 lemon, sliced, plus additional wedges for serving

1. Preheat the Ninja Foodi cooker to 190°C. 2. In a small bowl, toss the carrot, parsnip, and swede with olive oil and 1 teaspoon salt. 3. Lightly season the sea bass with the remaining 1 teaspoon of salt and the onion powder, then place it into the cook & crisp basket in a single layer. 4. Spread the garlic over the top of each fillet, then cover with lemon slices. 5. Pour the prepared vegetables into the basket around and on top of the fish. Roast for 15 minutes. 6. Serve with additional lemon wedges if desired.

Prawns Pasta with Basil and Mushrooms

Prep time: 10 minutes | Cook time: 10 minutes | Serves 6

455 g small prawns, peeled and deveined
120 ml olive oil plus 1 tablespoon, divided
¼ teaspoon garlic powder
¼ teaspoon cayenne
455 g whole grain pasta
5 garlic cloves, minced
230 g baby mushrooms, sliced
45 g Parmesan, plus more for serving (optional)
1 teaspoon salt
½ teaspoon black pepper
½ cup fresh basil

1. Preheat the Ninja Foodi cooker to 190°C. 2. In a small bowl, combine the prawns, 1 tablespoon olive oil, garlic powder, and cayenne. Toss to coat the prawns. 3. Place the prawns into the cook & crisp basket and roast for 5 minutes. Remove the prawns and set aside. 4. Cook the pasta according to package directions. Once done cooking, reserve ½ cup pasta water, then drain. 5. Meanwhile, in a large skillet, heat 120 ml of olive oil over medium heat. Add the garlic and mushrooms and cook down for 5 minutes. 6. Pour the pasta, reserved pasta water, Parmesan, salt, pepper, and basil into the skillet with the vegetable-and-oil mixture, and stir to coat the pasta. 7. Toss in the prawns and remove from heat, then let the mixture sit for 5 minutes before serving with additional Parmesan, if desired.

Chili and Turmeric Haddock

Prep time: 10 minutes | Cook time: 5 minutes | Serves 4

1 chili pepper, minced
450 g haddock, chopped
½ teaspoon ground turmeric
120 ml fish stock
240 ml water

1. In the mixing bowl mix up chili pepper, ground turmeric, and fish stock. 2. Then add chopped haddock and transfer the mixture in the baking mold. 3. Pour water in the Ninja Foodi cooker and insert the reversible rack. 4. Place the baking mold with fish on the reversible rack and close the lid. 5. Cook the meal on High Pressure for 5 minutes. Make a quick pressure release.

Tuna Stuffed Poblano Peppers

Prep time: 15 minutes | Cook time: 12 minutes | Serves 4

200 g canned tuna, shredded
1 teaspoon cream cheese
¼ teaspoon minced garlic
60 g Provolone cheese, grated
4 poblano pepper
240 ml water, for cooking

1. Remove the seeds from poblano peppers. 2. In the mixing bowl, mix up shredded tuna, cream cheese, minced garlic, and grated cheese. 3. Then fill the peppers with tuna mixture and put it in the baking pan. 4. Pour water and insert the baking pan in the Ninja Foodi cooker. 5. Cook the meal on High Pressure for 12 minutes. Then make a quick pressure release.

Lemon Butter Mahi Mahi

Prep time: 10 minutes | Cook time: 9 minutes | Serves 4

450 g mahi-mahi fillet
1 teaspoon grated lemon zest
1 tablespoon lemon juice
1 tablespoon butter, softened
½ teaspoon salt
240 ml water, for cooking

1. Cut the fish on 4 servings and sprinkle with lemon zest, lemon juice, salt, and rub with softened butter. 2. Then put the fish in the baking pan in one layer. 3. Pour water and insert the steamer rack in the Ninja Foodi cooker. 4. Put the mold with fish on the rack. Close and seal the lid. 5. Cook the Mahi Mahi on High Pressure for 9 minutes. Make a quick pressure release.

Perch Fillets with Red Curry

Prep time: 5 minutes | Cook time: 6 minutes | Serves 4

240 ml water
2 sprigs rosemary
1 large-sized lemon, sliced
450 g perch fillets

1 teaspoon cayenne pepper
Sea salt and ground black pepper, to taste
1 tablespoon red curry paste
1 tablespoons butter

1. Add the water, rosemary, and lemon slices to the Ninja Foodi cooker and insert a reversible rack. 2. Season the perch fillets with the cayenne pepper, salt, and black pepper. Spread the red curry paste and butter over the fillets. 3. Arrange the fish fillets on the reversible rack. 4. Lock the lid. Set the cooking time for 6 minutes at Low Pressure. 5. When the timer beeps, perform a quick pressure release. Carefully remove the lid. Serve with your favorite keto sides.

Trout Amandine with Lemon Butter Sauce

Prep time: 20 minutes | Cook time:8 minutes | Serves 4

Trout Amandine:
65 g toasted almonds
30 g grated Parmesan cheese
1 teaspoon salt
½ teaspoon freshly ground black pepper
2 tablespoons butter, melted
4 trout fillets, or salmon fillets, 110 g each
Cooking spray

Lemon Butter Sauce:
8 tablespoons butter, melted
2 tablespoons freshly squeezed lemon juice
½ teaspoon Worcestershire sauce
½ teaspoon salt
½ teaspoon freshly ground black pepper
¼ teaspoon hot sauce

1. In a blender or food processor, pulse the almonds for 5 to 10 seconds until finely processed. Transfer to a shallow bowl and whisk in the Parmesan cheese, salt, and pepper. Place the melted butter in another shallow bowl. 2. One at a time, dip the fish in the melted butter, then the almond mixture, coating thoroughly. 3. Preheat the Ninja Foodi cooker to 150ºC. Line the cook & crisp basket with baking paper. 4. Place the coated fish on the baking paper and spritz with oil. 5. Bake for 4 minutes. Flip the fish, spritz it with oil, and bake for 4 minutes more until the fish flakes easily with a fork. 6. In a small bowl, whisk the butter, lemon juice, Worcestershire sauce, salt, pepper, and hot sauce until blended. 7. Serve with the fish.

Buffalo Crispy Chicken Strips

Prep time: 15 minutes | Cook time: 13 to 17 minutes per batch | Serves 4

90 g all-purpose flour
2 eggs
2 tablespoons water
120 g seasoned panko bread crumbs
2 teaspoons granulated garlic
1 teaspoon salt
1 teaspoon freshly ground black

pepper
16 chicken breast strips, or 3 large boneless, skinless chicken breasts, cut into 1-inch strips
Olive oil spray
60 ml Buffalo sauce, plus more as needed

1. Put the flour in a small bowl. 2. In another small bowl, whisk the eggs and the water. 3. In a third bowl, stir together the panko, granulated garlic, salt, and pepper. 4. Dip each chicken strip in the flour, in the egg, and in the panko mixture to coat. Press the crumbs onto the chicken with your fingers. 5. Insert the crisper plate into the basket and the basket into the unit. Preheat the unit by selecting AIR CRISP, setting the temperature to 190°C, and setting the time to 3 minutes. Press START/STOP to begin. 6. Once the unit is preheated, place a parchment paper liner into the basket. Working in batches if needed, place the chicken strips into the basket. Do not stack unless using a wire rack for the second layer. Spray the top of the chicken with olive oil. 7. Select AIR CRISP, set the temperature to 190°C, and set the time to 17 minutes. Press START/STOP to begin. 8. After 10 or 12 minutes, remove the basket, flip the chicken, and spray again with olive oil. Reinsert the basket to resume cooking. 9. When the cooking is complete, the chicken should be golden brown and crispy and a food thermometer inserted into the chicken should register 75°C. 10. Repeat steps 6, 7, and 8 with any remaining chicken. 11. Transfer the chicken to a large bowl. Drizzle the Buffalo sauce over the top of the cooked chicken, toss to coat, and serve.

Turmeric Chicken Nuggets

Prep time: 10 minutes | Cook time: 9 minutes | Serves 5

230 g chicken fillet
1 teaspoon ground turmeric
½ teaspoon ground coriander

120 ml almond flour
2 eggs, beaten
120 ml butter

1. Chop the chicken fillet roughly into the medium size pieces. 2. In the mixing bowl, mix up ground turmeric, ground coriander, and almond flour. 3. Then dip the chicken pieces in the beaten egg and coat in the almond flour mixture. 4. Toss the butter in the Ninja Foodi cooker and melt it on Sauté mode for 4 minutes. 5. Then put the coated chicken in the hot butter and cook for 5 minutes or until the nuggets are golden brown.

Chicken Enchilada Bowl

Prep time: 10 minutes | Cook time: 35 minutes | Serves 4

2 (170 g) boneless, skinless chicken breasts
2 teaspoons chili powder
½ teaspoon garlic powder
½ teaspoon salt
¼ teaspoon pepper
2 tablespoons coconut oil
180 ml red enchilada sauce

60 ml chicken broth
1 (110 g) can green chilies
60 ml diced onion
480 ml cooked cauliflower rice
1 avocado, diced
120 ml sour cream
240 ml shredded Cheddar cheese

1. Sprinkle the chili powder, garlic powder, salt, and pepper on chicken breasts. 2. Set your Ninja Foodi cooker to Sauté and melt the coconut oil. Add the chicken breasts and sear each side for about 5 minutes until golden brown. 3. Pour the enchilada sauce and broth over the chicken. Using a wooden spoon or rubber spatula, scrape the bottom of pot to make sure nothing is sticking. Stir in the chilies and onion. 4. Secure the lid. Set the cooking time for 25 minutes at High Pressure. 5. Once cooking is complete, do a quick pressure release. Carefully open the lid. 6. Remove the chicken and shred with two forks. Serve the chicken over the cauliflower rice and place the avocado, sour cream, and Cheddar cheese on top.

Pecan Turkey Cutlets

Prep time: 10 minutes | Cook time: 10 to 12 minutes per batch | Serves 4

90 g panko bread crumbs
¼ teaspoon salt
¼ teaspoon pepper
¼ teaspoon mustard powder
¼ teaspoon poultry seasoning
50 g pecans

30 g cornflour
1 egg, beaten
450 g turkey cutlets, ½-inch thick
Salt and pepper, to taste
Oil for misting or cooking spray

1. Place the panko crumbs, ¼ teaspoon salt, ¼ teaspoon pepper, mustard, and poultry seasoning in food processor. Process until crumbs are finely crushed. Add pecans and process in short pulses just until nuts are finely chopped. Go easy so you don't overdo it! 2. Preheat the Ninja Foodi cooker to 180°C. 3. Place cornflour in one shallow dish and beaten egg in another. Transfer coating mixture from food processor into a third shallow dish. 4. Sprinkle turkey cutlets with salt and pepper to taste. 5. Dip cutlets in cornflour and shake off excess. Then dip in beaten egg and roll in crumbs, pressing to coat well. Spray both sides with oil or cooking spray. 6. Place 2 cutlets in cook & crisp basket in a single layer and cook for 10 to 12 minutes or until juices run clear. 7. Repeat step 6 to cook remaining cutlets.

Chicken Pesto Pizzas

Prep time: 10 minutes | Cook time: 12 minutes | Serves 4

450 g chicken mince thighs
¼ teaspoon salt
⅛ teaspoon ground black pepper
20 g basil pesto

225 g shredded Mozzarella cheese
4 grape tomatoes, sliced

1. Cut four squares of parchment paper to fit into your cook & crisp basket. 2. Place chicken mince in a large bowl and mix with salt and pepper. Divide mixture into four equal sections. 3. Wet your hands with water to prevent sticking, then press each section into a 6-inch circle onto a piece of ungreased parchment. Place each chicken crust into cook & crisp basket, working in batches if needed. 4. Adjust the temperature to 180ºC and air crisp for 10 minutes, turning crusts halfway through cooking. 5. Spread 1 tablespoon pesto across the top of each crust, then sprinkle with ¼ of the Mozzarella and top with 1 sliced tomato. Continue cooking at 180ºC for 2 minutes. Cheese will be melted and brown when done. Serve warm.

Lemon Garlic Chicken

Prep time: 20 minutes | Cook time: 30 minutes | Serves 6

900 g skinless chicken thighs
1 tablespoon avocado oil
1 teaspoon minced garlic
½ teaspoon ground coriander

1 teaspoon lemon zest
1 teaspoon lemon juice
80 ml chicken broth
240 ml water

1. Pour water and insert the steamer rack in the Ninja Foodi cooker. Pour water and chicken broth in the Ninja Foodi cooker bowl. 2. Put the chicken thighs in the bowl and sprinkle them with avocado oil, minced garlic, ground coriander, lemon zest, and lemon juice. 3. Then shake the chicken thighs gently and transfer them on the steamer rack. 4. Close and seal the lid. 5. Cook the chicken for 15 minutes on High Pressure. Then make a quick pressure release and transfer the chicken thighs on the plate.

Ann's Chicken Cacciatore

Prep time: 25 minutes | Cook time: 3 to 9 minutes | Serves 8

1 large onion, thinly sliced
1.4 kg chicken, cut up, skin removed, trimmed of fat
2 cans (170 g each) tomato paste
110 g canned sliced mushrooms, drained
1 teaspoon salt

60 ml dry white wine
¼ teaspoons pepper
1–2 garlic cloves, minced
1–2 teaspoons dried oregano
½ teaspoon dried basil
½ teaspoon celery seed, optional
1 bay leaf

1. In the inner pot of the Ninja Foodi cooker, place the onion and chicken. 2. Combine remaining ingredients and pour over the chicken. 3. Secure the lid and make sure vent is at sealing. Cook on Slow Cook mode, low 7–9 hours, or high 3–4 hours.

Chili Lime Turkey Burgers

Prep time: 10 minutes | Cook time: 3 minutes | Serves 4

Burgers:
900 g minced turkey
40 g diced red onion
2 cloves garlic, minced
1½ teaspoons minced coriander
1½ teaspoons salt
1 teaspoon Mexican chili powder

Juice and zest of 1 lime
120 ml water
Dipping Sauce:
120 ml sour cream
4 teaspoons sriracha
1 tablespoon chopped coriander, plus more for garnish
1 teaspoon lime juice

1. Make the burgers: In a large bowl, add the turkey, onion, garlic, coriander, salt, chili powder, and lime juice and zest. Use a wooden spoon to mix until the ingredients are well distributed. 2. Divide the meat into four 230 g balls. Use a kitchen scale to measure for accuracy. Pat the meat into thick patties, about 1 inch thick. 3. Add the water and reversible rack to the Ninja Foodi cooker. Place the turkey patties on top of the reversible rack, overlapping if necessary. 4. Close the lid and seal the vent. Cook on High Pressure for 3 minutes. Quick release the steam. 5. Remove the patties from the pot. 6. Make the dipping sauce: In a small bowl, whisk together the sour cream, sriracha, coriander, and lime juice. 7. Top each patty with 2 tablespoons of the sauce and garnish with fresh coriander.

Chicken Jalfrezi

Prep time: 15 minutes | Cook time: 15 minutes | Serves 4

Chicken:
450 g boneless, skinless chicken thighs, cut into 2 or 3 pieces each
1 medium onion, chopped
1 large green bell pepper, stemmed, seeded, and chopped
2 tablespoons olive oil
1 teaspoon ground turmeric
1 teaspoon garam masala

1 teaspoon kosher salt
½ to 1 teaspoon cayenne pepper
Sauce:
55 g tomato sauce
1 tablespoon water
1 teaspoon garam masala
½ teaspoon kosher salt
½ teaspoon cayenne pepper
Side salad, rice, or naan bread, for serving

1. For the chicken: In a large bowl, combine the chicken, onion, bell pepper, oil, turmeric, garam masala, salt, and cayenne. Stir and toss until well combined. 2. Place the chicken and vegetables in the cook & crisp basket. Set the Ninja Foodi cooker to 180ºC for 15 minutes, stirring and tossing halfway through the cooking time. Use a meat thermometer to ensure the chicken has reached an internal temperature of 75ºC. 3. Meanwhile, for the sauce: In a small microwave-safe bowl, combine the tomato sauce, water, garam masala, salt, and cayenne. Microwave on high for 1 minute. Remove and stir. Microwave for another minute; set aside. 4. When the chicken is cooked, remove and place chicken and vegetables in a large bowl. Pour the sauce over all. Stir and toss to coat the chicken and vegetables evenly. 5. Serve with rice, naan, or a side salad.

Thai Coconut Chicken

Prep time: 10 minutes | Cook time: 15 minutes | Serves 4

1 tablespoon coconut oil	1 tomato, peeled and chopped
450 g chicken, cubed	240 ml vegetable broth
2 cloves garlic, minced	80 ml unsweetened coconut
1 shallot, peeled and chopped	milk
1 teaspoon Thai chili, minced	2 tablespoons coconut aminos
1 teaspoon fresh ginger root,	1 teaspoon Thai curry paste
julienned	Salt and freshly ground black
1/3 teaspoon cumin powder	pepper, to taste

1. Set your Ninja Foodi cooker to Sauté and heat the coconut oil. 2. Brown the chicken cubes for 2 to 3 minutes, stirring frequently. Reserve the chicken in a bowl. 3. Add the garlic and shallot and sauté for 2 minutes until tender. Add a splash of vegetable broth to the pot, if needed. 4. Stir in the Thai chili, ginger, and cumin powder and cook for another 1 minute or until fragrant. 5. Add the cooked chicken, tomato, vegetable broth, milk, coconut aminos, and curry paste to the Ninja Foodi cooker and stir well. 6. Lock the lid. Set the cooking time for 10 minutes at High Pressure. 7. When the timer beeps, perform a quick pressure release. Carefully remove the lid. Season with salt and pepper to taste and serve.

Chicken Reuben Bake

Prep time: 10 minutes | Cook time: 6 to 8 hours | Serves 6

4 boneless, skinless chicken-	cheese
breast halves	180 ml fat-free Thousand Island
60 ml water	salad dressing
450 g bag sauerkraut, drained	2 tablespoons chopped fresh
and rinsed	parsley
4-5 (30 g each) slices Swiss	

1. Place chicken and water in inner pot of the Ninja Foodi cooker along with 60 ml water. Layer sauerkraut over chicken. Add cheese. Top with salad dressing. Sprinkle with parsley. 2. Secure the lid and cook on the Slow Cook setting on low 6–8 hours.

Chicken Shawarma

Prep time: 30 minutes | Cook time: 15 minutes | Serves 4

Shawarma Spice:	Chicken:
2 teaspoons dried oregano	450 g boneless, skinless chicken
1 teaspoon ground cinnamon	thighs, cut into large bite-size
1 teaspoon ground cumin	chunks
1 teaspoon ground coriander	2 tablespoons vegetable oil
1 teaspoon kosher salt	For Serving:
1/2 teaspoon ground allspice	Tzatziki
1/2 teaspoon cayenne pepper	Pita bread

1. For the shawarma spice: In a small bowl, combine the oregano, cayenne, cumin, coriander, salt, cinnamon, and allspice. 2. For the chicken: In a large bowl, toss together the chicken, vegetable oil,

and shawarma spice to coat. Marinate at room temperature for 30 minutes or cover and refrigerate for up to 24 hours. 3. Place the chicken in the cook & crisp basket. Set the Ninja Foodi cooker to 180ºC for 15 minutes, or until the chicken reaches an internal temperature of 75ºC. 4. Transfer the chicken to a serving platter. Serve with tzatziki and pita bread.

Crunchy Chicken Tenders

Prep time: 5 minutes | Cook time: 12 minutes | Serves 4

1 egg	1/2 teaspoon dried thyme
60 ml unsweetened almond milk	1/2 teaspoon dried sage
30 g whole wheat flour	1/2 teaspoon garlic powder
30 g whole wheat bread crumbs	450 g chicken tenderloins
1/2 teaspoon salt	1 lemon, quartered
1/2 teaspoon black pepper	

1. Preheat the Ninja Foodi cooker to 185ºC. 2. In a shallow bowl, beat together the egg and almond milk until frothy. 3. In a separate shallow bowl, whisk together the flour, bread crumbs, salt, pepper, thyme, sage, and garlic powder. 4. Dip each chicken tenderloin into the egg mixture, then into the bread crumb mixture, coating the outside with the crumbs. Place the breaded chicken tenderloins into the bottom of the cook & crisp basket in an even layer, making sure that they don't touch each other. 5. Cook for 6 minutes, then turn and cook for an additional 5 to 6 minutes. Serve with lemon slices.

African Chicken Peanut Stew

Prep time: 10 minutes | Cook time: 10 minutes | Serves 6

240 ml chopped onion	1 tablespoon sugar-free tomato
2 tablespoons minced garlic	paste
1 tablespoon minced fresh	450 g boneless, skinless chicken
ginger	breasts or thighs, cut into large
1 teaspoon salt	chunks
1/2 teaspoon ground cumin	700 ml - 1 L chopped Swiss
1/2 teaspoon ground coriander	chard
1/2 teaspoon freshly ground black	240 ml cubed raw pumpkin
pepper	120 ml water
1/2 teaspoon ground cinnamon	240 ml chunky peanut butter
1/8 teaspoon ground cloves	

1. In the inner cooking pot of the Ninja Foodi cooker, stir together the onion, garlic, ginger, salt, cumin, coriander, pepper, cinnamon, cloves, and tomato paste. Add the chicken, chard, pumpkin, and water. 2. Lock the lid into place. Adjust the pressure to High. Cook for 10 minutes. When the cooking is complete, let the pressure release naturally. Unlock the lid. 3. Mix in the peanut butter a little at a time. Taste with each addition, as your reward for cooking. The final sauce should be thick enough to coat the back of a spoon in a thin layer. 4. Serve over mashed cauliflower, cooked courgette noodles, steamed vegetables, or with a side salad.

Simply Terrific Turkey Meatballs

Prep time: 10 minutes | Cook time: 7 to 10 minutes | Serves 4

1 red bell pepper, seeded and coarsely chopped
2 cloves garlic, coarsely chopped
15 g chopped fresh parsley
680 g 85% lean turkey mince
1 egg, lightly beaten
45 g grated Parmesan cheese
1 teaspoon salt
½ teaspoon freshly ground black pepper

1. Preheat the Ninja Foodi cooker to 200°C. 2. In a food processor fitted with a metal blade, combine the bell pepper, garlic, and parsley. Pulse until finely chopped. Transfer the vegetables to a large mixing bowl. 3. Add the turkey, egg, Parmesan, salt, and black pepper. Mix gently until thoroughly combined. Shape the mixture into 1¼-inch meatballs. 4. Working in batches if necessary, arrange the meatballs in a single layer in the cook & crisp basket; coat lightly with olive oil spray. Pausing halfway through the cooking time to shake the basket, air crisp for 7 to 10 minutes, until lightly browned and a thermometer inserted into the centre of a meatball registers 75°C.

Fajita-Stuffed Chicken Breast

Prep time: 15 minutes | Cook time: 25 minutes | Serves 4

2 (170 g) boneless, skinless chicken breasts
¼ medium white onion, peeled and sliced
1 medium green bell pepper,
seeded and sliced
1 tablespoon coconut oil
2 teaspoons chili powder
1 teaspoon ground cumin
½ teaspoon garlic powder

1. Slice each chicken breast completely in half lengthwise into two even pieces. Using a meat tenderizer, pound out the chicken until it's about ¼-inch thickness. 2. Lay each slice of chicken out and place three slices of onion and four slices of green pepper on the end closest to you. Begin rolling the peppers and onions tightly into the chicken. Secure the roll with either toothpicks or a couple pieces of butcher's twine. 3. Drizzle coconut oil over chicken. Sprinkle each side with chili powder, cumin, and garlic powder. Place each roll into the cook & crisp basket. 4. Adjust the temperature to 180°C and air crisp for 25 minutes. 5. Serve warm.

Spice-Rubbed Turkey Breast

Prep time: 5 minutes | Cook time: 45 to 55 minutes | Serves 10

1 tablespoon sea salt
1 teaspoon paprika
1 teaspoon onion powder
1 teaspoon garlic powder
½ teaspoon freshly ground black
pepper
1.8 kg bone-in, skin-on turkey breast
2 tablespoons unsalted butter, melted

1. In a small bowl, combine the salt, paprika, onion powder, garlic powder, and pepper. 2. Sprinkle the seasonings all over the turkey. Brush the turkey with some of the melted butter. 3. Set the Ninja Foodi cooker to 180°C. Place the turkey in the cook & crisp basket, skin-side down, and roast for 25 minutes. 4. Flip the turkey and brush it with the remaining butter. Continue cooking for another 20 to 30 minutes, until an instant-read thermometer reads 70°C. 5. Remove the turkey breast from the Ninja Foodi cooker. Tent a piece of aluminum foil over the turkey, and allow it to rest for about 5 minutes before serving.

Barbecue Chicken and Coleslaw Tostadas

Prep time: 15 minutes | Cook time: 40 minutes | Makes 4 tostadas

Coleslaw:
60 g sour cream
25 g small green cabbage, finely chopped
½ tablespoon white vinegar
½ teaspoon garlic powder
½ teaspoon salt
¼ teaspoon ground black pepper

Tostadas:
280 g pulled rotisserie chicken
120 ml barbecue sauce
4 corn tortillas
110 g shredded Mozzarella cheese
Cooking spray

Make the Coleslaw: 1. Combine the ingredients for the coleslaw in a large bowl. Toss to mix well. 2. Refrigerate until ready to serve. Make the Tostadas: 1. Preheat the Ninja Foodi cooker to 190°C. Spritz the cook & crisp basket with cooking spray. 2. Toss the chicken with barbecue sauce in a separate large bowl to combine well. Set aside. 3. Place one tortilla in the preheated Ninja Foodi cooker and spritz with cooking spray. Work in batches to avoid overcrowding. 4. Air crisp the tortilla for 5 minutes or until lightly browned, then spread a quarter of the barbecue chicken and cheese over. 5. Air crisp for another 5 minutes or until the cheese melts. Repeat with remaining tortillas, chicken, and cheese. 6. Serve the tostadas with coleslaw on top.

Fried Chicken Breasts

Prep time: 30 minutes | Cook time: 12 to 14 minutes | Serves 4

450 g boneless, skinless chicken breasts
180 ml dill pickle juice
70 g finely ground blanched almond flour
70 g finely grated Parmesan
cheese
½ teaspoon sea salt
½ teaspoon freshly ground black pepper
2 large eggs
Avocado oil spray

1. Place the chicken breasts in a zip-top bag or between two pieces of plastic wrap. Using a meat mallet or heavy skillet, pound the chicken to a uniform ½-inch thickness. 2. Place the chicken in a large bowl with the pickle juice. Cover and allow to brine in the refrigerator for up to 2 hours. 3. In a shallow dish, combine the almond flour, Parmesan cheese, salt, and pepper. In a separate, shallow bowl, beat the eggs. 4. Drain the chicken and pat it dry with paper towels. Dip in the eggs and then in the flour mixture, making sure to press the coating into the chicken. Spray both sides of the coated breasts with oil. 5. Spray the cook & crisp basket with oil and put the chicken inside. Set the temperature to 200°C and air crisp for 6 to 7 minutes. 6. Carefully flip the breasts with a spatula. Spray the breasts again with oil and continue cooking for 6 to 7 minutes more, until golden and crispy.

Chicken with Tomatoes and Spinach

Prep time: 5 minutes | Cook time: 18 minutes | Serves 4

4 boneless, skinless chicken breasts (about 900 g)
70 g sun-dried tomatoes, coarsely chopped (about 2 tablespoons)
60 ml chicken broth
2 tablespoons creamy, no-sugar-added balsamic vinegar dressing

1 tablespoon whole-grain mustard
2 cloves garlic, minced
1 teaspoon salt
230 g fresh spinach
60 ml sour cream
30 g cream cheese, softened

1. Place the chicken breasts in the Ninja Foodi cooker. Add the tomatoes, broth, and dressing. 2. Close the lid and seal the vent. Cook on High Pressure for 10 minutes. Quick release the steam. Press Start/Stop. 3. Remove the chicken from the pot and place on a plate. Cover with aluminium foil to keep warm while you make the sauce. 4. Turn the pot to Sauté mode. Whisk in the mustard, garlic, and salt and then add the spinach. Stir the spinach continuously until it is completely cooked down, 2 to 3 minutes. The spinach will absorb the sauce but will release it again as it continues to cook down. 5. Once the spinach is completely wilted, add the sour cream and cream cheese. Whisk until completed incorporated. 6. Let the sauce simmer to thicken and reduce by about one-third, about 5 minutes. Stir occasionally to prevent burning. Press Start/Stop. 7. Pour the sauce over the chicken. Serve.

Chicken and Spiced Freekeh with coriander and Preserved Lemon

Prep time: 20 minutes | Cook time: 11 minutes | Serves 4

2 tablespoons extra-virgin olive oil, plus extra for drizzling
1 onion, chopped fine
4 garlic cloves, minced
1½ teaspoons smoked paprika
¼ teaspoon ground cardamom
¼ teaspoon red pepper flakes
540 ml chicken broth
360 ml cracked freekeh, rinsed
2 (340 g) bone-in split chicken

breasts, halved crosswise and trimmed
½ teaspoon table salt
¼ teaspoon pepper
60 ml chopped fresh coriander
2 tablespoons sesame seeds, toasted
½ preserved lemon, pulp and white pith removed, rind rinsed and minced (2 tablespoons)

1. Using highest sauté function, heat oil in Ninja Foodi cooker until shimmering. Add onion and cook until softened, about 5 minutes. Stir in garlic, paprika, cardamom, and pepper flakes and cook until fragrant, about 30 seconds. Stir in broth and freekeh. Sprinkle chicken with salt and pepper. Nestle skin side up into freekeh mixture. Lock lid in place and close pressure release valve. Select high pressure and cook for 5 minutes. 2. Turn off Ninja Foodi cooker and quick-release pressure. Carefully remove lid, allowing steam to escape away from you. Transfer chicken to serving dish and discard skin, if desired. Tent with aluminium foil and let rest while finishing freekeh. 3. Gently fluff freekeh with fork. Lay clean dish towel over pot, replace lid, and let sit for 5 minutes. Season with salt and pepper to taste. Transfer freekeh to serving dish with chicken and sprinkle with coriander, sesame seeds, and preserved lemon. Drizzle with extra oil and serve.

Shredded Buffalo Chicken

Prep time: 10 minutes | Cook time: 20 minutes | Serves 8

2 tablespoons avocado oil
120 ml finely chopped onion
1 celery stalk, finely chopped
1 large carrot, chopped
80 ml mild hot sauce (such as Frank's RedHot)

½ tablespoon apple cider vinegar
¼ teaspoon garlic powder
2 bone-in, skin-on chicken breasts (about 900 g)

1. Set the electric pressure cooker to the Sauté setting. When the pot is hot, pour in the avocado oil. 2. Sauté the onion, celery, and carrot for 3 to 5 minutes or until the onion begins to soften. Hit Start/Stop. 3. Stir in the hot sauce, vinegar, and garlic powder. Place the chicken breasts in the sauce, meat-side down. 4. Close and lock the lid of the pressure cooker. Set the valve to sealing. 5. Cook on high pressure for 20 minutes. 6. When cooking is complete, hit Start/Stop and quick release the pressure. Once the pin drops, unlock and remove the lid. 7. Using tongs, transfer the chicken breasts to a cutting board. When the chicken is cool enough to handle, remove the skin, shred the chicken and return it to the pot. Let the chicken soak in the sauce for at least 5 minutes. 8. Serve immediately.

Smoky Whole Chicken

Prep time: 20 minutes | Cook time: 21 minutes | Serves 6

2 tablespoons extra-virgin olive oil
1 tablespoon rock salt
1½ teaspoons smoked paprika
1 teaspoon freshly ground black pepper
½ teaspoon herbes de Provence
¼ teaspoon cayenne pepper
1 (1.6 kg) whole chicken, rinsed and patted dry, giblets removed
1 large lemon, halved
6 garlic cloves, peeled and

crushed with the flat side of a knife
1 large onion, cut into 8 wedges, divided
240 ml Chicken Bone Broth, store-bought chicken broth, or water
2 large carrots, each cut into 4 pieces
2 celery stalks, each cut into 4 pieces

1. In a small bowl, combine the olive oil, salt, paprika, pepper, herbes de Provence, and cayenne. 2. Place the chicken on a cutting board and rub the olive oil mixture under the skin and all over the outside. Stuff the cavity with the lemon halves, garlic cloves, and 3 to 4 wedges of onion. 3. Pour the broth into the electric pressure cooker. Add the remaining onion wedges, carrots, and celery. Insert a wire rack or reversible rack on top of the vegetables. 4. Place the chicken, breast-side up, on the rack. 5. Close and lock the lid of the pressure cooker. Set the valve to sealing. 6. Cook on high pressure for 21 minutes. 7. When the cooking is complete, hit Start/Stop and allow the pressure to release naturally for 15 minutes, then quick release any remaining pressure. 8. Once the pin drops, unlock and remove the lid. 9. Carefully remove the chicken to a clean cutting board. Remove the skin and cut the chicken into pieces or shred/chop the meat, and serve.

Chicken Escabèche

Prep time: 5 minutes | Cook time: 15 minutes | Serves 4

240 ml filtered water
450 g chicken, mixed pieces
3 garlic cloves, smashed
2 bay leaves
1 onion, chopped
120 ml red wine vinegar

½ teaspoon coriander
½ teaspoon ground cumin
½ teaspoon mint, finely chopped
½ teaspoon rock salt
½ teaspoon freshly ground black pepper

1. Pour the water into the Ninja Foodi cooker and insert the reversible rack. 2. Thoroughly combine the chicken, garlic, bay leaves, onion, vinegar, coriander, cumin, mint, salt, and black pepper in a large bowl. 3. Put the bowl on the reversible rack and cover loosely with aluminium foil. 4. Secure the lid. Set the cooking time for 15 minutes at High Pressure. 5. Once cooking is complete, do a natural pressure release for 10 minutes, then release any remaining pressure. Carefully open the lid. 6. Remove the dish from the Ninja Foodi cooker and cool for 5 to 10 minutes before serving.

Apricot-Glazed Turkey Tenderloin

Prep time: 20 minutes | Cook time: 30 minutes | Serves 4

Olive oil
80 g sugar-free apricot preserves
½ tablespoon spicy brown mustard

680 g turkey breast tenderloin
Salt and freshly ground black pepper, to taste

1. Spray the cook & crisp basket lightly with olive oil. 2. In a small bowl, combine the apricot preserves and mustard to make a paste. 3. Season the turkey with salt and pepper. Spread the apricot paste all over the turkey. 4. Place the turkey in the cook & crisp basket and lightly spray with olive oil. 5. Air crisp at 190°C for 15 minutes. Flip the turkey over and lightly spray with olive oil. Air crisp until the internal temperature reaches at least 80°C, an additional 10 to 15 minutes. 6. Let the turkey rest for 10 minutes before slicing and serving.

Sweet Chili Spiced Chicken

Prep time: 10 minutes | Cook time: 43 minutes | Serves 4

Spice Rub:
2 tablespoons brown sugar
2 tablespoons paprika
1 teaspoon dry mustard powder
1 teaspoon chili powder
2 tablespoons coarse sea salt or

kosher salt
2 teaspoons coarsely ground black pepper
1 tablespoon vegetable oil
1 (1.6 kg) chicken, cut into 8 pieces

1. Prepare the spice rub by combining the brown sugar, paprika, mustard powder, chili powder, salt and pepper. Rub the oil all over the chicken pieces and then rub the spice mix onto the chicken, covering completely. This is done very easily in a zipper sealable bag. You can do this ahead of time and let the chicken marinate in

the refrigerator, or just proceed with cooking right away. 2. Preheat the Ninja Foodi cooker to 190°C. 3. Air crisp the chicken in two batches. Place the two chicken thighs and two drumsticks into the cook & crisp basket. Air crisp at 190°C for 10 minutes. Then, gently turn the chicken pieces over and air crisp for another 10 minutes. Remove the chicken pieces and let them rest on a plate while you cook the chicken breasts. Air crisp the chicken breasts, skin side down for 8 minutes. Turn the chicken breasts over and air crisp for another 12 minutes. 4. Lower the temperature of the Ninja Foodi cooker to 170°C. Place the first batch of chicken on top of the second batch already in the basket and air crisp for a final 3 minutes. 5. Let the chicken rest for 5 minutes and serve warm with some mashed potatoes and a green salad or vegetables.

Buttermilk-Fried Drumsticks

Prep time: 10 minutes | Cook time: 25 minutes | Serves 2

1 egg
120 g buttermilk
90 g self-rising flour
90 g seasoned panko bread crumbs

1 teaspoon salt
¼ teaspoon ground black pepper (to mix into coating)
4 chicken drumsticks, skin on
Oil for misting or cooking spray

1. Beat together egg and buttermilk in shallow dish. 2. In a second shallow dish, combine the flour, panko crumbs, salt, and pepper. 3. Sprinkle chicken legs with additional salt and pepper to taste. 4. Dip legs in buttermilk mixture, then roll in panko mixture, pressing in crumbs to make coating stick. Mist with oil or cooking spray. 5. Spray the cook & crisp basket with cooking spray. 6. Cook drumsticks at 180°C for 10 minutes. Turn pieces over and cook an additional 10 minutes. 7. Turn pieces to check for browning. If you have any white spots that haven't begun to brown, spritz them with oil or cooking spray. Continue cooking for 5 more minutes or until crust is golden brown and juices run clear. Larger, meatier drumsticks will take longer to cook than small ones.

Marjoram Chicken Wings with Cream Cheese

Prep time: 7 minutes | Cook time: 10 minutes | Serves 2

1 teaspoon marjoram
1 teaspoon cream cheese
½ green pepper
½ teaspoon salt

½ teaspoon ground black pepper
400 g chicken wings
180 ml water
1 teaspoon coconut oil

1. Rub the chicken wings with the marjoram, salt, and ground black pepper. 2. Blend the green pepper until you get a purée. 3. Rub the chicken wings in the green pepper purée. 4. Then toss the coconut oil in the Ninja Foodi cooker bowl and preheat it on the Sauté mode. 5. Add the chicken wings and cook them for 3 minutes from each side or until light brown. 6. Then add cream cheese and water. 7. Cook the meal for 4 minutes at High Pressure. 8. When the time is over, make a quick pressure release. 9. Let the cooked chicken wings chill for 1 to 2 minutes and serve them!

Shredded Chicken

Prep time: 5 minutes | Cook time: 14 minutes | Serves 4

½ teaspoon salt
½ teaspoon pepper
½ teaspoon dried oregano
½ teaspoon dried basil
½ teaspoon garlic powder

2 (170 g) boneless, skinless chicken breasts
1 tablespoon coconut oil
240 ml water

1. In a small bowl, combine the salt, pepper, oregano, basil, and garlic powder. Rub this mix over both sides of the chicken. 2. Set your Ninja Foodi cooker to Sauté and heat the coconut oil until sizzling. 3. Add the chicken and sear for 3 to 4 minutes until golden on both sides. 4. Remove the chicken and set aside. 5. Pour the water into the Ninja Foodi cooker and use a wooden spoon or rubber spatula to make sure no seasoning is stuck to bottom of pot. 6. Add the reversible rack to the Ninja Foodi cooker and place the chicken on top. 7. Secure the lid. Set the cooking time for 10 minutes at High Pressure. 8. Once cooking is complete, do a natural pressure release for 5 minutes, then release any remaining pressure. Carefully open the lid. 9. Remove the chicken and shred, then serve.

Chicken Thighs with Feta

Prep time: 7 minutes | Cook time: 15 minutes | Serves 2

4 lemon slices
2 chicken thighs
1 tablespoon Greek seasoning

110 g feta, crumbled
1 teaspoon butter
120 ml water

1. Rub the chicken thighs with Greek seasoning. 2. Then spread the chicken with butter. 3. Pour water in the Ninja Foodi cooker and place the reversible rack. 4. Place the chicken on the foil and top with the lemon slices. Top it with feta. 5. Wrap the chicken in the foil and transfer on the reversible rack. 6. Cook on the Sauté mode for 10 minutes. Then make a quick pressure release for 5 minutes. 7. Discard the foil from the chicken thighs and serve!

Coriander Lime Chicken Thighs

Prep time: 15 minutes | Cook time: 22 minutes | Serves 4

4 bone-in, skin-on chicken thighs
1 teaspoon baking powder
½ teaspoon garlic powder

2 teaspoons chili powder
1 teaspoon cumin
2 medium limes
5 g chopped fresh coriander

1. Pat chicken thighs dry and sprinkle with baking powder. 2. In a small bowl, mix garlic powder, chili powder, and cumin and sprinkle evenly over thighs, gently rubbing on and under chicken skin. 3. Cut one lime in half and squeeze juice over thighs. Place chicken into the cook & crisp basket. 4. Adjust the temperature to 190ºC and roast for 22 minutes. 5. Cut other lime into four wedges for serving and garnish cooked chicken with wedges and coriander.

Broccoli Chicken Divan

Prep time: 15 minutes | Cook time: 10 minutes | Serves 4

240 ml chopped broccoli
2 tablespoons cream cheese
120 ml double cream
1 tablespoon curry powder

60 ml chicken broth
120 ml grated Cheddar cheese
170 g chicken fillet, cooked and chopped

1. Mix up broccoli and curry powder and put the mixture in the Ninja Foodi cooker. 2. Add double cream and cream cheese. 3. Then add chicken and mix up the ingredients. 4. Then add chicken broth and double cream. 5. Top the mixture with Cheddar cheese. Close and seal the lid. 6. Cook the meal on High Pressure for 10 minutes. Allow the natural pressure release for 5 minutes, open the lid and cool the meal for 10 minutes.

Sesame Chicken with Broccoli

Prep time: 15 minutes | Cook time: 12 minutes | Serves 2

½ teaspoon five spices
½ teaspoon sesame seeds
120 ml chopped broccoli
170 g chicken fillet, sliced

120 ml chicken broth
1 teaspoon coconut aminos
1 tablespoon avocado oil

1. In the mixing bowl, mix up avocado oil, coconut aminos, and sesame seeds. 2. Add five spices. 3. After this, mix up sliced chicken fillet and coconut aminos mixture. 4. Put the chicken in the Ninja Foodi cooker. Add chicken broth and broccoli. 5. Close and seal the lid. 6. Cook the meal on High Pressure for 12 minutes. Make a quick pressure release.

Mexican Turkey Tenderloin

Prep time: 5 minutes | Cook time: 8 minutes | Serves 6

240 ml Salsa or bottled salsa
1 teaspoon chili powder
½ teaspoon ground cumin
¼ teaspoon dried oregano
680 g unseasoned turkey

tenderloin or boneless turkey breast, cut into 6 pieces
Freshly ground black pepper
120 ml shredded Monterey Jack cheese or Mexican cheese blend

1. In a small bowl or measuring cup, combine the salsa, chili powder, cumin, and oregano. Pour half of the mixture into the electric pressure cooker. 2. Nestle the turkey into the sauce. Grind some pepper onto each piece of turkey. Pour the remaining salsa mixture on top. 3. Close and lock the lid of the pressure cooker. Set the valve to sealing. 4. Cook on high pressure for 8 minutes. 5. When the cooking is complete, hit Start/Stop. Allow the pressure to release naturally for 10 minutes, then quick release any remaining pressure. 6. Once the pin drops, unlock and remove the lid. 7. Sprinkle the cheese on top, and put the lid back on for a few minutes to let the cheese melt. 8. Serve immediately.

Lettuce-Wrapped Turkey and Mushroom Meatballs

Prep time: 10 minutes | Cook time: 15 minutes | Serves 6

Sauce:
2 tablespoons tamari
2 tablespoons tomato sauce
1 tablespoon lime juice
¼ teaspoon peeled and grated fresh ginger
1 clove garlic, smashed to a paste
120 ml chicken broth
70 g sugar
2 tablespoons toasted sesame oil
Cooking spray
Meatballs:
900 g turkey mince
75 g finely chopped button mushrooms

2 large eggs, beaten
1½ teaspoons tamari
15 g finely chopped green onions, plus more for garnish
2 teaspoons peeled and grated fresh ginger
1 clove garlic, smashed
2 teaspoons toasted sesame oil
2 tablespoons sugar
For Serving:
Lettuce leaves, for serving
Sliced red chilies, for garnish (optional)
Toasted sesame seeds, for garnish (optional)

1. Preheat the Ninja Foodi cooker to 180ºC. Spritz a baking pan with cooking spray. 2. Combine the ingredients for the sauce in a small bowl. Stir to mix well. Set aside. 3. Combine the ingredients for the meatballs in a large bowl. Stir to mix well, then shape the mixture in twelve 1½-inch meatballs. 4. Arrange the meatballs in a single layer on the baking pan, then baste with the sauce. You may need to work in batches to avoid overcrowding. 5. Arrange the pan in the Ninja Foodi cooker. Air crisp for 15 minutes or until the meatballs are golden brown. Flip the balls halfway through the cooking time. 6. Unfold the lettuce leaves on a large serving plate, then transfer the cooked meatballs on the leaves. Spread the red chilies and sesame seeds over the balls, then serve.

Chicken Breasts with Asparagus, Beans, and Rocket

Prep time: 20 minutes | Cook time: 25 minutes | Serves 2

160 g canned cannellini beans, rinsed
1½ tablespoons red wine vinegar
1 garlic clove, minced
2 tablespoons extra-virgin olive oil, divided
Salt and ground black pepper, to taste

½ red onion, sliced thinly
230 g asparagus, trimmed and cut into 1-inch lengths
2 (230 g) boneless, skinless chicken breasts, trimmed
¼ teaspoon paprika
½ teaspoon ground coriander
60 g baby rocket, rinsed and drained

1. Preheat the Ninja Foodi cooker to 200ºC. 2. Warm the beans in microwave for 1 minutes and combine with red wine vinegar, garlic, 1 tablespoon of olive oil, ¼ teaspoon of salt, and ¼ teaspoon of ground black pepper in a bowl. Stir to mix well. 3. Combine the onion with ⅛ teaspoon of salt, ⅛ teaspoon of ground black pepper, and 2 teaspoons of olive oil in a separate bowl. Toss to coat well. 4. Place the onion in the Ninja Foodi cooker and air crisp for 2 minutes, then add the asparagus and air crisp for 8 more minutes or until the asparagus is tender. Shake the basket halfway through. Transfer the onion and asparagus to the bowl with beans. Set aside. 5. Toss the chicken breasts with remaining ingredients, except for the baby rocket, in a large bowl. 6. Put the chicken breasts in the Ninja Foodi cooker and air crisp for 14 minutes or until the internal temperature of the chicken reaches at least 75ºC. Flip the breasts halfway through. 7. Remove the chicken from the Ninja Foodi cooker and serve on an aluminum foil with asparagus, beans, onion, and rocket. Sprinkle with salt and ground black pepper. Toss to serve.

Gochujang Chicken Wings

Prep time: 15 minutes | Cook time: 25 minutes | Serves 4

Wings:
900 g chicken wings
1 teaspoon kosher salt
1 teaspoon black pepper or gochugaru (Korean red pepper)
Sauce:
2 tablespoons gochujang (Korean chili paste)
1 tablespoon mayonnaise
1 tablespoon toasted sesame oil

1 tablespoon minced fresh ginger
1 tablespoon minced garlic
1 teaspoon sugar
1 teaspoon agave nectar or honey
For Serving
1 teaspoon sesame seeds
25 g chopped spring onions

1. For the wings: Season the wings with the salt and pepper and place in the cook & crisp basket. Set the Ninja Foodi cooker to 200ºC for 20 minutes, turning the wings halfway through the cooking time. 2. Meanwhile, for the sauce: In a small bowl, combine the gochujang, mayonnaise, sesame oil, ginger, garlic, sugar, and agave; set aside. 3. As you near the 20-minute mark, use a meat thermometer to check the meat. When the wings reach 70ºC, transfer them to a large bowl. Pour about half the sauce on the wings; toss to coat (serve the remaining sauce as a dip). 4. Return the wings to the cook & crisp basket and cook for 5 minutes, until the sauce has glazed. 5. Transfer the wings to a serving platter. Sprinkle with the sesame seeds and spring onions. Serve with the reserved sauce on the side for dipping.

Pecan-Crusted Chicken Tenders

Prep time: 10 minutes | Cook time: 12 minutes | Serves 4

2 tablespoons mayonnaise
1 teaspoon Dijon mustard
455 g boneless, skinless chicken tenders

½ teaspoon salt
¼ teaspoon ground black pepper
75 g chopped roasted pecans, finely ground

1. In a small bowl, whisk mayonnaise and mustard until combined. Brush mixture onto chicken tenders on both sides, then sprinkle tenders with salt and pepper. 2. Place pecans in a medium bowl and press each tender into pecans to coat each side. 3. Place tenders into ungreased cook & crisp basket in a single layer, working in batches if needed. Adjust the temperature to (190ºC and roast for 12 minutes, turning tenders halfway through cooking. Tenders will be golden brown and have an internal temperature of at least 75ºC when done. Serve warm.

Chipotle Drumsticks

Prep time: 15 minutes | Cook time: 20 minutes | Serves 4

1 tablespoon tomato paste
½ teaspoon chipotle powder
¼ teaspoon apple cider vinegar
¼ teaspoon garlic powder
8 chicken drumsticks
½ teaspoon salt
⅛ teaspoon ground black pepper

1. In a small bowl, combine tomato paste, chipotle powder, vinegar, and garlic powder. 2. Sprinkle drumsticks with salt and pepper, then place into a large bowl and pour in tomato paste mixture. Toss or stir to evenly coat all drumsticks in mixture. 3. Place drumsticks into ungreased cook & crisp basket. Adjust the temperature to 200ºC and air crisp for 25 minutes, turning drumsticks halfway through cooking. Drumsticks will be dark red with an internal temperature of at least 75ºC when done. Serve warm.

Coconut Chicken Meatballs

Prep time: 10 minutes | Cook time: 14 minutes | Serves 4

450 g chicken mince
2 spring onions, finely chopped
20 g chopped fresh corinader leaves
20 g unsweetened shredded coconut
1 tablespoon hoisin sauce
1 tablespoon soy sauce
2 teaspoons Sriracha or other hot sauce
1 teaspoon toasted sesame oil
½ teaspoon kosher salt
1 teaspoon black pepper

1. In a large bowl, gently mix the chicken, spring onions, coriander, coconut, hoisin, soy sauce, Sriracha, sesame oil, salt, and pepper until thoroughly combined (the mixture will be wet and sticky). 2. Place a sheet of parchment paper in the cook & crisp basket. Using a small scoop or teaspoon, drop rounds of the mixture in a single layer onto the parchment paper. 3. Set the Ninja Foodi cooker to 180ºC for 10 minutes, turning the meatballs halfway through the cooking time. Raise the Ninja Foodi cooker temperature to 200ºC and cook for 4 minutes more to brown the outsides of the meatballs. Use a meat thermometer to ensure the meatballs have reached an internal temperature of 75ºC. 4. Transfer the meatballs to a serving platter. Repeat with any remaining chicken mixture.

Chicken Enchiladas

Prep time: 10 minutes | Cook time: 8 minutes | Serves 4

Oil, for spraying
420 g shredded cooked chicken
1 package taco seasoning
8 flour tortillas, at room temperature
60 g canned black beans, rinsed
and drained
1 (115 g) can diced green chilies, drained
1 (280 g) can red or green enchilada sauce
235 g shredded Cheddar cheese

1. Line the cook & crisp basket with parchment and spray lightly with oil. (Do not skip the step of lining the basket; the parchment will keep the sauce and cheese from dripping through the holes.)

2. In a small bowl, mix together the chicken and taco seasoning. 3. Divide the mixture among the tortillas. Top with the black beans and green chilis. Carefully roll up each tortilla. 4. Place the enchiladas, seam-side down, in the prepared basket. You may need to work in batches, depending on the size of your Ninja Foodi cooker. 5. Spoon the enchilada sauce over the enchiladas. Use just enough sauce to keep them from drying out. You can add more sauce when serving. Sprinkle the cheese on top. 6. Air crisp at 180ºC for 5 to 8 minutes, or until heated through and the cheese is melted. 7. Place 2 enchiladas on each plate and top with more enchilada sauce, if desired.

Garlic Parmesan Drumsticks

Prep time: 5 minutes | Cook time: 25 minutes | Serves 4

8 (115 g) chicken drumsticks
½ teaspoon salt
⅛ teaspoon ground black pepper
½ teaspoon garlic powder
2 tablespoons salted butter, melted
45 g grated Parmesan cheese
1 tablespoon dried parsley

1. Sprinkle drumsticks with salt, pepper, and garlic powder. Place drumsticks into ungreased cook & crisp basket. 2. Adjust the temperature to 200ºC and air crisp for 25 minutes, turning drumsticks halfway through cooking. Drumsticks will be golden and have an internal temperature of at least 75ºC when done. 3. Transfer drumsticks to a large serving dish. Pour butter over drumsticks, and sprinkle with Parmesan and parsley. Serve warm.

Korean Flavour Glazed Chicken Wings

Prep time: 10 minutes | Cook time: 25 minutes | Serves 4

Wings:
900 g chicken wings
1 teaspoon salt
1 teaspoon ground black pepper
Sauce:
2 tablespoons gochujang
1 tablespoon mayonnaise
1 tablespoon minced ginger
1 tablespoon minced garlic
1 teaspoon agave nectar
2 packets Splenda
1 tablespoon sesame oil
For Garnish:
2 teaspoons sesame seeds
15 g chopped green onions

1. Preheat the Ninja Foodi cooker to 200ºC. Line a baking pan with aluminum foil, then arrange the rack on the pan. 2. On a clean work surface, rub the chicken wings with salt and ground black pepper, then arrange the seasoned wings on the rack. 3. Air crisp for 20 minutes or until the wings are well browned. Flip the wings halfway through. You may need to work in batches to avoid overcrowding. 4. Meanwhile, combine the ingredients for the sauce in a small bowl. Stir to mix well. Reserve half of the sauce in a separate bowl until ready to serve. 5. Remove the air fried chicken wings from the Ninja Foodi cooker and toss with remaining half of the sauce to coat well. 6. Place the wings back to the Ninja Foodi cooker and air crisp for 5 more minutes or until the internal temperature of the wings reaches at least 75ºC. 7. Remove the wings from the Ninja Foodi cooker and place on a large plate. Sprinkle with sesame seeds and green onions. Serve with reserved sauce.

Bacon Lovers' Stuffed Chicken

Prep time: 15 minutes | Cook time: 10 minutes | Serves 4

4 (140 g) boneless, skinless chicken breasts, pounded to ¼ inch thick
2 (150 g) packages Boursin cheese (or Kite Hill brand chive cream cheese style spread,
softened, for dairy-free)
8 slices thin-cut bacon or beef bacon
Sprig of fresh coriander, for garnish (optional)

1. Spray the cook & crisp basket with avocado oil. Preheat the Ninja Foodi cooker to 200ºC. 2. Place one of the chicken breasts on a cutting board. With a sharp knife held parallel to the cutting board, make a 1-inch-wide incision at the top of the breast. Carefully cut into the breast to form a large pocket, leaving a ½-inch border along the sides and bottom. Repeat with the other 3 chicken breasts. 3. Snip the corner of a large resealable plastic bag to form a ¾-inch hole. Place the Boursin cheese in the bag and pipe the cheese into the pockets in the chicken breasts, dividing the cheese evenly among them. 4. Wrap 2 slices of bacon around each chicken breast and secure the ends with toothpicks. Place the bacon-wrapped chicken in the cook & crisp basket and air crisp until the bacon is crisp and the chicken's internal temperature reaches 75ºC, about 18 to 20 minutes, flipping after 10 minutes. Garnish with a sprig of coriander before serving, if desired. 5. Store leftovers in an airtight container in the refrigerator for up to 4 days. Reheat in a preheated 200ºC Ninja Foodi cooker for 5 minutes, or until warmed through.

Israeli Chicken Schnitzel

Prep time: 5 minutes | Cook time: 10 minutes | Serves 4

2 large boneless, skinless chicken breasts, each weighing about 450 g
125 g all-purpose flour
2 teaspoons garlic powder
2 teaspoons kosher salt
1 teaspoon black pepper
1 teaspoon paprika
2 eggs beaten with 2 tablespoons water
250 g panko bread crumbs
Vegetable oil spray
Lemon juice, for serving

1. Preheat the Ninja Foodi cooker to 190ºC. 2. Place 1 chicken breast between 2 pieces of plastic wrap. Use a mallet or a rolling pin to pound the chicken until it is ¼ inch thick. Set aside. Repeat with the second breast. Whisk together the flour, garlic powder, salt, pepper, and paprika on a large plate. Place the panko in a separate shallow bowl or pie plate. 3. Dredge 1 chicken breast in the flour, shaking off any excess, then dip it in the egg mixture. Dredge the chicken breast in the panko, making sure to coat it completely. Shake off any excess panko. Place the battered chicken breast on a plate. Repeat with the second chicken breast. 4. Spray the cook & crisp basket with oil spray. Place 1 of the battered chicken breasts in the basket and spray the top with oil spray. Air crisp until the top is browned, about 5 minutes. Flip the chicken and spray the second side with oil spray. Air crisp until the second side is browned and crispy and the internal temperature reaches 75ºC. Remove the first chicken breast from the Ninja Foodi cooker and repeat with the second chicken breast. 5. Serve hot with lemon juice.

Ethiopian Chicken with Cauliflower

Prep time: 15 minutes | Cook time: 28 minutes | Serves 6

2 handful fresh Italian parsley, roughly chopped
20 g fresh chopped chives
2 sprigs thyme
6 chicken drumsticks
1½ small-sized head cauliflower, broken into large-sized florets
2 teaspoons mustard powder
⅓ teaspoon porcini powder
1½ teaspoons berbere spice
⅓ teaspoon sweet paprika
½ teaspoon shallot powder
1teaspoon granulated garlic
1 teaspoon freshly cracked pink peppercorns
½ teaspoon sea salt

1. Simply combine all items for the berbere spice rub mix. After that, coat the chicken drumsticks with this rub mix on all sides. Transfer them to the baking dish. 2. Now, lower the cauliflower onto the chicken drumsticks. Add thyme, chives and Italian parsley and spritz everything with a pan spray. Transfer the baking dish to the preheated Ninja Foodi cooker. 3. Next step, set the timer for 28 minutes; roast at 180ºC, turning occasionally. Bon appétit!

Cider Chicken with Pecans

Prep time: 10 minutes | Cook time: 15 minutes | Serves 2

170 g chicken fillet, cubed
2 pecans, chopped
1 teaspoon coconut aminos
½ bell pepper, chopped
1 tablespoon coconut oil
60 ml apple cider vinegar
60 ml chicken broth

1. Melt coconut oil on Sauté mode and add chicken cubes. 2. Add bell pepper, and pecans. 3. Sauté the ingredients for 10 minutes and add apple cider vinegar, chicken broth, and coconut aminos. 4. Sauté the chicken for 5 minutes more.

Crispy Dill Chicken Strips

Prep time: 30 minutes | Cook time: 10 minutes | Serves 4

2 whole boneless, skinless chicken breasts (about 450 g each), halved lengthwise
230 ml Italian dressing
110 g finely crushed crisps
1 tablespoon dried dill weed
1 tablespoon garlic powder
1 large egg, beaten
1 to 2 tablespoons oil

1. In a large resealable bag, combine the chicken and Italian dressing. Seal the bag and refrigerate to marinate at least 1 hour. 2. In a shallow dish, stir together the potato chips, dill, and garlic powder. Place the beaten egg in a second shallow dish. 3. Remove the chicken from the marinade. Roll the chicken pieces in the egg and the crisp mixture, coating thoroughly. 4. Preheat the Ninja Foodi cooker to 170ºC. Line the cook & crisp basket with parchment paper. 5. Place the coated chicken on the parchment and spritz with oil. 6. Cook for 5 minutes. Flip the chicken, spritz it with oil, and cook for 5 minutes more until the outsides are crispy and the insides are no longer pink.

Chicken with Pineapple and Peach

Prep time: 10 minutes | Cook time: 14 to 15 minutes | Serves 4

1 (450 g) low-sodium boneless, skinless chicken breasts, cut into 1-inch pieces
1 medium red onion, chopped
1 (230 g) can pineapple chunks, drained, 60 ml juice reserved
1 tablespoon peanut oil or

safflower oil
1 peach, peeled, pitted, and cubed
1 tablespoon cornflour
½ teaspoon ground ginger
¼ teaspoon ground allspice
Brown rice, cooked (optional)

1. Preheat the Ninja Foodi cooker to 195°C. 2. In a medium metal bowl, mix the chicken, red onion, pineapple, and peanut oil. Bake in the Ninja Foodi cooker for 9 minutes. Remove and stir. 3. Add the peach and return the bowl to the Ninja Foodi cooker. Bake for 3 minutes more. Remove and stir again. 4. In a small bowl, whisk the reserved pineapple juice, the cornflour, ginger, and allspice well. Add to the chicken mixture and stir to combine. 5. Bake for 2 to 3 minutes more, or until the chicken reaches an internal temperature of 75°C on a meat thermometer and the sauce is slightly thickened. 6. Serve immediately over hot cooked brown rice, if desired.

Nashville Hot Chicken

Prep time: 20 minutes | Cook time: 24 to 28 minutes | Serves 8

1.4 kg bone-in, skin-on chicken pieces, breasts halved crosswise
1 tablespoon sea salt
1 tablespoon freshly ground black pepper
140 g finely ground blanched almond flour
130 g grated Parmesan cheese
1 tablespoon baking powder
2 teaspoons garlic powder, divided

120 g heavy (whipping) cream
2 large eggs, beaten
1 tablespoon vinegar-based hot sauce
Avocado oil spray
115 g unsalted butter
120 ml avocado oil
1 tablespoon cayenne pepper (more or less to taste)
2 tablespoons Xylitol

1. Sprinkle the chicken with the salt and pepper. 2. In a large shallow bowl, whisk together the almond flour, Parmesan cheese, baking powder, and 1 teaspoon of the garlic powder. 3. In a separate bowl, whisk together the heavy cream, eggs, and hot sauce. 4. Dip the chicken pieces in the egg, then coat each with the almond flour mixture, pressing the mixture into the chicken to adhere. Allow to sit for 15 minutes to let the breading set. 5. Set the Ninja Foodi cooker to 200°C. Place the chicken in a single layer in the cook & crisp basket, being careful not to overcrowd the pieces, working in batches if necessary. Spray the chicken with oil and roast for 13 minutes. 6. Carefully flip the chicken and spray it with more oil. Reduce the Ninja Foodi cooker temperature to 180°C. Roast for another 11 to 15 minutes, until an instant-read thermometer reads 70°C. 7. While the chicken cooks, heat the butter, avocado oil, cayenne pepper, xylitol, and remaining 1 teaspoon of garlic powder in a saucepan over medium-low heat. Cook until the butter is melted and the sugar substitute has dissolved. 8. Remove the chicken from the Ninja Foodi cooker. Use tongs to dip the chicken in the sauce. Place the coated chicken on a rack over a baking sheet, and allow it to rest for 5 minutes before serving.

Pesto Chicken

Prep time: 5 minutes | Cook time: 25 minutes | Serves 2

2 (170 g) boneless, skinless chicken breasts, butterflied
½ teaspoon salt
¼ teaspoon pepper
¼ teaspoon dried parsley
¼ teaspoon garlic powder
2 tablespoons coconut oil

240 ml water
60 ml whole-milk ricotta cheese
60 ml pesto
60 ml shredded whole-milk Mozzarella cheese
Chopped parsley, for garnish (optional)

1. Sprinkle the chicken breasts with salt, pepper, parsley, and garlic powder. 2. Set your Ninja Foodi cooker to Sauté and melt the coconut oil. 3. Add the chicken and brown for 3 to 5 minutes. Remove the chicken from the pot to a 7-cup glass bowl. 4. Pour the water into the Ninja Foodi cooker and use a wooden spoon or rubber spatula to make sure no seasoning is stuck to bottom of pot. 5. Scatter the ricotta cheese on top of the chicken. Pour the pesto over chicken, and sprinkle the Mozzarella cheese over chicken. Cover with aluminium foil. Add the reversible rack to the Ninja Foodi cooker and place the bowl on the reversible rack. 6. Secure the lid. Set the cooking time for 20 minutes at High Pressure. 7. Once cooking is complete, do a natural pressure release for 10 minutes, then release any remaining pressure. Carefully open the lid. 8. Serve the chicken garnished with the chopped parsley, if desired.

Italian Chicken Thighs

Prep time: 5 minutes | Cook time: 20 minutes | Serves 2

4 bone-in, skin-on chicken thighs
2 tablespoons unsalted butter, melted
1 teaspoon dried parsley

1 teaspoon dried basil
½ teaspoon garlic powder
¼ teaspoon onion powder
¼ teaspoon dried oregano

1. Brush chicken thighs with butter and sprinkle remaining ingredients over thighs. Place thighs into the cook & crisp basket. 2. Adjust the temperature to 190°C and roast for 20 minutes. 3. Halfway through the cooking time, flip the thighs. 4. When fully cooked, internal temperature will be at least 75°C and skin will be crispy. Serve warm.

Chicken and Kale Sandwiches

Prep time: 10 minutes | Cook time: 10 minutes | Serves 2

110 g kale leaves
230 g chicken fillet
1 tablespoon butter

30 g lemon
60 ml water

1. Dice the chicken fillet. 2. Squeeze the lemon juice over the poultry. 3. Transfer the poultry into the Ninja Foodi cooker; add water and butter. 4. Close the lid and cook the chicken on the Poultry mode for 10 minutes. 5. When the chicken is cooked, place it on the kale leaves to make the medium sandwiches.

Bacon-Wrapped Chicken Breasts Rolls

Prep time: 10 minutes | Cook time: 15 minutes | Serves 4

15 g chopped fresh chives
2 tablespoons lemon juice
1 teaspoon dried sage
1 teaspoon fresh rosemary leaves
15 g fresh parsley leaves
4 cloves garlic, peeled
1 teaspoon ground fennel
3 teaspoons sea salt
½ teaspoon red pepper flakes
4 (115 g) boneless, skinless chicken breasts, pounded to ¼ inch thick
8 slices bacon
Sprigs of fresh rosemary, for garnish
Cooking spray

1. Preheat the Ninja Foodi cooker to 170°C. Spritz the cook & crisp basket with cooking spray. 2. Put the chives, lemon juice, sage, rosemary, parsley, garlic, fennel, salt, and red pepper flakes in a food processor, then pulse to purée until smooth. 3. Unfold the chicken breasts on a clean work surface, then brush the top side of the chicken breasts with the sauce. 4. Roll the chicken breasts up from the shorter side, then wrap each chicken rolls with 2 bacon slices to cover. Secure with toothpicks. 5. Arrange the rolls in the preheated Ninja Foodi cooker, then cook for 10 minutes. Flip the rolls halfway through. 6. Increase the heat to 200°C and air crisp for 5 more minutes or until the bacon is browned and crispy. 7. Transfer the rolls to a large plate. Discard the toothpicks and spread with rosemary sprigs before serving.

Piri-Piri Chicken Thighs

Prep time: 5 minutes | Cook time: 25 minutes | Serves 4

60 ml piri-piri sauce
1 tablespoon freshly squeezed lemon juice
2 tablespoons brown sugar, divided
2 cloves garlic, minced
1 tablespoon extra-virgin olive oil
4 bone-in, skin-on chicken thighs, each weighing approximately 200 to 230 g
½ teaspoon cornflour

1. To make the marinade, whisk together the piri-piri sauce, lemon juice, 1 tablespoon of brown sugar, and the garlic in a small bowl. While whisking, slowly pour in the oil in a steady stream and continue to whisk until emulsified. Using a skewer, poke holes in the chicken thighs and place them in a small glass dish. Pour the marinade over the chicken and turn the thighs to coat them with the sauce. Cover the dish and refrigerate for at least 15 minutes and up to 1 hour. 2. Preheat the Ninja Foodi cooker to 190°C. Remove the chicken thighs from the dish, reserving the marinade, and place them skin-side down in the cook & crisp basket. Air crisp until the internal temperature reaches 75°C, 15 to 20 minutes. 3. Meanwhile, whisk the remaining brown sugar and the cornflour into the marinade and microwave it on high power for 1 minute until it is bubbling and thickened to a glaze. 4. Once the chicken is cooked, turn the thighs over and brush them with the glaze. Air crisp for a few additional minutes until the glaze browns and begins to char in spots. 5. Remove the chicken to a platter and serve with additional piri-piri sauce, if desired.

Potato-Crusted Chicken

Prep time: 15 minutes | Cook time: 22 to 25 minutes | Serves 4

60 g buttermilk
1 large egg, beaten
180 g instant potato flakes
20 g grated Parmesan cheese
1 teaspoon salt
½ teaspoon freshly ground black
pepper
2 whole boneless, skinless chicken breasts (about 450 g each), halved
1 to 2 tablespoons oil

1. In a shallow bowl, whisk the buttermilk and egg until blended. In another shallow bowl, stir together the potato flakes, cheese, salt, and pepper. 2. One at a time, dip the chicken pieces in the buttermilk mixture and the potato flake mixture, coating thoroughly. 3. Preheat the Ninja Foodi cooker to 200°C. Line the cook & crisp basket with parchment paper. 4. Place the coated chicken on the parchment and spritz with oil. 5. Cook for 15 minutes. Flip the chicken, spritz it with oil, and cook for 7 to 10 minutes more until the outside is crispy and the inside is no longer pink.

Mushroom Chicken Alfredo

Prep time: 15 minutes | Cook time: 10 minutes | Serves 4

120 ml sliced cremini mushrooms
60 ml chopped leek
1 tablespoon sesame oil
1 teaspoon chili flakes
240 ml double cream
450 g chicken fillet, chopped
1 teaspoon Italian seasoning
1 tablespoon cream cheese

1. Brush the Ninja Foodi cooker boil with sesame oil from inside. 2. Put the chicken in the Ninja Foodi cooker in one layer. 3. Then top it with mushrooms and leek. 4. Sprinkle the ingredients with chili flakes, double cream, Italian seasoning, and cream cheese. 5. Close and seal the lid. 6. Cook the meal on High Pressure for 10 minutes. 7. When the time is finished, allow the natural pressure release for 10 minutes.

Lemon-Basil Turkey Breasts

Prep time: 30 minutes | Cook time: 58 minutes | Serves 4

2 tablespoons olive oil
900 g turkey breasts, bone-in, skin-on
Coarse sea salt and ground
black pepper, to taste
1 teaspoon fresh basil leaves, chopped
2 tablespoons lemon zest, grated

1. Rub olive oil on all sides of the turkey breasts; sprinkle with salt, pepper, basil, and lemon zest. 2. Place the turkey breasts skin side up on the parchment-lined cook & crisp basket. 3. Cook in the preheated Ninja Foodi cooker at 170°C for 30 minutes. Now, turn them over and cook an additional 28 minutes. 4. Serve with lemon wedges, if desired. Bon appétit!

Tex-Mex Chicken Breasts

Prep time: 10 minutes | Cook time: 17 to 20 minutes | Serves 4

450 g low-sodium boneless, skinless chicken breasts, cut into 1-inch cubes
1 medium onion, chopped
1 red bell pepper, chopped
1 jalapeño pepper, minced

2 teaspoons olive oil
115 g canned low-sodium black beans, rinsed and drained
130 g low-sodium salsa
2 teaspoons chili powder

1. Preheat the Ninja Foodi cooker to 200°C. 2. In a medium metal bowl, mix the chicken, onion, bell pepper, jalapeño, and olive oil. Roast for 10 minutes, stirring once during cooking. 3. Add the black beans, salsa, and chili powder. Roast for 7 to 10 minutes more, stirring once, until the chicken reaches an internal temperature of 75°C on a meat thermometer. Serve immediately.

Dijon Turkey

Prep time: 15 minutes | Cook time: 14 minutes | Serves 4

400 g minced turkey
1 tablespoon Dijon mustard
120 ml coconut flour
1 teaspoon onion powder

1 teaspoon salt
120 ml chicken broth
1 tablespoon avocado oil

1. In the mixing bowl, mix up minced turkey, Dijon mustard, coconut flour, onion powder, and salt. 2. Make the meatballs with the help of the fingertips. 3. Then pour avocado oil in the Ninja Foodi cooker and heat it up for 1 minute. 4. Add the meatballs and cook them for 2 minutes from each side. 5. Then add chicken broth. Close and seal the lid. 6. Cook the meatballs for 10 minutes. Make a quick pressure release.

Poblano Chicken

Prep time: 10 minutes | Cook time: 29 minutes | Serves 4

2 Poblano peppers, sliced
450 g chicken fillet
½ teaspoon salt

120 ml coconut cream
1 tablespoon butter
½ teaspoon chili powder

1. Heat up the butter on Sauté mode for 3 minutes. 2. Add Poblano and cook them for 3 minutes. 3. Meanwhile, cut the chicken fillet into the strips and sprinkle with salt and chili powder. 4. Add the chicken strips to the Ninja Foodi cooker. 5. Then add coconut cream and close the lid. Cook the meal on Sauté mode for 20 minutes.

Chapter 7 Beef, Pork, and Lamb

Southern Chili

Prep time: 20 minutes | Cook time: 25 minutes | Serves 4

450 g beef mince (85% lean)
235 ml minced onion
1 (794 g) can tomato purée
1 (425 g) can diced tomatoes

1 (425 g) can red kidney beans, rinsed and drained
60 ml Chili seasoning

1. Preheat the Ninja Foodi cooker to 205°C. 2. In a baking pan, mix the mince and onion. Place the pan in the Ninja Foodi cooker. 3. Cook for 4 minutes. Stir and cook for 4 minutes more until browned. Remove the pan from the fryer. Drain the meat and transfer to a large bowl. 4. Reduce the Ninja Foodi cooker temperature to 175°C. 5. To the bowl with the meat, add in the tomato purée, diced tomatoes, kidney beans, and Chili seasoning. Mix well. Pour the mixture into the baking pan. 6. Cook for 25 minutes, stirring every 10 minutes, until thickened.

Steak with Bell Pepper

Prep time: 30 minutes | Cook time: 20 to 23 minutes | Serves 6

60 ml avocado oil
60 ml freshly squeezed lime juice
2 teaspoons minced garlic
1 tablespoon chili powder
½ teaspoon ground cumin
Sea salt and freshly ground black pepper, to taste

450 g top rump steak or bavette or skirt steak, thinly sliced against the grain
1 red pepper, cored, seeded, and cut into ½-inch slices
1 green pepper, cored, seeded, and cut into ½-inch slices
1 large onion, sliced

1. In a small bowl or blender, combine the avocado oil, lime juice, garlic, chili powder, cumin, and salt and pepper to taste. 2. Place the sliced steak in a zip-top bag or shallow dish. Place the peppers and onion in a separate zip-top bag or dish. Pour half the marinade over the steak and the other half over the vegetables. Seal both bags and let the steak and vegetables marinate in the refrigerator for at least 1 hour or up to 4 hours. 3. Line the cook & crisp basket with an Ninja Foodi cooker liner or aluminum foil. Remove the vegetables from their bag or dish and shake off any excess marinade. Set the Ninja Foodi cooker to 205°C. Place the vegetables in the cook & crisp basket and cook for 13 minutes. 4. Remove the steak from its bag or dish and shake off any excess marinade. Place the steak on top of the vegetables in the Ninja Foodi cooker, and cook for 7 to 10 minutes or until an instant-read thermometer reads 50°C for medium-rare (or cook to your desired doneness). 5. Serve with desired fixings, such as keto tortillas, lettuce, sour cream, avocado slices, shredded Cheddar cheese, and coriander.

Beef Steak with Cheese Mushroom Sauce

Prep time: 6 minutes | Cook time: 30 minutes | Serves 6

1 tablespoon olive oil
680 g beef blade steak
240 ml stock
2 garlic cloves, minced
Sea salt and ground black pepper, to taste
½ teaspoon cayenne pepper
1 tablespoon coconut aminos

Sauce:
1 tablespoon butter, softened
480 ml sliced Porcini mushrooms
120 ml thinly sliced onions
120 ml sour cream
110 g goat cheese, crumbled

1. Press the Sauté button to heat up the Ninja Foodi cooker. Then, heat the olive oil until sizzling. Once hot, cook the blade steak approximately 3 minutes or until delicately browned. 2. Add the stock, garlic, salt, black pepper, cayenne pepper, and coconut aminos. 3. Secure the lid. Choose High Pressure; cook for 20 minutes. Once cooking is complete, use a quick pressure release; carefully remove the lid. 4. Take the meat out of the Ninja Foodi cooker. Allow it to cool slightly and then, slice it into strips. 5. Press the Sauté button again and add the butter, mushrooms and onions to the Ninja Foodi cooker. Let it cook for 5 minutes longer or until the mushrooms are fragrant and the onions are softened. 6. Add sour cream and goat cheese; continue to simmer for a couple of minutes more or until everything is thoroughly heated. 7. Return the meat to the Ninja Foodi cooker and serve. Bon appétit!

Herbed Lamb Steaks

Prep time: 30 minutes | Cook time: 15 minutes | Serves 4

½ medium onion
2 tablespoons minced garlic
2 teaspoons ground ginger
1 teaspoon ground cinnamon
1 teaspoon onion granules

1 teaspoon cayenne pepper
1 teaspoon salt
4 (170 g) boneless lamb sirloin steaks
Oil, for spraying

1. In a blender, combine the onion, garlic, ginger, cinnamon, onion granules, cayenne pepper, and salt and pulse until the onion is minced. 2. Place the lamb steaks in a large bowl or zip-top plastic bag and sprinkle the onion mixture over the top. Turn the steaks until they are evenly coated. Cover with plastic wrap or seal the bag and refrigerate for 30 minutes. 3. Preheat the Ninja Foodi cooker to 165°C. Line the cook & crisp basket with parchment and spray lightly with oil. 4. Place the lamb steaks in a single layer in the prepared basket, making sure they don't overlap. You may need to work in batches, depending on the size of your Ninja Foodi cooker. 5. Cook for 8 minutes, flip, and cook for another 7 minutes, or until the internal temperature reaches 68°C.

Herbed Beef

Prep time: 5 minutes | Cook time: 22 minutes | Serves 6

1 teaspoon dried dill
1 teaspoon dried thyme
1 teaspoon garlic powder
900 g beef steak
3 tablespoons butter

1. Preheat the Ninja Foodi cooker to 180ºC. 2. Combine the dill, thyme, and garlic powder in a small bowl, and massage into the steak. 3. Air crisp the steak in the Ninja Foodi cooker for 20 minutes, then remove, shred, and return to the Ninja Foodi cooker. 4. Add the butter and air crisp the shredded steak for a further 2 minutes at 185ºC. Make sure the beef is coated in the butter before serving.

Spinach and Beef Braciole

Prep time: 25 minutes | Cook time: 1 hour 32 minutes | Serves 4

½ onion, finely chopped
1 teaspoon olive oil
80 ml red wine
475 ml crushed tomatoes
1 teaspoon Italian seasoning
½ teaspoon garlic powder
¼ teaspoon crushed red pepper flakes
2 tablespoons chopped fresh parsley
2 bavette or skirt steaks (about
680 g)
salt and freshly ground black pepper
475 ml fresh spinach, chopped
1 clove minced garlic
120 ml roasted red peppers, julienned
120 ml grated pecorino cheese
60 ml pine nuts, toasted and roughly chopped
2 tablespoons olive oil

1. Preheat the Ninja Foodi cooker to 205ºC. 2. Toss the onions and olive oil together in a baking pan or casserole dish. Air crisp at 205ºC for 5 minutes, stirring a couple times during the cooking process. Add the red wine, crushed tomatoes, Italian seasoning, garlic powder, red pepper flakes and parsley and stir. Cover the pan tightly with aluminum foil, lower the Ninja Foodi cooker temperature to 175ºC and continue to air crisp for 15 minutes. 3. While the sauce is simmering, prepare the beef. Using a meat mallet, pound the beef until it is ¼-inch thick. Season both sides of the beef with salt and pepper. Combine the spinach, garlic, red peppers, pecorino cheese, pine nuts and olive oil in a medium bowl. Season with salt and freshly ground black pepper. Disperse the mixture over the steaks. Starting at one of the short ends, roll the beef around the filling, tucking in the sides as you roll to ensure the filling is completely enclosed. Secure the beef rolls with toothpicks. 4. Remove the baking pan with the sauce from the Ninja Foodi cooker and set it aside. Preheat the Ninja Foodi cooker to 205ºC. 5. Brush or spray the beef rolls with a little olive oil and air crisp at 205ºC for 12 minutes, rotating the beef during the cooking process for even browning. When the beef is browned, submerge the rolls into the sauce in the baking pan, cover the pan with foil and return it to the Ninja Foodi cooker. Reduce the temperature of the Ninja Foodi cooker to 120ºC and air crisp for 60 minutes. 6. Remove the beef rolls from the sauce. Cut each roll into slices and serve, ladling some sauce overtop.

Rosemary Pork Belly

Prep time: 10 minutes | Cook time: 75 minutes | Serves 4

280 g pork belly
1 teaspoon dried rosemary
½ teaspoon dried thyme
¼ teaspoon ground cinnamon
1 teaspoon salt
240 ml water

1. Rub the pork belly with dried rosemary, thyme, ground cinnamon, and salt and transfer in the Ninja Foodi cooker bowl. 2. Add water, close and seal the lid. 3. Cook the pork belly on High Pressure for 75 minutes. 4. Remove the cooked pork belly from the Ninja Foodi cooker and slice it into servings.

Braised Pork Belly

Prep time: 15 minutes | Cook time: 37 minutes | Serves 4

450 g pork belly
1 tablespoon olive oil
Salt and ground black pepper to taste
1 clove garlic, minced
240 ml dry white wine
Rosemary sprig

1. Select the Sauté mode on the Ninja Foodi cooker and heat the oil. 2. Add the pork belly and sauté for 2 minutes per side, until starting to brown. 3. Season the meat with salt and pepper, add the garlic. 4. Pour in the wine and add the rosemary sprig. Bring to a boil. 5. Set the cooking time for 35 minutes at High pressure. 6. Once cooking is complete, use a natural pressure release for 10 minutes, then release any remaining pressure. Open the lid. 7. Slice the meat and serve.

Beef Carne Guisada

Prep time: 10 minutes | Cook time: 20 minutes | Serves 4

2 tomatoes, chopped
1 red bell pepper, chopped
½ onion, chopped
3 garlic cloves, chopped
1 teaspoon ancho chili powder
1 tablespoon ground cumin
½ teaspoon dried oregano
1 teaspoons salt
1 teaspoon freshly ground black pepper
1 teaspoon smoked paprika
450 g beef chuck, cut into large pieces
180 ml water, plus 2 tablespoons
¼ teaspoon xanthan gum

1. In a blender, purée the tomatoes, bell pepper, onion, garlic, chili powder, cumin, oregano, salt, pepper, and paprika. 2. Put the beef pieces in the Ninja Foodi cooker. Pour in the blended mixture. 3. Use 180 ml of water to wash out the blender and pour the liquid into the pot. 4. Lock the lid. Set cooking time for 20 minutes on High Pressure. 5. When cooking is complete, quick release the pressure. Unlock the lid. 6. Switch the pot to Sauté mode. Bring the stew to a boil. 7. Put the xanthan gum and 2 tablespoons of water into the boiling stew and stir until it thickens. 8. Serve immediately.

Cardamom Pork Ribs

Prep time: 15 minutes | Cook time: 25 minutes | Serves 3

¼ teaspoon ground cardamom
½ teaspoon minced ginger
4 tablespoons apple cider vinegar
¼ teaspoon sesame seeds
280 g pork ribs, chopped
¼ teaspoon chili flakes
1 tablespoon avocado oil

1. In the mixing bowl, mix up ground cardamom. Minced ginger, apple cider vinegar, sesame seeds, chili flakes, and avocado oil. 2. Then brush the pork ribs with the cardamom mixture and leave for 10 minutes to marinate. 3. After this, heat up the Ninja Foodi cooker on Sauté mode for 2 minutes. 4. Add the marinated pork ribs and all remaining marinade. 5. Cook the pork ribs on Sauté mode for 25 minutes. Flip the ribs on another side every 5 minutes.

Cardamom Beef Stew Meat with Broccoli

Prep time: 10 minutes | Cook time: 50 minutes | Serves 2

255 g beef stew meat, chopped
1 teaspoon ground cardamom
½ teaspoon salt
240 ml chopped broccoli
240 ml water

1. Preheat the Ninja Foodi cooker on the Sauté mode. 2. When the title "Hot" is displayed, add chopped beef stew meat and cook it for 4 minutes (for 2 minutes from each side). 3. Then add the ground cardamom, salt, and broccoli. 4. Add water and close the Ninja Foodi cooker lid. 5. Sauté the stew for 45 minutes to get the tender taste. 6. Enjoy!

Reuben Beef Rolls with Thousand Island Sauce

Prep time: 15 minutes | Cook time: 10 minutes per batch | Makes 10 rolls

230 g cooked salt beef, chopped
120 ml drained and chopped sauerkraut
1 (230 g) package cream cheese, softened
120 ml shredded Swiss cheese
20 slices prosciutto
Cooking spray

Thousand Island Sauce:
60 ml chopped dill pickles
60 ml tomato ketchup
180 ml mayonnaise
Fresh thyme leaves, for garnish
2 tablespoons sugar
⅛ teaspoon fine sea salt
Ground black pepper, to taste

1. Preheat the Ninja Foodi cooker to 205ºC and spritz with cooking spray. 2. Combine the beef, sauerkraut, cream cheese, and Swiss cheese in a large bowl. Stir to mix well. 3. Unroll a slice of prosciutto on a clean work surface, then top with another slice of prosciutto crosswise. Scoop up 4 tablespoons of the beef mixture in the center. 4. Fold the top slice sides over the filling as the ends of the roll, then roll up the long sides of the bottom prosciutto and make it into a roll shape. Overlap the sides by about 1 inch. Repeat with remaining filling and prosciutto. 5. Arrange the rolls in the preheated Ninja Foodi cooker, seam side down, and spritz with cooking spray. 6. Air crisp for 10 minutes or until golden and crispy. Flip the rolls halfway through. Work in batches to avoid overcrowding. 7. Meanwhile, combine the ingredients for the sauce in a small bowl. Stir to mix well. 8. Serve the rolls with the dipping sauce.

Fajita Meatball Lettuce Wraps

Prep time: 10 minutes | Cook time: 10 minutes | Serves 4

450 g beef mince (85% lean)
120 ml salsa, plus more for serving if desired
60 ml chopped onions
60 ml diced green or red peppers
1 large egg, beaten
1 teaspoon fine sea salt
½ teaspoon chili powder
½ teaspoon ground cumin
1 clove garlic, minced
For Serving (Optional):
8 leaves butterhead lettuce
Pico de gallo or salsa
Lime slices

1. Spray the cook & crisp basket with avocado oil. Preheat the Ninja Foodi cooker to 175ºC. 2. In a large bowl, mix together all the ingredients until well combined. 3. Shape the meat mixture into eight 1-inch balls. Place the meatballs in the cook & crisp basket, leaving a little space between them. Air crisp for 10 minutes, or until cooked through and no longer pink inside and the internal temperature reaches 65ºC. 4. Serve each meatball on a lettuce leaf, topped with pico de gallo or salsa, if desired. Serve with lime slices if desired. 5. Store leftovers in an airtight container in the fridge for 3 days or in the freezer for up to a month. Reheat in a preheated 175ºC Ninja Foodi cooker for 4 minutes, or until heated through.

Cheese Wine Pork Loin

Prep time: 30 minutes | Cook time: 15 minutes | Serves 2

235 ml water
235 ml red wine
1 tablespoon sea salt
2 pork loin steaks
60 ml ground almonds
60 ml flaxseed meal
½ teaspoon baking powder
1 teaspoon onion granules
½ teaspoon porcini powder
Sea salt and ground black pepper, to taste
1 egg
60 ml yoghurt
1 teaspoon wholegrain or English mustard
80 ml Parmesan cheese, grated

1. In a large ceramic dish, combine the water, wine and salt. Add the pork and put for 1 hour in the refrigerator. 2. In a shallow bowl, mix the ground almonds, flaxseed meal, baking powder, onion granules, porcini powder, salt, and ground pepper. In another bowl, whisk the eggs with yoghurt and mustard. 3. In a third bowl, place the grated Parmesan cheese. 4. Dip the pork in the seasoned flour mixture and toss evenly; then, in the egg mixture. Finally, roll them over the grated Parmesan cheese. 5. Spritz the bottom of the cook & crisp basket with cooking oil. Add the breaded pork and cook at 200ºC and for 10 minutes. 6. Flip and cook for 5 minutes more on the other side. Serve warm.

Saucy Beef Fingers

Prep time: 30 minutes | Cook time: 14 minutes | Serves 4

680 g rump steak
60 ml red wine
60 ml fresh lime juice
1 teaspoon garlic powder
1 teaspoon onion granules
1 teaspoon celery salt
1 teaspoon mustard seeds

Coarse sea salt and ground
black pepper, to taste
1 teaspoon red pepper flakes
2 eggs, lightly whisked
235 ml Parmesan cheese
1 teaspoon paprika

1. Place the steak, red wine, lime juice, garlic powder, onion granules, celery salt, mustard seeds, salt, black pepper, and red pepper in a large ceramic bowl; let it marinate for 3 hours. 2. Tenderize the steak by pounding with a mallet; cut into 1-inch strips. 3. In a shallow bowl, whisk the eggs. In another bowl, mix the Parmesan cheese and paprika. 4. Dip the beef pieces into the whisked eggs and coat on all sides. Now, dredge the beef pieces in the Parmesan mixture. 5. Cook at 205°C for 14 minutes, flipping halfway through the cooking time. 6. Meanwhile, make the sauce by heating the reserved marinade in a saucepan over medium heat; let it simmer until thoroughly warmed. Serve the steak fingers with the sauce on the side. Enjoy!

Swedish Meatloaf

Prep time: 10 minutes | Cook time: 35 minutes | Serves 8

680 g beef mince (85% lean)
110 g pork mince
1 large egg (omit for egg-free)
120 ml minced onions
60 ml tomato sauce
2 tablespoons mustard powder
2 cloves garlic, minced
2 teaspoons fine sea salt
1 teaspoon ground black pepper, plus more for garnish

Sauce:
120 ml (1 stick) unsalted butter
120 ml shredded Swiss or mild Cheddar cheese (about 60 g)
60 g cream cheese (60 ml), softened
80 ml beef stock
⅛ teaspoon ground nutmeg
Halved cherry tomatoes, for serving (optional)

1. Preheat the Ninja Foodi cooker to 200°C. 2. In a large bowl, combine the beef, pork, egg, onions, tomato sauce, mustard powder, garlic, salt, and pepper. Using your hands, mix until well combined. 3. Place the meatloaf mixture in a loaf pan and place it in the Ninja Foodi cooker. Bake for 35 minutes, or until cooked through and the internal temperature reaches 65°C. Check the meatloaf after 25 minutes; if it's getting too brown on the top, cover it loosely with foil to prevent burning. 4. While the meatloaf cooks, make the sauce: Heat the butter in a saucepan over medium-high heat until it sizzles and brown flecks appear, stirring constantly to keep the butter from burning. Turn the heat down to low and whisk in the Swiss cheese, cream cheese, stock, and nutmeg. Simmer for at least 10 minutes. The longer it simmers, the more the flavors open up. 5. When the meatloaf is done, transfer it to a serving tray and pour the sauce over it. Garnish with ground black pepper and serve with cherry tomatoes, if desired. Allow the meatloaf to rest for 10 minutes before slicing so it doesn't crumble apart. 6. Store leftovers in an airtight container in the fridge for 3 days or in the freezer for up to a month. Reheat in a preheated 175°C Ninja Foodi cooker for 4 minutes, or until heated through.

Italian Sausage Links

Prep time: 10 minutes | Cook time: 24 minutes | Serves 4

1 pepper (any color), sliced
1 medium onion, sliced
1 tablespoon avocado oil
1 teaspoon Italian seasoning

Sea salt and freshly ground
black pepper, to taste
450 g Italian-seasoned sausage
links

1. Place the pepper and onion in a medium bowl, and toss with the avocado oil, Italian seasoning, and salt and pepper to taste. 2. Set the Ninja Foodi cooker to 205°C. Put the vegetables in the cook & crisp basket and cook for 12 minutes. 3. Push the vegetables to the side of the basket and arrange the sausage links in the bottom of the basket in a single layer. Spoon the vegetables over the sausages. Cook for 12 minutes, tossing halfway through, until an instant-read thermometer inserted into the sausage reads 70°C.

Fruited Ham

Prep time: 15 minutes | Cook time: 8 to 10 minutes | Serves 4

235 ml orange marmalade
60 ml packed light brown sugar
¼ teaspoon ground cloves
½ teaspoon mustard powder
1 to 2 tablespoons oil

450 g cooked ham, cut into
1-inch cubes
120 ml canned mandarin
oranges, drained and chopped

1. In a small bowl, stir together the orange marmalade, brown sugar, cloves, and mustard powder until blended. Set aside. 2. Preheat the Ninja Foodi cooker to 160°C. Spritz a baking pan with oil. 3. Place the ham cubes in the prepared pan. Pour the marmalade sauce over the ham to glaze it. 4. Cook for 4 minutes. Stir and cook for 2 minutes more. 5. Add the mandarin oranges and cook for 2 to 4 minutes more until the sauce begins to thicken and the ham is tender.

Beef Burgundy

Prep time: 30 minutes | Cook time: 30 minutes | Serves 6

2 tablespoons olive oil
900 g stewing meat, cubed,
trimmed of fat
2½ tablespoons flour
5 medium onions, thinly sliced
230 g fresh mushrooms, sliced

1 teaspoon salt
¼ teaspoon dried marjoram
¼ teaspoon dried thyme
⅛ teaspoon pepper
180 ml beef broth
360 ml burgundy

1. Press Sauté on the Ninja Foodi cooker and add in the olive oil. 2. Dredge meat in flour, then brown in batches in the Ninja Foodi cooker. Set aside the meat. Sauté the onions and mushrooms in the remaining oil and drippings for about 3–4 minutes, then add the meat back in. Press Start/Stop. 3. Add the salt, marjoram, thyme, pepper, broth, and wine to the Ninja Foodi cooker. 4. Secure the lid and make sure the vent is set to sealing. Set to 30 minutes. 5. When cook time is up, let the pressure release naturally for 15 minutes, then perform a quick release. 6. Serve over cooked noodles.

Sweet and Spicy Country-Style Ribs

Prep time: 10 minutes | Cook time: 25 minutes | Serves 4

2 tablespoons brown sugar
2 tablespoons smoked paprika
1 teaspoon garlic powder
1 teaspoon onion granules
1 teaspoon mustard powder
1 teaspoon ground cumin
1 teaspoon coarse or flaky salt
1 teaspoon black pepper
¼ to ½ teaspoon cayenne pepper
680 g boneless pork steaks
235 ml barbecue sauce

1. In a small bowl, stir together the brown sugar, paprika, garlic powder, onion granules, mustard powder, cumin, salt, black pepper, and cayenne. Mix until well combined. 2. Pat the ribs dry with a paper towel. Generously sprinkle the rub evenly over both sides of the ribs and rub in with your fingers. 3. Place the ribs in the cook & crisp basket. Set the Ninja Foodi cooker to 175ºC for 15 minutes. Turn the ribs and brush with 120 ml of the barbecue sauce. Cook for an additional 10 minutes. Use a meat thermometer to ensure the pork has reached an internal temperature of 65ºC. 4. Serve with remaining barbecue sauce.

Cheesesteak Meatloaf

Prep time: 15 minutes | Cook time: 40 minutes | Serves 4

240 ml minced pork
120 ml shredded Cheddar cheese
2 tablespoons almond flour
1 tablespoon chopped chives
1 teaspoon pork seasoning
1 egg, beaten
240 ml water, for cooking

1. Put the minced pork in the bowl. 2. Add almond flour, chives, pork seasoning, and egg. 3. Mix up the mixture until smooth. 4. After this, place ½ part of the mixture in the loaf mold, flatten it well and top with ½ part of all Cheddar cheese. 5. Then add remaining minced pork mixture and cheese. 6. Pour water and insert the steamer rack in the Ninja Foodi cooker. 7. Place the meatloaf on the rack. Close and seal the lid. 8. Cook the meal on High Pressure for 40 minutes. Make a quick pressure release.

London Broil with Herb Butter

Prep time: 30 minutes | Cook time: 20 to 25 minutes | Serves 4

680 g bavette or skirt steak
60 ml olive oil
2 tablespoons balsamic vinegar
1 tablespoon Worcestershire sauce
4 cloves garlic, minced
Herb Butter:
6 tablespoons unsalted butter,
softened
1 tablespoon chopped fresh parsley
¼ teaspoon salt
¼ teaspoon dried ground rosemary or thyme
¼ teaspoon garlic powder
Pinch of red pepper flakes

1. Place the beef in a gallon-size resealable bag. In a small bowl, whisk together the olive oil, balsamic vinegar, Worcestershire sauce, and garlic. Pour the marinade over the beef, massaging gently to coat, and seal the bag. Let sit at room temperature for an hour or refrigerate overnight. 2. To make the herb butter: In a small bowl, mix the butter with the parsley, salt, rosemary, garlic powder, and red pepper flakes until smooth. Cover and refrigerate until ready to use. 3. Preheat the Ninja Foodi cooker to 205ºC. 4. Remove the beef from the marinade (discard the marinade) and place the beef in the cook & crisp basket. Pausing halfway through the cooking time to turn the meat, air crisp for 20 to 25 minutes, until a thermometer inserted into the thickest part indicates the desired doneness, 50ºC (rare) to 65ºC (medium). Let the beef rest for 10 minutes before slicing. Serve topped with the herb butter.

Greek Lamb Pitta Pockets

Prep time: 15 minutes | Cook time: 6 minutes | Serves 4

Dressing:
235 ml plain yogurt
1 tablespoon lemon juice
1 teaspoon dried dill, crushed
1 teaspoon ground oregano
½ teaspoon salt
Meatballs:
230 g lamb mince
1 tablespoon diced onion
1 teaspoon dried parsley
1 teaspoon dried dill, crushed
¼ teaspoon oregano
¼ teaspoon coriander
¼ teaspoon ground cumin
¼ teaspoon salt
4 pitta halves
Suggested Toppings:
1 red onion, slivered
1 medium cucumber, deseeded, thinly sliced
Crumbled feta cheese
Sliced black olives
Chopped fresh peppers

1. Preheat the Ninja Foodi cooker to 200ºC. 2. Stir the dressing ingredients together in a small bowl and refrigerate while preparing lamb. 3. Combine all meatball ingredients in a large bowl and stir to distribute seasonings. 4. Shape meat mixture into 12 small meatballs, rounded or slightly flattened if you prefer. 5. Transfer the meatballs in the preheated Ninja Foodi cooker and air crisp for 6 minutes, until well done. Remove and drain on paper towels. 6. To serve, pile meatballs and the choice of toppings in pitta pockets and drizzle with dressing.

Vietnamese Grilled Pork

Prep time: 30 minutes | Cook time: 20 minutes | Serves 6

60 ml minced brown onion
2 tablespoons sugar
2 tablespoons vegetable oil
1 tablespoon minced garlic
1 tablespoon fish sauce
1 tablespoon minced fresh lemongrass
2 teaspoons dark soy sauce
½ teaspoon black pepper
680 g boneless pork shoulder, cut into ½-inch-thick slices
60 ml chopped salted roasted peanuts
2 tablespoons chopped fresh coriander or parsley

1. In a large bowl, combine the onion, sugar, vegetable oil, garlic, fish sauce, lemongrass, soy sauce, and pepper. Add the pork and toss to coat. Marinate at room temperature for 30 minutes, or cover and refrigerate for up to 24 hours. 2. Arrange the pork slices in the cook & crisp basket; discard the marinade. Set the Ninja Foodi cooker to 205ºC for 20 minutes, turning the pork halfway through the cooking time. 3. Transfer the pork to a serving platter. Sprinkle with the peanuts and coriander and serve.

Rosemary Lamb Chops

Prep time: 25 minutes | Cook time: 2 minutes | Serves 4

680 g lamb chops (4 small chops)
1 teaspoon rock salt
Leaves from 1 (6-inch) rosemary sprig

2 tablespoons avocado oil
1 shallot, peeled and cut in quarters
1 tablespoon tomato paste
240 ml beef broth

1. Place the lamb chops on a cutting board. Press the salt and rosemary leaves into both sides of the chops. Let rest at room temperature for 15 to 30 minutes. 2. Set the electric pressure cooker to Sauté/More setting. When hot, add the avocado oil. 3. Brown the lamb chops, about 2 minutes per side. (If they don't all fit in a single layer, brown them in batches.) 4. Transfer the chops to a plate. In the pot, combine the shallot, tomato paste, and broth. Cook for about a minute, scraping up the brown bits from the bottom. Hit Start/Stop. 5. Add the chops and any accumulated juices back to the pot. 6. Close and lock the lid of the pressure cooker. Set the valve to sealing. 7. Cook on high pressure for 2 minutes. 8. When the cooking is complete, hit Start/Stop and quick release the pressure. 9. Once the pin drops, unlock and remove the lid. 10. Place the lamb chops on plates and serve immediately.

Ginger Beef Flank Steak

Prep time: 8 minutes | Cook time: 13 minutes | Serves 2

400 g beef flank steak, sliced
1 tablespoon almond flour
½ teaspoon minced ginger

30 g spring onions, sliced
1 tablespoon coconut oil
180 ml water

1. Toss the beef strips in the almond flour and shake well. 2. Toss the coconut oil in the Ninja Foodi cooker bowl and set the Sauté mode. 3. When the coconut oil is melted, add the beef flank steak slices and cook them for 3 minutes. Stir them from time to time. 4. Add minced ginger. 5. Pour the water over the meat and lock the Ninja Foodi cooker lid. 6. Select the High Pressure and set the timer for 10 minutes. 7. Make a quick pressure release. 8. Top the cooked beef with sliced spring onions.

Lemon Pork with Marjoram

Prep time: 5 minutes | Cook time: 10 minutes | Serves 4

1 (450 g) pork tenderloin, cut into ½-inch-thick slices
1 tablespoon extra-virgin olive oil
1 tablespoon freshly squeezed lemon juice
1 tablespoon honey

½ teaspoon grated lemon zest
½ teaspoon dried marjoram leaves
Pinch salt
Freshly ground black pepper, to taste
Cooking oil spray

1. Put the pork slices in a medium bowl. 2. In a small bowl, whisk the olive oil, lemon juice, honey, lemon zest, marjoram, salt, and pepper until combined. Pour this marinade over the tenderloin slices and gently massage with your hands to work it into the pork. 3. Insert the crisper plate into the basket and the basket into the unit. Preheat the unit by selecting AIR ROAST, setting the temperature to 205°C, and setting the time to 3 minutes. Press START/STOP to begin. 4. Once the unit is preheated, spray the crisper plate with cooking oil. Place the pork into the basket. 5. Select AIR ROAST, set the temperature to 205°C, and set the time to 10 minutes. Press START/STOP to begin. 6. When the cooking is complete, a food thermometer inserted into the pork should register at least 65°C. Let the pork stand for 5 minutes and serve.

Green Pepper Cheeseburgers

Prep time: 5 minutes | Cook time: 30 minutes | Serves 4

2 green peppers
680 g 85% lean beef mince
1 clove garlic, minced
1 teaspoon salt
½ teaspoon freshly ground black

pepper
4 slices Cheddar cheese (about 85 g)
4 large lettuce leaves

1. Preheat the Ninja Foodi cooker to 205°C. 2. Arrange the peppers in the basket of the Ninja Foodi cooker. Pausing halfway through the cooking time to turn the peppers, air crisp for 20 minutes, or until they are softened and beginning to char. Transfer the peppers to a large bowl and cover with a plate. When cool enough to handle, peel off the skin, remove the seeds and stems, and slice into strips. Set aside. 3. Meanwhile, in a large bowl, combine the beef with the garlic, salt, and pepper. Shape the beef into 4 patties. 4. Lower the heat on the Ninja Foodi cooker to 180°C. Arrange the burgers in a single layer in the basket of the Ninja Foodi cooker. Pausing halfway through the cooking time to turn the burgers, air crisp for 10 minutes, or until a thermometer inserted into the thickest part registers 70°C. 5. Top the burgers with the cheese slices and continue baking for a minute or two, just until the cheese has melted. Serve the burgers on a lettuce leaf topped with the roasted peppers.

Pigs in a Blanket

Prep time: 10 minutes | Cook time: 7 minutes | Serves 2

120 ml shredded Mozzarella cheese
2 tablespoons blanched finely ground almond flour

30 g full-fat cream cheese
2 (110 g) beef smoked sausage, cut in two
½ teaspoon sesame seeds

1. Place Mozzarella, almond flour, and cream cheese in a large microwave-safe bowl. Microwave for 45 seconds and stir until smooth. Roll dough into a ball and cut in half. 2. Press each half out into a 4 × 5-inch rectangle. Roll one sausage up in each dough half and press seams closed. Sprinkle the top with sesame seeds. 3. Place each wrapped sausage into the cook & crisp basket. 4. Adjust the temperature to 205°C and air crisp for 7 minutes. 5. The outside will be golden when completely cooked. Serve immediately.

Parmesan-Crusted Pork Chops

Prep time: 5 minutes | Cook time: 12 minutes | Serves 4

1 large egg
120 ml grated Parmesan cheese
4 (110 g) boneless pork chops
½ teaspoon salt
¼ teaspoon ground black pepper

1. Whisk egg in a medium bowl and place Parmesan in a separate medium bowl. 2. Sprinkle pork chops on both sides with salt and pepper. Dip each pork chop into egg, then press both sides into Parmesan. 3. Place pork chops into ungreased cook & crisp basket. Adjust the temperature to 205°C and air crisp for 12 minutes, turning chops halfway through cooking. Pork chops will be golden and have an internal temperature of at least 65°C when done. Serve warm.

Bone-in Pork Chops

Prep time: 5 minutes | Cook time: 10 to 12 minutes | Serves 2

450 g bone-in pork chops
1 tablespoon avocado oil
1 teaspoon smoked paprika
½ teaspoon onion granules
¼ teaspoon cayenne pepper
Sea salt and freshly ground black pepper, to taste

1. Brush the pork chops with the avocado oil. In a small dish, mix together the smoked paprika, onion granules, cayenne pepper, and salt and black pepper to taste. Sprinkle the seasonings over both sides of the pork chops. 2. Set the Ninja Foodi cooker to 205°C. Place the chops in the cook & crisp basket in a single layer, working in batches if necessary. Air crisp for 10 to 12 minutes, until an instant-read thermometer reads 65°C at the chops' thickest point. 3. Remove the chops from the Ninja Foodi cooker and allow them to rest for 5 minutes before serving.

Beef Ribs with Radishes

Prep time: 20 minutes | Cook time: 56 minutes | Serves 4

¼ teaspoon ground coriander
¼ teaspoon ground cumin
1 teaspoon rock salt, plus more to taste
½ teaspoon smoked paprika
Pinch of ground allspice (optional)
4 (227 g each) bone-in beef
short ribs
2 tablespoons avocado oil
240 ml water
2 radishes, ends trimmed, leaves rinsed and roughly chopped
Freshly ground black pepper, to taste

1. In a small bowl, mix together the coriander, cumin, salt, paprika, and allspice. Rub the spice mixture all over the short ribs. 2. Set the Ninja Foodi cooker to Sauté mode and add the oil to heat. Add the short ribs, bone side up. Brown for 4 minutes on each side. 3. Pour the water into the Ninja Foodi cooker. Secure the lid. Set cooking time for 45 minutes on High Pressure. 4. When timer beeps, allow the pressure to release naturally for 10 minutes, then release any remaining pressure. Open the lid. 5. Remove the short ribs to a serving plate. 6. Add the radishes to the sauce in the pot. Place a metal steaming basket directly on top of the radishes and place the radish leaves in the basket. 7. Secure the lid. Set cooking time for 3 minutes on High Pressure. 8. When timer beeps, quick release the pressure. Open the lid. Transfer the leaves to a serving bowl. Sprinkle with with salt and pepper. 9. Remove the radishes and place on top of the leaves. Serve hot with the short ribs.

Low Carb Pork Tenderloin

Prep time: 15 minutes | Cook time: 30 minutes | Serves 2

255 g pork tenderloin
1 teaspoon sweetener
½ teaspoon dried dill
½ teaspoon white pepper
1 garlic clove, minced
3 tablespoons butter
60 ml water

1. Rub the pork tenderloin with sweetener, dried dill, white pepper, and minced garlic. 2. Then melt the butter in the Ninja Foodi cooker on Sauté mode. 3. Add pork tenderloin and cook it for 8 minutes from each side (use Sauté mode). 4. Then add water and close the lid. 5. Cook the meat on Sauté mode for 10 minutes. 6. Cool the cooked tenderloin for 10 to 15 minutes and slice.

Bacon-Wrapped Pork Bites

Prep time: 15 minutes | Cook time: 20 minutes | Serves 4

3 tablespoons butter
280 g pork tenderloin, cubed
170 g bacon, sliced
½ teaspoon white pepper
180 ml chicken stock

1. Melt the butter on Sauté mode in the Ninja Foodi cooker. 2. Meanwhile, wrap the pork tenderloin cubes in the sliced bacon and sprinkle with white pepper. Secure with toothpicks, if necessary. 3. Put the wrapped pork tenderloin in the melted butter and cook for 3 minutes on each side. 4. Add the chicken stock and close the lid. 5. Set cooking time for 14 minutes on High Pressure. 6. When timer beeps, use a natural pressure release for 5 minutes, then release any remaining pressure. Open the lid. 7. Discard the toothpicks and serve immediately.

Vietnamese Pork Tenderloin

Prep time: 10 minutes | Cook time: 20 minutes | Serves 2

170 g pork tenderloin
120 ml water
¼ teaspoon ground clove
¼ teaspoon minced ginger
1 teaspoon coconut aminos
1 teaspoon olive oil

1. Heat up olive oil on Sauté mode. 2. Then chop the pork tenderloin roughly and add it in the Ninja Foodi cooker. 3. Cook the meat for 2 minutes and flip it on another side. 4. After this, add coconut aminos, minced ginger, ground clove, and water. 5. Close and seal the lid and cook the meat on High Pressure for 15 minutes. 6. Allow the natural pressure release for 10 minutes and transfer the meat in the bowls.

Bulgogi Burgers

Prep time: 30 minutes | Cook time: 10 minutes | Serves 4

Burgers:
450 g 85% lean beef mince
60 ml chopped spring onionspring onions
2 tablespoons gochujang (Korean red chili paste)
1 tablespoon dark soy sauce
2 teaspoons minced garlic
2 teaspoons minced fresh ginger
2 teaspoons sugar
1 tablespoon toasted sesame oil

½ teaspoon coarse or flaky salt
Gochujang Mayonnaise:
60 ml mayonnaise
60 ml chopped spring onionspring onions
1 tablespoon gochujang (Korean red chili paste)
1 tablespoon toasted sesame oil
2 teaspoons sesame seeds
4 hamburger buns

1. For the burgers: In a large bowl, mix the ground beef, spring onionspring onions, gochujang, soy sauce, garlic, ginger, sugar, sesame oil, and salt. Marinate at room temperature for 30 minutes, or cover and refrigerate for up to 24 hours. 2. Divide the meat into four portions and form them into round patties. Make a slight depression in the middle of each patty with your thumb to prevent them from puffing up into a dome shape while cooking. 3. Place the patties in a single layer in the cook & crisp basket. Set the Ninja Foodi cooker to 175ºC for 10 minutes. 4. Meanwhile, for the gochujang mayonnaise: Stir together the mayonnaise, spring onionspring onions, gochujang, sesame oil, and sesame seeds. 5. At the end of the cooking time, use a meat thermometer to ensure the burgers have reached an internal temperature of 70ºC (medium). 6. To serve, place the burgers on the buns and top with the mayonnaise.

Cantonese BBQ Pork

Prep time: 30 minutes | Cook time: 15 minutes | Serves 4

60 ml honey
2 tablespoons dark soy sauce
1 tablespoon sugar
1 tablespoon Shaoxing wine (rice cooking wine)
1 tablespoon hoisin sauce

2 teaspoons minced garlic
2 teaspoons minced fresh ginger
1 teaspoon Chinese five-spice powder
450 g fatty pork shoulder, cut into long, 1-inch-thick pieces

1. In a small microwave-safe bowl, combine the honey, soy sauce, sugar, wine, hoisin, garlic, ginger, and five-spice powder. Microwave in 10-second intervals, stirring in between, until the honey has dissolved. 2. Use a fork to pierce the pork slices to allow the marinade to penetrate better. Place the pork in a large bowl or resealable plastic bag and pour in half the marinade; set aside the remaining marinade to use for the sauce. Toss to coat. Marinate the pork at room temperature for 30 minutes, or cover and refrigerate for up 24 hours. 3. Place the pork in a single layer in the cook & crisp basket. Set the Ninja Foodi cooker to 205ºC for 15 minutes, turning and basting the pork halfway through the cooking time. 4. While the pork is cooking, microwave the reserved marinade on high for 45 to 60 seconds, stirring every 15 seconds, to thicken it slightly to the consistency of a sauce. 5. Transfer the pork to a cutting board and let rest for 10 minutes. Brush with the sauce and serve.

Beef and Broccoli with Cheddar

Prep time: 5 minutes | Cook time: 10 minutes | Serves 4

450 g 85% lean minced beef
1 teaspoon salt
½ teaspoon garlic powder
½ teaspoon dried parsley
¼ teaspoon dried oregano
2 tablespoons butter

180 ml beef broth
480 ml broccoli florets
60 ml double cream
240 ml shredded mild Cheddar cheese

1. Press the Sauté button and brown minced beef in Ninja Foodi cooker until there's no more pink. Press the Start/Stop button. Sprinkle seasonings over meat and add butter, broth, and broccoli. Click lid closed. 2. Set time for 2 minutes. When timer beeps, press the Start/Stop button. Stir in double cream and Cheddar until completely melted.

Basil and Thyme Pork Loin

Prep time: 10 minutes | Cook time: 17 minutes | Serves 4

450 g pork loin
1 teaspoon dried basil
1 tablespoon avocado oil
1 teaspoon dried thyme

½ teaspoon salt
2 tablespoons apple cider vinegar
240 ml water, for cooking

1. In the shallow bowl, mix up dried basil, avocado oil, thyme, salt, and apple cider vinegar. 2. Then rub the pork loin with the spice mixture and leave the meat for 10 minutes to marinate. 3. Wrap the meat in foil and put on the steamer rack. 4. Pour water and transfer the steamer rack with meat in the Ninja Foodi cooker. 5. Close and seal the lid. Cook the meat on High Pressure for 20 minutes. Allow the natural pressure release for 5 minutes. 6. Slice the cooked pork loin.

Easy Lamb Chops with Asparagus

Prep time: 10 minutes | Cook time: 15 minutes | Serves 4

4 asparagus spears, trimmed
2 tablespoons olive oil, divided
450 g lamb chops
1 garlic clove, minced

2 teaspoons chopped fresh thyme, for serving
Salt and ground black pepper, to taste

1. Preheat the Ninja Foodi cooker to 205ºC. Spritz the cook & crisp basket with cooking spray. 2. On a large plate, brush the asparagus with 1 tablespoon olive oil, then sprinkle with salt. Set aside. 3. On a separate plate, brush the lamb chops with remaining olive oil and sprinkle with salt and ground black pepper. 4. Arrange the lamb chops in the preheated Ninja Foodi cooker. Air crisp for 10 minutes. 5. Flip the lamb chops and add the asparagus and garlic. Air crisp for 5 more minutes or until the lamb is well browned and the asparagus is tender. 6. Serve them on a plate with thyme on top.

Cheddar Bacon Burst with Spinach

Prep time: 5 minutes | Cook time: 60 minutes | Serves 8

30 slices bacon
1 tablespoon Chipotle chilli powder
2 teaspoons Italian seasoning
120 ml Cheddar cheese
1 L raw spinach

1. Preheat the Ninja Foodi cooker to 190°C. 2. Weave the bacon into 15 vertical pieces and 12 horizontal pieces. Cut the extra 3 in half to fill in the rest, horizontally. 3. Season the bacon with Chipotle chilli powder and Italian seasoning. 4. Add the cheese to the bacon. 5. Add the spinach and press down to compress. 6. Tightly roll up the woven bacon. 7. Line a baking sheet with kitchen foil and add plenty of salt to it. 8. Put the bacon on top of a cooling rack and put that on top of the baking sheet. 9. Bake for 60 minutes. 10. Let cool for 15 minutes before slicing and serving.

Bacon Cheddar Cheese Stuffed Burgers

Prep time: 10 minutes | Cook time: 9 minutes | Serves 4

450 g minced beef
170 g shredded Cheddar cheese
5 slices bacon, coarsely chopped
2 teaspoons Worcestershire sauce
1 teaspoon salt
½ teaspoon liquid smoke
½ teaspoon black pepper
½ teaspoon garlic powder
240 ml water

1. In a large bowl, add the beef, cheese, bacon, Worcestershire sauce, salt, liquid smoke, pepper, and garlic powder. Gently work everything into the meat. Do not overwork the meat, or it will become tough when it cooks. 2. Separate the meat into four equal portions. Use a food scale to measure evenly. 3. Shape each piece into a ball. Use your thumb to make a crater in the middle of the patty but make sure the round shape is retained. 4. Wrap each patty loosely in aluminium foil. Place them on top of the reversible rack in the pot. They will overlap. 5. Add the water to the bottom of the pot. Close the lid and seal the vent. Cook on High Pressure for 9 minutes. Quick release the steam. Remove the foil packets from the pot and set them on a large plate. Carefully unwrap the burgers. There will be juices in the bottom of the foil.

Pork Chops in Creamy Mushroom Gravy

Prep time: 5 minutes | Cook time: 15 minutes | Serves 4

4 (140 g each) pork chops
1 teaspoon salt
½ teaspoon pepper
2 tablespoons avocado oil
240 ml chopped button mushrooms
½ medium onion, sliced
1 clove garlic, minced
240 ml chicken broth
60 ml double cream
4 tablespoons butter
¼ teaspoon xanthan gum
1 tablespoon chopped fresh parsley

1. Sprinkle pork chops with salt and pepper. Place avocado oil and mushrooms in Ninja Foodi cooker and press the Sauté button. Sauté 3 to 5 minutes until mushrooms begin to soften. Add onions and pork chops. Sauté additional 3 minutes until pork chops reach a golden brown. 2. Add garlic and broth to Ninja Foodi cooker. Click lid closed. Adjust time for 15 minutes. When timer beeps, allow a 10-minute natural release. Quick-release the remaining pressure. 3. Remove lid and place pork chops on plate. Press the Sauté button and add double cream, butter, and xanthan gum. Reduce for 5 to 10 minutes or until sauce begins to thicken. Add pork chops back into pot. Serve warm topped with mushroom sauce and parsley.

Aubergine Pork Lasagna

Prep time: 20 minutes | Cook time: 30 minutes | Serves 6

2 aubergines, sliced
1 teaspoon salt
280 g minced pork
240 ml Mozzarella, shredded
1 tablespoon unsweetened tomato purée
1 teaspoon butter, softened
240 ml chicken stock

1. Sprinkle the aubergines with salt and let sit for 10 minutes, then pat dry with paper towels. 2. In a mixing bowl, mix the minced pork, butter, and tomato purée. 3. Make a layer of the sliced aubergines in the bottom of the Ninja Foodi cooker and top with minced pork mixture. 4. Top the minced pork with Mozzarella and repeat with remaining ingredients. 5. Pour in the chicken stock. Close the lid. Set cooking time for 30 minutes on High Pressure. 6. When timer beeps, use a natural pressure release for 10 minutes, then release the remaining pressure and open the lid. 7. Cool for 10 minutes and serve.

Air Fried Beef Satay with Peanut Dipping Sauce

Prep time: 30 minutes | Cook time: 5 to 7 minutes | Serves 4

230 g bavette or skirt steak, sliced into 8 strips
2 teaspoons curry powder
½ teaspoon coarse or flaky salt
Cooking spray
Peanut Dipping sauce:
2 tablespoons creamy peanut butter
1 tablespoon reduced-salt soy sauce
2 teaspoons rice vinegar
1 teaspoon honey
1 teaspoon grated ginger
Special Equipment:
4 bamboo skewers, cut into halves and soaked in water for 20 minutes to keep them from burning while cooking

1. Preheat the Ninja Foodi cooker to 180°C. Spritz the cook & crisp basket with cooking spray. 2. In a bowl, place the steak strips and sprinkle with the curry powder and coarse or flaky salt to season. Thread the strips onto the soaked skewers. 3. Arrange the skewers in the prepared cook & crisp basket and spritz with cooking spray. Air crisp for 5 to 7 minutes, or until the beef is well browned, turning halfway through. 4. In the meantime, stir together the peanut butter, soy sauce, rice vinegar, honey, and ginger in a bowl to make the dipping sauce. 5. Transfer the beef to the serving dishes and let rest for 5 minutes. Serve with the peanut dipping sauce on the side.

Goat Cheese-Stuffed Bavette Steak

Prep time: 10 minutes | Cook time: 14 minutes | Serves 6

450 g bavette or skirt steak
1 tablespoon avocado oil
½ teaspoon sea salt
½ teaspoon garlic powder
¼ teaspoon freshly ground black pepper
60 g goat cheese, crumbled
235 ml baby spinach, chopped

1. Place the steak in a large zip-top bag or between two pieces of plastic wrap. Using a meat mallet or heavy-bottomed skillet, pound the steak to an even ¼-inch thickness. 2. Brush both sides of the steak with the avocado oil. 3. Mix the salt, garlic powder, and pepper in a small dish. Sprinkle this mixture over both sides of the steak. 4. Sprinkle the goat cheese over top, and top that with the spinach. 5. Starting at one of the long sides, roll the steak up tightly. Tie the rolled steak with kitchen string at 3-inch intervals. 6. Set the Ninja Foodi cooker to 205ºC. Place the steak roll-up in the cook & crisp basket. Air crisp for 7 minutes. Flip the steak and cook for an additional 7 minutes, until an instant-read thermometer reads 50ºC for medium-rare (adjust the cooking time for your desired doneness).

Pork Chops with Caramelized Onions

Prep time: 20 minutes | Cook time: 23 to 34 minutes | Serves 4

4 bone-in pork chops (230 g each)
1 to 2 tablespoons oil
2 tablespoons Cajun seasoning,
divided
1 brown onion, thinly sliced
1 green pepper, thinly sliced
2 tablespoons light brown sugar

1. Spritz the pork chops with oil. Sprinkle 1 tablespoon of Cajun seasoning on one side of the chops. 2. Preheat the Ninja Foodi cooker to 205ºC. Line the cook & crisp basket with parchment paper and spritz the parchment with oil. 3. Place 2 pork chops, spice-side up, on the paper. 4. Cook for 4 minutes. Flip the chops, sprinkle with the remaining 1 tablespoon of Cajun seasoning, and cook for 4 to 8 minutes more until the internal temperature reaches 65ºC, depending on the chops' thickness. Remove and keep warm while you cook the remaining 2 chops. Set the chops aside. 5. In a baking pan, combine the onion, pepper, and brown sugar, stirring until the vegetables are coated. Place the pan in the cook & crisp basket and cook for 4 minutes. 6. Stir the vegetables. Cook for 3 to 6 minutes more to your desired doneness. Spoon the vegetable mixture over the chops to serve.

Fillet with Crispy Shallots

Prep time: 30 minutes | Cook time: 18 to 20 minutes | Serves 6

680 g beef fillet steaks
Sea salt and freshly ground black pepper, to taste
4 medium shallots
1 teaspoon olive oil or avocado oil

1. Season both sides of the steaks with salt and pepper, and let them sit at room temperature for 45 minutes. 2. Set the Ninja Foodi cooker to 205ºC and let it preheat for 5 minutes. 3. Working in batches if necessary, place the steaks in the cook & crisp basket in a single layer and air crisp for 5 minutes. Flip and cook for 5 minutes longer, until an instant-read thermometer inserted in the center of the steaks registers 50ºC for medium-rare (or as desired). Remove the steaks and tent with aluminum foil to rest. 4. Set the Ninja Foodi cooker to 150ºC. In a medium bowl, toss the shallots with the oil. Place the shallots in the basket and air crisp for 5 minutes, then give them a toss and cook for 3 to 5 minutes more, until crispy and golden brown. 5. Place the steaks on serving plates and arrange the shallots on top.

Mojito Lamb Chops

Prep time: 30 minutes | Cook time: 5 minutes | Serves 2

Marinade:
2 teaspoons grated lime zest
120 ml lime juice
60 ml avocado oil
60 ml chopped fresh mint leaves
4 cloves garlic, roughly chopped
2 teaspoons fine sea salt
½ teaspoon ground black pepper
4 (1-inch-thick) lamb chops
Sprigs of fresh mint, for garnish (optional)
Lime slices, for serving (optional)

1. Make the marinade: Place all the ingredients for the marinade in a food processor or blender and purée until mostly smooth with a few small chunks. Transfer half of the marinade to a shallow dish and set the other half aside for serving. Add the lamb to the shallow dish, cover, and place in the refrigerator to marinate for at least 2 hours or overnight. 2. Spray the cook & crisp basket with avocado oil. Preheat the Ninja Foodi cooker to 200ºC. 3. Remove the chops from the marinade and place them in the cook & crisp basket. Air crisp for 5 minutes, or until the internal temperature reaches 65ºC for medium doneness. 4. Allow the chops to rest for 10 minutes before serving with the rest of the marinade as a sauce. Garnish with fresh mint leaves and serve with lime slices, if desired. Best served fresh.

Panko Crusted Calf's Liver Strips

Prep time: 15 minutes | Cook time: 23 to 25 minutes | Serves 4

450 g sliced calf's liver, cut into ½-inch wide strips
2 eggs
2 tablespoons milk
120 ml whole wheat flour
475 ml panko breadcrumbs
Salt and ground black pepper, to taste
Cooking spray

1. Preheat the Ninja Foodi cooker to 200ºC and spritz with cooking spray. 2. Rub the calf's liver strips with salt and ground black pepper on a clean work surface. 3. Whisk the eggs with milk in a large bowl. Pour the flour in a shallow dish. Pour the panko on a separate shallow dish. 4. Dunk the liver strips in the flour, then in the egg mixture. Shake the excess off and roll the strips over the panko to coat well. 5. Arrange half of the liver strips in a single layer in the preheated Ninja Foodi cooker and spritz with cooking spray. 6. Air crisp for 5 minutes or until browned. Flip the strips halfway through. Repeat with the remaining strips. 7. Serve immediately.

Sesame Beef Lettuce Tacos

60 ml soy sauce or tamari

60 ml avocado oil

2 tablespoons cooking sherry

1 tablespoon granulated sweetener

1 tablespoon ground cumin

1 teaspoon minced garlic

Sea salt and freshly ground black pepper, to taste

450 g bavette or skirt steak

8 butterhead lettuce leaves

2 spring onions, sliced

1 tablespoon toasted sesame seeds

Hot sauce, for serving

Lime wedges, for serving

Flaky sea salt (optional)

1. In a small bowl, whisk together the soy sauce, avocado oil, cooking sherry, sweetener, cumin, garlic, and salt and pepper to taste. 2. Place the steak in a shallow dish. Pour the marinade over the beef. Cover the dish with plastic wrap and let it marinate in the refrigerator for at least 2 hours or overnight. 3. Remove the flank steak from the dish and discard the marinade. 4. Set the Ninja Foodi cooker to 205°C. Place the steak in the cook & crisp basket and air crisp for 4 to 6 minutes. Flip the steak and cook for 4 minutes more, until an instant-read thermometer reads 50°C at the thickest part (or cook it to your desired doneness). Allow the steak to rest for 10 minutes, then slice it thinly against the grain. 5. Stack 2 lettuce leaves on top of each other and add some sliced meat. Top with spring onions and sesame seeds. Drizzle with hot sauce and lime juice, and finish with a little flaky salt (if using). Repeat with the remaining lettuce leaves and fillings.

Chapter 8 Desserts

Protein Powder Doughnut Holes

Prep time: 25 minutes | Cook time: 6 minutes | Makes 12 holes

50 g blanched finely ground almond flour	½ teaspoon baking powder
60 g low-carb vanilla protein powder	1 large egg
	5 tablespoons unsalted butter, melted
100 g granulated sweetener	½ teaspoon vanilla extract

1. Mix all ingredients in a large bowl. Place into the freezer for 20 minutes. 2. Wet your hands with water and roll the dough into twelve balls. 3. Cut a piece of baking paper to fit your cook & crisp basket. Working in batches as necessary, place doughnut holes into the cook & crisp basket on top of baking paper. 4. Adjust the temperature to 190°C and air crisp for 6 minutes. 5. Flip doughnut holes halfway through the cooking time. 6. Let cool completely before serving.

Chocolate Pecan Clusters

Prep time: 5 minutes | Cook time: 5 minutes | Makes 8 clusters

3 tablespoons butter	240 ml chopped pecans
60 ml double cream	60 ml low-carb chocolate chips
1 teaspoon vanilla extract	

1. Press the Sauté button and add butter to Ninja Foodi cooker. Allow butter to melt and begin to turn golden brown. Once it begins to brown, immediately add double cream. Press the Start/Stop button. 2. Add vanilla and chopped pecans to Ninja Foodi cooker. Allow to cool for 10 minutes, stirring occasionally. Spoon mixture onto parchment-lined baking sheet to form eight clusters, and scatter chocolate chips over clusters. Place in fridge to cool.

Chocolate Chip Brownies

Prep time: 10 minutes | Cook time: 33 minutes | Serves 8

360 ml almond flour	2 eggs
80 ml unsweetened cocoa powder	1 tablespoon vanilla extract
180 ml granulated sweetener	5 tablespoons butter, melted
1 teaspoon baking powder	60 ml sugar-free chocolate chips
	120 ml water

1. In a large bowl, add the almond flour, cocoa powder, sweetener, and baking powder. Use a hand mixer on low speed to combine and smooth out any lumps. 2. Add the eggs and vanilla and mix until well combined. 3. Add the butter and mix on low speed until well combined. Scrape the bottom and sides of the bowl and mix again if needed. Fold in the chocolate chips. 4. Grease a baking dish with cooking spray. Pour the batter into the dish and smooth with a spatula. Cover tightly with aluminium foil. 5. Pour the water into the pot. Place the reversible rack in the pot and carefully lower the baking dish onto the reversible rack. 6. Close the lid. Set cooking time for 33 minutes on High Pressure. 7. When timer beeps, use a quick pressure release and open the lid. 8. Use the handles to carefully remove the reversible rack from the pot. Remove the foil from the dish. 9. Let the brownies cool for 10 minutes before turning out onto a plate.

Oatmeal Raisin Bars

Prep time: 15 minutes | Cook time: 15 minutes | Serves 8

40 g plain flour	50 g granulated sugar
¼ teaspoon kosher, or coarse sea salt	120 ml canola, or rapeseed oil
¼ teaspoon baking powder	1 large egg
¼ teaspoon ground cinnamon	1 teaspoon vanilla extract
50 g light brown sugar, lightly packed	110 g quick-cooking oats
	60 g raisins

1. Preheat the Ninja Foodi cooker to 185°C. 2. In a large bowl, combine the plain flour, kosher salt, baking powder, ground cinnamon, light brown sugar, granulated sugar, canola oil, egg, vanilla extract, quick-cooking oats, and raisins. 3. Spray a baking pan with nonstick cooking spray, then pour the oat mixture into the pan and press down to evenly distribute. Place the pan in the Ninja Foodi cooker and bake for 15 minutes or until golden brown. 4. Remove from the Ninja Foodi cooker and allow to cool in the pan on a wire rack for 20 minutes before slicing and serving.

Butter Flax Cookies

Prep time: 25 minutes | Cook time: 20 minutes | Serves 4

225 g almond meal	A pinch of coarse salt
2 tablespoons flaxseed meal	1 large egg, room temperature.
30 g monk fruit, or equivalent sweetener	110 g unsalted butter, room temperature
1 teaspoon baking powder	1 teaspoon vanilla extract
A pinch of grated nutmeg	

1. Mix the almond meal, flaxseed meal, monk fruit, baking powder, grated nutmeg, and salt in a bowl. 2. In a separate bowl, whisk the egg, butter, and vanilla extract. 3. Stir the egg mixture into dry mixture; mix to combine well or until it forms a nice, soft dough. 4. Roll your dough out and cut out with a cookie cutter of your choice. Bake in the preheated Ninja Foodi cooker at 175°C for 10 minutes. Decrease the temperature to 165°C and cook for 10 minutes longer. Bon appétit!

Pumpkin Pudding with Vanilla Wafers

Prep time: 10 minutes | Cook time: 12 to 17 minutes | Serves 4

250 g canned no-salt-added pumpkin purée (not pumpkin pie filling)
50 g packed brown sugar
3 tablespoons plain flour
1 egg, whisked
2 tablespoons milk

1 tablespoon unsalted butter, melted
1 teaspoon pure vanilla extract
4 low-fat vanilla, or plain wafers, crumbled
Nonstick cooking spray

1. Preheat the Ninja Foodi cooker to 175ºC. Coat a baking pan with nonstick cooking spray. Set aside. 2. Mix the pumpkin purée, brown sugar, flour, whisked egg, milk, melted butter, and vanilla in a medium bowl and whisk to combine. Transfer the mixture to the baking pan. 3. Place the baking pan in the cook & crisp basket and bake for 12 to 17 minutes until set. 4. Remove the pudding from the basket to a wire rack to cool. 5. Divide the pudding into four bowls and serve with the vanilla wafers sprinkled on top.

Fast Chocolate Mousse

Prep time: 10 minutes | Cook time: 4 minutes | Serves 1

1 egg yolk
1 teaspoon sweetener
1 teaspoon cocoa powder

2 tablespoons coconut milk
1 tablespoon cream cheese
240 ml water, for cooking

1. Pour water and insert the steamer rack in the Ninja Foodi cooker. 2. Then whisk the egg yolk with sweetener. 3. When the mixture turns into lemon colour, add coconut milk, cream cheese, and cocoa powder. Whisk the mixture until smooth. 4. Then pour it in the glass jar and place it on the steamer rack. 5. Close and seal the lid. 6. Cook the dessert on High Pressure for 4 minutes. Make a quick pressure release.

Nutmeg Cupcakes

Prep time: 5 minutes | Cook time: 30 minutes | Serves 7

Cake:
480 ml blanched almond flour
2 tablespoons grass-fed butter, softened
2 eggs
120 ml unsweetened almond milk
120 ml granulated sweetener, or more to taste
½ teaspoon ground nutmeg
½ teaspoon baking powder

Frosting:
110 g full-fat cream cheese, softened
4 tablespoons grass-fed butter, softened
480 ml heavy whipping cream
1 teaspoon vanilla extract
120 ml granulated sweetener, or more to taste
6 tablespoons sugar-free chocolate chips (optional)

1. Pour 240 ml of filtered water into the inner pot of the Ninja Foodi cooker, then insert the reversible rack. In a large bowl, combine the flour, butter, eggs, almond milk, granulated sweetener, nutmeg, and baking powder. Mix thoroughly. Working in batches

if needed, transfer this mixture into a well-greased, Ninja Foodi cooker-friendly muffin (or egg bites) mold. 2. Place the molds onto the reversible rack, and cover loosely with aluminium foil. Close the lid, set the pressure release to Sealing. Set the Ninja Foodi cooker to 30 minutes on High Pressure, and let cook. 3. While you wait, in a large bowl, combine the cream cheese, butter, whipping cream, vanilla, granulated sweetener, and chocolate chips. Use an electric hand mixer until you achieve a light and fluffy texture. Place frosting in refrigerator. 4. Once the cupcakes are cooked, let the pressure release naturally, for about 10 minutes. Then, switch the pressure release to Venting. Open the Ninja Foodi cooker, and remove the food. Let cool, top each cupcake evenly with a scoop of frosting.

Cocoa Cookies

Prep time: 15 minutes | Cook time: 25 minutes | Serves 4

120 ml coconut flour
3 tablespoons cream cheese
1 teaspoon cocoa powder
1 tablespoon sweetener

¼ teaspoon baking powder
1 teaspoon apple cider vinegar
1 tablespoon butter
240 ml water, for cooking

1. Make the dough: Mix up coconut flour, cream cheese, cocoa powder, sweetener, baking powder, apple cider vinegar, and butter. Knead the dough, 2. Then transfer the dough in the baking pan and flatten it in the shape of a cookie. 3. Pour water and insert the steamer rack in the Ninja Foodi cooker. 4. Put the pan with a cookie in the Ninja Foodi cooker. Close and seal the lid. 5. Cook the cookie on High Pressure for 25 minutes. Make a quick pressure release. Cool the cookie well.

Ultimate Chocolate Cheesecake

Prep time: 10 minutes | Cook time: 50 minutes | Serves 12

480 ml pecans
2 tablespoons butter
450 g cream cheese, softened
240 ml granulated sweetener
60 ml sour cream
2 tablespoons cocoa powder

2 teaspoons vanilla extract
480 ml low-carb chocolate chips
1 tablespoon coconut oil
2 eggs
480 ml water

1. Preheat oven to 205ºC. Place pecans and butter into food processor. Pulse until dough-like consistency. Press into bottom of 7-inch springform pan. Bake for 10 minutes then set aside to cool. 2. While crust bakes, mix cream cheese, sweetener, sour cream, cocoa powder, and vanilla together in large bowl using a rubber spatula. Set aside. 3. In medium bowl, combine chocolate chips and coconut oil. Microwave in 20-second increments until chocolate begins to melt and then stir until smooth. Gently fold chocolate mixture into cheesecake mixture. 4. Add eggs and gently fold in, careful not to overmix. Pour mixture over cooled pecan crust. Cover with foil. 5. Pour water into Ninja Foodi cooker and place steam rack on bottom. Place cheesecake on steam rack and click lid closed. Adjust time for 40 minutes. When timer beeps, allow a natural release. Carefully remove and let cool completely. Serve chilled.

Keto Brownies

Prep time: 15 minutes | Cook time: 15 minutes | Serves 8

240 ml coconut flour	1 teaspoon apple cider vinegar
1 tablespoon cocoa powder	80 ml butter, melted
1 tablespoon coconut oil	1 tablespoon sweetener
1 teaspoon vanilla extract	240 ml water, for cooking
1 teaspoon baking powder	

1. In the mixing bowl, mix up sweetener, melted butter, apple cider vinegar, baking powder, vanilla extract, coconut oil, cocoa powder, and coconut flour. 2. Whisk the mixture until smooth and pour it in the baking pan. Flatten the surface of the batter. 3. Pour water and insert the steamer rack in the Ninja Foodi cooker. 4. Put the pan with brownie batter on the rack. Close and seal the lid. 5. Cook the brownie on High Pressure for 15 minutes. 6. Then allow the natural pressure release for 5 minutes. 7. Cut the cooked brownies into the bars.

Lemon Raspberry Muffins

Prep time: 5 minutes | Cook time: 15 minutes | Serves 6

220 g almond flour	¼ teaspoon salt
75 g powdered sweetener	2 eggs
1¼ teaspoons baking powder	240 ml sour cream
⅓ teaspoon ground allspice	120 ml coconut oil
⅓ teaspoon ground star anise	60 g raspberries
½ teaspoon grated lemon zest	

1. Preheat the Ninja Foodi cooker to 175ºC. Line a muffin pan with 6 paper cases. 2. In a mixing bowl, mix the almond flour, sweetener, baking powder, allspice, star anise, lemon zest, and salt. 3. In another mixing bowl, beat the eggs, sour cream, and coconut oil until well mixed. Add the egg mixture to the flour mixture and stir to combine. Mix in the raspberries. 4. Scrape the batter into the prepared muffin cups, filling each about three-quarters full. 5. Bake for 15 minutes, or until the tops are golden and a toothpick inserted in the middle comes out clean. 6. Allow the muffins to cool for 10 minutes in the muffin pan before removing and serving.

Pears with Honey-Lemon Ricotta

Prep time: 10 minutes | Cook time: 8 minutes | Serves 4

2 large Bartlett pears	125 g full-fat ricotta cheese
3 tablespoons butter, melted	1 tablespoon honey, plus
3 tablespoons brown sugar	additional for drizzling
½ teaspoon ground ginger	1 teaspoon pure almond extract
¼ teaspoon ground cardamom	1 teaspoon pure lemon extract

1. Peel each pear and cut in half, lengthwise. Use a melon baller to scoop out the core. Place the pear halves in a medium bowl, add the melted butter, and toss. Add the brown sugar, ginger, and cardamom; toss to coat. 2. Place the pear halves, cut side down, in the cook & crisp basket. Set the Ninja Foodi cooker to 190ºC

cooking for 8 to 10 minutes, or until the pears are lightly browned and tender, but not mushy. 3. Meanwhile, in a medium bowl, combine the ricotta, honey, and almond and lemon extracts. Beat with an electric mixer on medium speed until the mixture is light and fluffy, about 1 minute. 4. To serve, divide the ricotta mixture among four small shallow bowls. Place a pear half, cut side up, on top of the cheese. Drizzle with additional honey and serve.

Mini Cheesecake

Prep time: 10 minutes | Cook time: 15 minutes | Serves 2

50 g walnuts	softened
2 tablespoons salted butter	1 large egg
2 tablespoons granulated	½ teaspoon vanilla extract
sweetener	35 g powdered sweetener
110 g full-fat cream cheese,	

1. Place walnuts, butter, and granulated sweetener in a food processor. Pulse until ingredients stick together and a dough forms. 2. Press dough into a springform pan then place the pan into the cook & crisp basket. 3. Adjust the temperature to 205ºC and bake for 5 minutes. 4. When done, remove the crust and let cool. 5. In a medium bowl, mix cream cheese with egg, vanilla extract, and powdered sweetener until smooth. 6. Spoon mixture on top of baked walnut crust and place into the cook & crisp basket. 7. Adjust the temperature to 150ºC and bake for 10 minutes. 8. Once done, chill for 2 hours before serving.

Hearty Crème Brûlée

Prep time: 5 minutes | Cook time: 30 minutes | Serves 4

5 egg yolks	360 ml double cream
5 tablespoons granulated	2 teaspoons vanilla extract
sweetener	480 ml water

1. In a small bowl, use a fork to break up the egg yolks. Stir in the sweetener. 2. Pour the cream into a small saucepan over medium-low heat and let it warm up for 3 to 4 minutes. Remove the saucepan from the heat. 3. Temper the egg yolks by slowly adding a small spoonful of the warm cream, keep whisking. Do this three times to make sure the egg yolks are fully tempered. 4. Slowly add the tempered eggs to the cream, whisking the whole time. Add the vanilla and whisk again. 5. Pour the cream mixture into the ramekins. Each ramekin should have 120 ml liquid. Cover each with aluminium foil. 6. Place the reversible rack inside the Ninja Foodi cooker. Add the water. Carefully place the ramekins on top of the reversible rack. 7. Close the lid. Set cooking time for 11 minutes on High Pressure. 8. When timer beeps, use a natural release for 15 minutes, then release any remaining pressure. Open the lid. 9. Carefully remove a ramekin from the pot. Remove the foil and check for doneness. The custard should be mostly set with a slightly jiggly center. 10. Place all the ramekins in the fridge for 2 hours to chill and set. Serve chilled.

Strawberry Cheesecake

Prep time: 20 minutes | Cook time: 10 minutes | Serves 2

1 tablespoon gelatin
4 tablespoon water (for gelatin)
4 tablespoon cream cheese
1 strawberry, chopped

60 ml coconut milk
1 tablespoon granulated sweetener

1. Mix up gelatin and water and leave the mixture for 10 minutes. 2. Meanwhile, pour coconut milk in the Ninja Foodi cooker. 3. Bring it to boil on Sauté mode, about 10 minutes. 4. Meanwhile, mash the strawberry and mix it up with cream cheese. 5. Add the mixture in the hot coconut milk and stir until smooth. 6. Cool the liquid for 10 minutes and add gelatin. Whisk it until gelatin is melted. 7. Then pour the cheesecake in the mold and freeze in the freezer for 3 hours.

Traditional Kentucky Butter Cake

Prep time: 5 minutes | Cook time: 35 minutes | Serves 4

480 ml almond flour
180 ml granulated sweetener
1½ teaspoons baking powder
4 eggs

1 tablespoon vanilla extract
120 ml butter, melted
Cooking spray
120 ml water

1. In a medium bowl, whisk together the almond flour, sweetener, and baking powder. Whisk well to remove any lumps. 2. Add the eggs and vanilla and whisk until combined. 3. Add the butter and whisk until the batter is mostly smooth and well combined. 4. Grease the pan with cooking spray and pour in the batter. Cover tightly with aluminium foil. 5. Add the water to the pot. Place the Bundt pan on the reversible rack and carefully lower it into the pot using. 6. Set the lid in place. Set the cooking time for 35 minutes on High Pressure. When the timer goes off, do a quick pressure release. Carefully open the lid. 7. Remove the pan from the pot. Let the cake cool in the pan before flipping out onto a plate.

Coconut Cupcakes

Prep time: 5 minutes | Cook time: 10 minutes | Serves 6

4 eggs, beaten
4 tablespoons coconut milk
4 tablespoons coconut flour
½ teaspoon vanilla extract

2 tablespoons sweetener
1 teaspoon baking powder
240 ml water

1. In the mixing bowl, mix up eggs, coconut milk, coconut flour, vanilla extract, sweetener, and baking powder. 2. Then pour the batter in the cupcake molds. 3. Pour the water and insert the reversible rack in the Ninja Foodi cooker. 4. Place the cupcakes on the reversible rack. 5. Lock the lid. Set the cooking time for 10 minutes on High Pressure. Once the timer goes off, perform a natural pressure release for 5 minutes, then release any remaining pressure. Carefully open the lid. 6. Serve immediately.

Almond-Roasted Pears

Prep time: 10 minutes | Cook time: 15 to 20 minutes | Serves 4

Yogurt Topping:
140-170 g pot vanilla Greek yogurt
¼ teaspoon almond flavoring

2 whole pears
4 crushed Biscoff biscuits
1 tablespoon flaked almonds
1 tablespoon unsalted butter

1. Stir the almond flavoring into yogurt and set aside while preparing pears. 2. Halve each pear and spoon out the core. 3. Place pear halves in cook & crisp basket, skin side down. 4. Stir together the crushed biscuits and almonds. Place a quarter of this mixture into the hollow of each pear half. 5. Cut butter into 4 pieces and place one piece on top of biscuit mixture in each pear. 6. Roast at 185°C for 15 to 20 minutes, or until pears have cooked through but are still slightly firm. 7. Serve pears warm with a dollop of yogurt topping.

Goat Cheese–Stuffed Pears

Prep time: 6 minutes | Cook time: 2 minutes | Serves 4

60 g goat cheese, at room temperature
2 teaspoons pure maple syrup
2 ripe, firm pears, halved

lengthwise and cored
2 tablespoons chopped pistachios, toasted

1. Pour 240 ml of water into the electric pressure cooker and insert a wire rack or reversible rack. 2. In a small bowl, combine the goat cheese and maple syrup. 3. Spoon the goat cheese mixture into the cored pear halves. Place the pears on the rack inside the pot, cut-side up. 4. Close and lock the lid of the pressure cooker. Set the valve to sealing. 5. Cook on high pressure for 2 minutes. 6. When the cooking is complete, hit Start/Stop and quick release the pressure. 7. Once the pin drops, unlock and remove the lid. 8. Using tongs, carefully transfer the pears to serving plates. 9. Sprinkle with pistachios and serve immediately.

Spiced Pear Applesauce

Prep time: 15 minutes | Cook time: 5 minutes | Makes: 840 ml

450 g pears, peeled, cored, and sliced
2 teaspoons apple pie spice or

cinnamon
Pinch rock salt
Juice of ½ small lemon

1. In the electric pressure cooker, combine the apples, pears, apple pie spice, salt, lemon juice, and 60 ml of water. 2. Close and lock the lid of the pressure cooker. Set the valve to sealing. 3. Cook on high pressure for 5 minutes. 4. When the cooking is complete, hit Start/Stop and let the pressure release naturally. 5. Once the pin drops, unlock and remove the lid. 6. Mash the apples and pears with a potato masher to the consistency you like. 7. Serve warm, or cool to room temperature and refrigerate.

Chocolate Croissants

Prep time: 5 minutes | Cook time: 24 minutes | Serves 8

1 sheet frozen puff pastry, thawed

100 g chocolate-hazelnut spread
1 large egg, beaten

1. On a lightly floured surface, roll puff pastry into a 14-inch square. Cut pastry into quarters to form 4 squares. Cut each square diagonally to form 8 triangles. 2. Spread 2 teaspoons chocolate-hazelnut spread on each triangle; from wider end, roll up pastry. Brush egg on top of each roll. 3. Preheat the Ninja Foodi cooker to 190°C. Air crisp rolls in batches, 3 or 4 at a time, 8 minutes per batch, or until pastry is golden brown. 4. Cool on a wire rack; serve while warm or at room temperature.

Pumpkin Cookie with Cream Cheese Frosting

Prep time: 10 minutes | Cook time: 7 minutes | Serves 6

50 g blanched finely ground almond flour
50 g powdered sweetener, divided
2 tablespoons butter, softened
1 large egg
½ teaspoon unflavored gelatin
½ teaspoon baking powder
½ teaspoon vanilla extract

½ teaspoon pumpkin pie spice
2 tablespoons pure pumpkin purée
½ teaspoon ground cinnamon, divided
40 g low-carb, sugar-free chocolate chips
85 g full-fat cream cheese, softened

1. In a large bowl, mix almond flour and 25 gsweetener. Stir in butter, egg, and gelatin until combined. 2. Stir in baking powder, vanilla, pumpkin pie spice, pumpkin purée, and ¼ teaspoon cinnamon, then fold in chocolate chips. 3. Pour batter into a round baking pan. Place pan into the cook & crisp basket. 4. Adjust the temperature to 150°C and bake for 7 minutes. 5. When fully cooked, the top will be golden brown, and a toothpick inserted in center will come out clean. Let cool at least 20 minutes. 6. To make the frosting: mix cream cheese, remaining ¼ teaspoon cinnamon, and remaining 25 g sweetener in a large bowl. Using an electric mixer, beat until it becomes fluffy. Spread onto the cooled cookie. Garnish with additional cinnamon if desired.

Crustless Key Lime Cheesecake

Prep time: 15 minutes | Cook time: 35 minutes | Serves 8

Nonstick cooking spray
450 g light cream cheese (Neufchâtel), softened
160 ml granulated sweetener
60 ml unsweetened Key lime juice (I like Nellie & Joe's Famous Key West Lime Juice)

½ teaspoon vanilla extract
60 ml plain Greek yoghurt
1 teaspoon grated lime zest
2 large eggs
Whipped cream, for garnish (optional)

1. Spray a 7-inch springform pan with nonstick cooking spray. Line the bottom and partway up the sides of the pan with foil. 2. Put the cream cheese in a large bowl. Use an electric mixer to whip the cream cheese until smooth, about 2 minutes. Add the sweetener, lime juice, vanilla, yoghurt, and zest, and blend until smooth. Stop the mixer and scrape down the sides of the bowl with a rubber spatula. With the mixer on low speed, add the eggs, one at a time, blending until just mixed. (Don't overbeat the eggs.) 3. Pour the mixture into the prepared pan. Drape a paper towel over the top of the pan, not touching the cream cheese mixture, and tightly wrap the top of the pan in foil. (Your goal here is to keep out as much moisture as possible.) 4. Pour 240 ml of water into the electric pressure cooker. 5. Place the foil-covered pan onto the wire rack and carefully lower it into the pot. 6. Close and lock the lid of the pressure cooker. Set the valve to sealing. 7. Cook on high pressure for 35 minutes. 8. When the cooking is complete, hit Start/Stop. Allow the pressure to release naturally for 20 minutes, then quick release any remaining pressure. 9. Once the pin drops, unlock and remove the lid. 10. Using the handles of the wire rack, carefully transfer the pan to a cooling rack. Cool to room temperature, then refrigerate for at least 3 hours. 11. When ready to serve, run a thin rubber spatula around the rim of the cheesecake to loosen it, then remove the ring. 12. Slice into wedges and serve with whipped cream (if using).

Apple Dutch Baby

Prep time: 30 minutes | Cook time: 16 minutes | Serves 2 to 3

Batter:
2 large eggs
30 g plain flour
¼ teaspoon baking powder
1½ teaspoons granulated sugar
Pinch kosher, or coarse sea salt
120 ml whole milk
1 tablespoon butter, melted
½ teaspoon pure vanilla extract
¼ teaspoon ground nutmeg

Apples:
2 tablespoon butter
4 tablespoons granulated sugar
¼ teaspoon ground cinnamon
¼ teaspoon ground nutmeg
1 small tart apple (such as Granny Smith), peeled, cored, and sliced
Vanilla ice cream (optional), for serving

1. For the batter: In a medium bowl, combine the eggs, flour, baking powder, sugar, and salt. Whisk lightly. While whisking continuously, slowly pour in the milk. Whisk in the melted butter, vanilla, and nutmeg. Let the batter stand for 30 minutes. (You can also cover and refrigerate overnight.) 2. For the apples: Place the butter in a baking pan. Place the pan in the cook & crisp basket. Set the Ninja Foodi cooker to 205°C and cook for 2 minutes. In a small bowl, combine 2 tablespoons of the sugar with the cinnamon and nutmeg and stir until well combined. 3. When the pan is hot and the butter is melted, brush some butter up the sides of the pan. Sprinkle the spiced sugar mixture over the butter. Arrange the apple slices in the pan in a single layer and sprinkle the remaining 2 tablespoons sugar over the apples. Keep the Ninja Foodi cooker at 205°C and cook for a further2 minutes, or until the mixture bubbles. 4. Gently pour the batter over the apples. Set the Ninja Foodi cooker to 175°C cooking for 12 minutes, or until the pancake is golden brown around the edges, the center is cooked through, and a toothpick emerges clean. 5. Serve immediately with ice cream, if desired.

Peanut Butter, Honey & Banana Toast

Prep time: 10 minutes | Cook time: 9 minutes | Serves 4

2 tablespoons unsalted butter, softened	2 bananas, peeled and thinly sliced
4 slices white bread	4 tablespoons honey
4 tablespoons peanut butter	1 teaspoon ground cinnamon

1. Spread butter on one side of each slice of bread, then peanut butter on the other side. Arrange the banana slices on top of the peanut butter sides of each slice (about 9 slices per toast). Drizzle honey on top of the banana and sprinkle with cinnamon. 2. Cut each slice in half lengthwise so that it will better fit into the cook & crisp basket. Arrange two pieces of bread, butter sides down, in the cook & crisp basket. Set the Ninja Foodi cooker to 190ºC cooking for 5 minutes. Then set the Ninja Foodi cooker to 205ºC and cook for an additional 4 minutes, or until the bananas have started to brown. Repeat with remaining slices. Serve hot.

Breaded Bananas with Chocolate Topping

Prep time: 10 minutes | Cook time: 10 minutes | Serves 6

40 g cornflour	3 bananas, halved crosswise
25 g plain breadcrumbs	Cooking spray
1 large egg, beaten	Chocolate sauce, for serving

1. Preheat the Ninja Foodi cooker to175ºC. 2. Place the cornflour, breadcrumbs, and egg in three separate bowls. 3. Roll the bananas in the cornstarch, then in the beaten egg, and finally in the breadcrumbs to coat well. 4. Spritz the cook & crisp basket with the cooking spray. 5. Arrange the banana halves in the basket and mist them with the cooking spray. Air crisp for 5 minutes. Flip the bananas and continue to air crisp for another 2 minutes. 6. Remove the bananas from the basket to a serving plate. Serve with the chocolate sauce drizzled over the top.

Chocolate Chip Pecan Biscotti

Prep time: 15 minutes | Cook time: 20 to 22 minutes | Serves 10

135 g finely ground blanched almond flour	1 large egg, beaten
¾ teaspoon baking powder	1 teaspoon pure vanilla extract
½ teaspoon xanthan gum	50 g chopped pecans
¼ teaspoon sea salt	40 g organic chocolate chips,
3 tablespoons unsalted butter, at room temperature	Melted organic chocolate chips and chopped pecans, for topping (optional)
35 g powdered sweetener	

1. In a large bowl, combine the almond flour, baking powder, xanthan gum, and salt. 2. Line a cake pan that fits inside your Ninja Foodi cooker with baking paper. 3. In the bowl of a stand mixer, beat together the butter and powdered sweetener. Add the beaten egg and vanilla and beat for about 3 minutes. 4. Add the almond flour mixture to the butter and egg mixture; beat until just combined. 5. Stir in the pecans and chocolate chips. 6. Transfer the dough to the prepared pan and press it into the bottom. 7. Set the Ninja Foodi cooker to 165ºC and bake for 12 minutes. Remove from the Ninja Foodi cooker and let cool for 15 minutes. Using a sharp knife, cut the cookie into thin strips, then return the strips to the cake pan with the bottom sides facing up. 8. Set the Ninja Foodi cooker to 150ºC. Bake for 8 to 10 minutes. 9. Remove from the Ninja Foodi cooker and let cool completely on a wire rack. If desired, dip one side of each biscotti piece into melted chocolate chips, and top with chopped pecans.

Crispy Pineapple Rings

Prep time: 5 minutes | Cook time: 6 to 8 minutes | Serves 6

240 ml rice milk	½ teaspoon vanilla essence
85 g plain flour	½ teaspoon ground cinnamon
120 ml water	¼ teaspoon ground star anise
25 g unsweetened flaked coconut	Pinch of kosher, or coarse sea salt
4 tablespoons granulated sugar	1 medium pineapple, peeled and sliced
½ teaspoon baking soda	
½ teaspoon baking powder	

1. Preheat the Ninja Foodi cooker to 190ºC. 2. In a large bowl, stir together all the ingredients except the pineapple. 3. Dip each pineapple slice into the batter until evenly coated. 4. Arrange the pineapple slices in the basket and air crisp for 6 to 8 minutes until golden brown. 5. Remove from the basket to a plate and cool for 5 minutes before serving warm

Lush Chocolate Chip Cookies

Prep time: 7 minutes | Cook time: 9 minutes | Serves 4

3 tablespoons butter, at room temperature	chocolate
65 g light brown sugar, plus 1 tablespoon	¼ teaspoon baking soda
	½ teaspoon vanilla extract
1 egg yolk	120 g semisweet chocolate chips
70 g plain flour	Nonstick flour-infused baking spray
2 tablespoons ground white	

1. In medium bowl, beat together the butter and brown sugar until fluffy. Stir in the egg yolk. 2. Add the flour, white chocolate, baking soda, and vanilla and mix well. Stir in the chocolate chips. 3. Line a 6-by-2-inch round baking pan with baking paper. Spray the baking paper with flour-infused baking spray. 4. Insert the crisper plate into the basket and the basket into the unit. Preheat the unit to 150ºC. 5. Spread the batter into the prepared pan, leaving a ½-inch border on all sides. 6. Once the unit is preheated, place the pan into the basket. 7. Bake to cookies for 9 minutes. 8. When the cooking is complete, the cookies should be light brown and just barely set. Remove the pan from the basket and let cool for 10 minutes. Remove the cookie from the pan, remove the baking paper, and let cool completely on a wire rack.

Gingerbread

Prep time: 5 minutes | Cook time: 20 minutes | Makes 1 loaf

Cooking spray
125 g plain flour
2 tablespoons granulated sugar
¾ teaspoon ground ginger
¼ teaspoon cinnamon
1 teaspoon baking powder
½ teaspoon baking soda

⅛ teaspoon salt
1 egg
70 g treacle
120 ml buttermilk
2 tablespoons coconut, or avocado oil
1 teaspoon pure vanilla extract

1. Preheat the Ninja Foodi cooker to 165°C. 2. Spray a baking dish lightly with cooking spray. 3. In a medium bowl, mix together all the dry ingredients. 4. In a separate bowl, beat the egg. Add treacle, buttermilk, oil, and vanilla and stir until well mixed. 5. Pour liquid mixture into dry ingredients and stir until well blended. 6. Pour batter into baking dish and bake for 20 minutes, or until toothpick inserted in center of loaf comes out clean.

Traditional Cheesecake

Prep time: 30 minutes | Cook time: 45 minutes | Serves 8

For Crust:
360 ml almond flour
4 tablespoons butter, melted
1 tablespoon granulated sweetener
1 tablespoon granulated sweetener
½ teaspoon ground cinnamon

For Filling:
450 g cream cheese, softened
120 ml granulated sweetener
2 eggs
1 teaspoon vanilla extract
½ teaspoon lemon extract
360 ml water

1. To make the crust: In a medium bowl, combine the almond flour, butter, granulated sweetener, sweetener, and cinnamon. Use a fork to press it all together. When completed, the mixture should resemble wet sand. 2. Spray the springform pan with cooking spray and line the bottom with baking paper. 3. Press the crust evenly into the pan. Work the crust up the sides of the pan, about halfway from the top, and make sure there are no bare spots on the bottom. 4. Place the crust in the freezer for 20 minutes while you make the filling. 5. To make the filling: In the bowl of a stand mixer using the whip attachment, combine the cream cheese and sweetener on medium speed until the cream cheese is light and fluffy, 2 to 3 minutes. 6. Add the eggs, vanilla extract, and lemon extract. Mix until well combined. 7. Remove the crust from the freezer and pour in the filling. Cover the pan tightly with aluminium foil and place it on the reversible rack. 8. Add the water to the pot and carefully lower the reversible rack into the pot. 9. Close the lid. Set cooking time for 45 minutes on High Pressure. 10. When timer beeps, use a quick pressure release and open the lid. 11. Remove the reversible rack and cheesecake from the pot. Remove the foil from the pan. The center of the cheesecake should still be slightly jiggly. If the cheesecake is still very jiggly in the center, cook for an additional 5 minutes on High pressure until the appropriate doneness is reached. 12. Let the cheesecake cool for 30 minutes on the counter before placing it in the refrigerator to set. Leave the cheesecake in the refrigerator for at least 6 hours before removing the sides of the pan, slicing, and serving.

Pecan Butter Cookies

Prep time: 5 minutes | Cook time: 24 minutes | Makes 12 cookies

125 g chopped pecans
110 g salted butter, melted
55 g coconut flour

150 g granulated sweetener, divided
1 teaspoon vanilla extract

1. In a food processor, blend together pecans, butter, flour, 100 g sweetener, and vanilla 1 minute until a dough forms. 2. Form dough into twelve individual cookie balls, about 1 tablespoon each. 3. Cut three pieces of baking paper to fit cook & crisp basket. Place four cookies on each ungreased baking paper and place one piece baking paper with cookies into cook & crisp basket. Adjust Ninja Foodi cooker temperature to 165°C and set the timer for 8 minutes. Repeat cooking with remaining batches. 4. When the timer goes off, allow cookies to cool 5 minutes on a large serving plate until cool enough to handle. While still warm, dust cookies with remaining granulated sweetener. Allow to cool completely, about 15 minutes, before serving.

Coconut Flour Cake

Prep time: 10 minutes | Cook time: 25 minutes | Serves 6

2 tablespoons salted butter, melted
35 g coconut flour
2 large eggs, whisked

100 g granulated sweetener
1 teaspoon baking powder
1 teaspoon vanilla extract
120 ml sour cream

1. Mix all ingredients in a large bowl. Pour batter into an ungreased round nonstick baking dish. 2. Place baking dish into cook & crisp basket. Adjust the temperature to 150°C and bake for 25 minutes. The cake will be dark golden on top, and a toothpick inserted in the center should come out clean when done. 3. Let cool in dish 15 minutes before slicing and serving.

Apple Wedges with Apricots

Prep time: 5 minutes | Cook time: 15 to 18 minutes | Serves 4

4 large apples, peeled and sliced into 8 wedges
2 tablespoons light olive oil
95 g dried apricots, chopped

1 to 2 tablespoons granulated sugar
½ teaspoon ground cinnamon

1. Preheat the Ninja Foodi cooker to 180°C. 2. Toss the apple wedges with the olive oil in a mixing bowl until well coated. 3. Place the apple wedges in the cook & crisp basket and air crisp for 12 to 15 minutes. 4. Sprinkle with the dried apricots and air crisp for another 3 minutes. 5. Meanwhile, thoroughly combine the sugar and cinnamon in a small bowl. 6. Remove the apple wedges from the basket to a plate. Serve sprinkled with the sugar mixture.

Pine Nut Mousse

Prep time: 5 minutes | Cook time: 35 minutes | Serves 8

1 tablespoon butter	240 ml granulated sweetener,
300 ml pine nuts	reserve 1 tablespoon
300 ml full-fat double cream	1 c water
2 large eggs	240 ml full-fat heavy whipping
1 teaspoon vanilla extract	cream

1. Butter the bottom and the side of a pie pan and set aside. 2. In a food processor, blend the pine nuts and double cream. Add the eggs, vanilla extract and granulated sweetener and pulse a few times to incorporate. 3. Pour the batter into the pan and loosely cover with aluminium foil. Pour the water in the Ninja Foodi cooker and place the reversible rack inside. Place the pan on top of the reversible rack. 4. Close the lid. Set the timer for 35 minutes on High pressure. 5. In a small mixing bowl, whisk the heavy whipping cream and 1 tablespoon of granulated sweetener until a soft peak forms. 6. When timer beeps, use a natural pressure release for 15 minutes, then release any remaining pressure and open the lid. 7. Serve immediately with whipped cream on top.

Vanilla Cream Pie

Prep time: 20 minutes | Cook time: 35 minutes | Serves 12

240 ml double cream	240 ml coconut flour
3 eggs, beaten	1 tablespoon butter, melted
1 teaspoon vanilla extract	240 ml water, for cooking
60 ml sweetener	

1. In the mixing bowl, mix up coconut flour, sweetener, vanilla extract, eggs, and double cream. 2. Grease the baking pan with melted butter. 3. Pour the coconut mixture in the baking pan. 4. Pour water and insert the steamer rack in the Ninja Foodi cooker. 5. Place the pie on the rack. Close and seal the lid. 6. Cook the pie on High Pressure for 35 minutes. 7. Allow the natural pressure release for 10 minutes.

Pecan Pumpkin Pie

Prep time: 5 minutes | Cook time: 40 minutes | Serves 5 to 6

Base:	80 ml heavy whipping cream
2 tablespoons grass-fed butter,	½ teaspoon ground cinnamon
softened	½ teaspoon ginger, finely grated
240 ml blanched almond flour	½ teaspoon ground nutmeg
120 ml chopped pecans	½ teaspoon ground cloves
Topping:	1 (400 g) can organic pumpkin
120 ml granulated sweetener, or	purée
more to taste	1 egg

1. Pour 240 ml of filtered water into the inner pot of the Ninja Foodi cooker, then insert the reversible rack. Using an electric mixer, combine the butter, almond flour, and pecans. Mix thoroughly. Transfer this mixture into a well-greased, Ninja Foodi cooker-friendly pan, and form a crust at the bottom of the pan, with a slight coating of the mixture also on the sides. Freeze for 15 minutes. In a large bowl, thoroughly combine the topping ingredients. 2. Take the pan from the freezer, add the topping evenly, and then place the pan onto the reversible rack. Cover loosely with aluminium foil. Close the lid, set the pressure release to Sealing. Set the Ninja Foodi cooker to 40 minutes on High Pressure, and let cook. 3. Once cooked, let the pressure naturally disperse from the Ninja Foodi cooker for about 10 minutes, then carefully switch the pressure release to Venting. 4. Open the Ninja Foodi cooker and remove the pan. Cool in the refrigerator for 4 to 5 hours, serve, and enjoy!

Berry Crumble

Prep time: 10 minutes | Cook time: 15 minutes | Serves 4

For the Filling:	20 g rolled oats
300 g mixed berries	1 tablespoon granulated sugar
2 tablespoons sugar	2 tablespoons cold unsalted
1 tablespoon cornflour	butter, cut into small cubes
1 tablespoon fresh lemon juice	Whipped cream or ice cream
For the Topping☐	(optional)
30 g plain flour	

1. Preheat the Ninja Foodi cooker to 205ºC. 2. For the filling: In a round baking pan, gently mix the berries, sugar, cornflour, and lemon juice until thoroughly combined. 3. For the topping: In a small bowl, combine the flour, oats, and sugar. Stir the butter into the flour mixture until the mixture has the consistency of breadcrumbs. 4. Sprinkle the topping over the berries. 5. Put the pan in the cook & crisp basket and air crisp for 15 minutes. Let cool for 5 minutes on a wire rack. 6. Serve topped with whipped cream or ice cream, if desired.

Coconut Almond Cream Cake

Prep time: 10 minutes | Cook time: 40 minutes | Serves 8

Nonstick cooking spray	1 teaspoon baking powder
240 ml almond flour	1 teaspoon apple pie spice
120 ml unsweetened desiccated	2 eggs, lightly whisked
coconut	60 ml unsalted butter, melted
80 ml granulated sweetener	120 ml heavy (whipping) cream

1. Grease a 6-inch round cake pan with the cooking spray. 2. In a medium bowl, mix together the almond flour, coconut, granulated sweetener, baking powder, and apple pie spice. 3. Add the eggs, then the butter, then the cream, mixing well after each addition. 4. Pour the batter into the pan and cover with aluminium foil. 5. Pour 480 ml of water into the inner cooking pot of the Ninja Foodi cooker, then place a reversible rack in the pot. Place the pan on the reversible rack. 6. Lock the lid into place. Adjust the pressure to High. Cook for 40 minutes. When the cooking is complete, let the pressure release naturally for 10 minutes, then quick-release any remaining pressure. Unlock the lid. 7. Carefully take out the pan and let it cool for 15 to 20 minutes. Invert the cake onto a plate. Sprinkle with desiccated coconut, almond slices, or granulated sweetener, if desired, and serve.

Baked Peaches with Yogurt and Blueberries

Prep time: 10 minutes | Cook time: 7 to 11 minutes | Serves 6

3 peaches, peeled, halved, and pitted
2 tablespoons packed brown sugar

285 g plain Greek yogurt
¼ teaspoon ground cinnamon
1 teaspoon pure vanilla extract
190 g fresh blueberries

1. Preheat the Ninja Foodi cooker to 190°C. 2. Arrange the peaches in the cook & crisp basket, cut side up. Top with a generous sprinkle of brown sugar. 3. Bake in the preheated Ninja Foodi cooker for 7 to 11 minutes, or until the peaches are lightly browned and caramelized. 4. Meanwhile, whisk together the yogurt, cinnamon, and vanilla in a small bowl until smooth. 5. Remove the peaches from the basket to a plate. Serve topped with the yogurt mixture and fresh blueberries.

Chocolate and Rum Cupcakes

Prep time: 5 minutes | Cook time: 15 minutes | Serves 6

150 g granulated sweetener
140 g almond flour
1 teaspoon unsweetened baking powder
3 teaspoons cocoa powder
½ teaspoon baking soda
½ teaspoon ground cinnamon
¼ teaspoon grated nutmeg

⅛ teaspoon salt
120 ml milk
110 g butter, at room temperature
3 eggs, whisked
1 teaspoon pure rum extract
70 g blueberries
Cooking spray

1. Preheat the Ninja Foodi cooker to 175°C. Spray a 6-cup muffin tin with cooking spray. 2. In a mixing bowl, combine the sweetener, almond flour, baking powder, cocoa powder, baking soda, cinnamon, nutmeg, and salt and stir until well blended. 3. In another mixing bowl, mix together the milk, butter, egg, and rum extract until thoroughly combined. Slowly and carefully pour this mixture into the bowl of dry mixture. Stir in the blueberries. 4. Spoon the batter into the greased muffin cups, filling each about three-quarters full. 5. Bake for 15 minutes, or until the center is springy and a toothpick inserted in the middle comes out clean. 6. Remove from the basket and place on a wire rack to cool. Serve immediately.

Cardamom Custard

Prep time: 10 minutes | Cook time: 25 minutes | Serves 2

240 ml whole milk
1 large egg
2 tablespoons granulated sugar, plus 1 teaspoon

¼ teaspoon vanilla bean paste or pure vanilla extract
¼ teaspoon ground cardamom, plus more for sprinkling

1. In a medium bowl, beat together the milk, egg, sugar, vanilla, and cardamom. 2. Place two ramekins in the cook & crisp basket. Divide the mixture between the ramekins. Sprinkle lightly with cardamom. Cover each ramekin tightly with aluminum foil. Set the Ninja Foodi cooker to 175°C and cook for 25 minutes, or

until a toothpick inserted in the center comes out clean. 3. Let the custards cool on a wire rack for 5 to 10 minutes. 4. Serve warm or refrigerate until cold and serve chilled.

Coconut Lemon Squares

Prep time: 5 minutes | Cook time: 40 minutes | Serves 5 to 6

3 eggs
2 tablespoons grass-fed butter, softened
120 ml full-fat coconut milk
½ teaspoon baking powder

½ teaspoon vanilla extract
120 ml granulated sweetener, or more to taste
60 ml lemon juice
240 ml blanched almond flour

1. In a large bowl, mix together the eggs, butter, coconut milk, baking powder, vanilla, granulated sweetener, lemon juice, and flour. Stir thoroughly, until a perfectly even mixture is obtained. 2. Next, pour 240 ml filtered water into the Ninja Foodi cooker, and insert the reversible rack. Transfer the mixture from the bowl into a well-greased, Ninja Foodi cooker-friendly pan (or dish). 3. Using a sling if desired, place the dish onto the reversible rack, and cover loosely with aluminium foil. Close the lid, set the pressure release to Sealing. Set the Ninja Foodi cooker to 40 minutes on High Pressure, and let cook. 4. Once cooked, let the pressure naturally disperse from the Ninja Foodi cooker for about 10 minutes, then carefully switch the pressure release to Venting. 5. Open the Ninja Foodi cooker, and remove the dish. Let cool, cut into 6 squares, serve, and enjoy!

Cocoa Custard

Prep time: 5 minutes | Cook time: 7 minutes | Serves 4

480 ml double cream (or full-fat coconut milk for dairy-free)
4 large egg yolks
60 ml granulated sweetener, or more to taste
1 tablespoon plus 1 teaspoon

unsweetened cocoa powder, or more to taste
½ teaspoon almond extract
Pinch of fine sea salt
240 ml cold water

1. Heat the cream in a pan over medium-high heat until hot, about 2 minutes. 2. Place the remaining ingredients except the water in a blender and blend until smooth. 3. While the blender is running, slowly pour in the hot cream. Taste and adjust the sweetness to your liking. Add more cocoa powder, if desired. 4. Scoop the custard mixture into four ramekins with a spatula. Cover the ramekins with aluminium foil. 5. Place a reversible rack in the Ninja Foodi cooker and pour in the water. Place the ramekins on the reversible rack. 6. Lock the lid. Set the cooking time for 5 minutes at High Pressure. 7. When the timer beeps, use a quick pressure release. Carefully remove the lid. 8. Remove the foil and set the foil aside. Let the custard cool for 15 minutes. Cover the ramekins with the foil again and place in the refrigerator to chill completely, about 2 hours. 9. Serve.

Baked Apples and Walnuts

Prep time: 6 minutes | Cook time: 20 minutes | Serves 4

4 small Granny Smith apples
50 g chopped walnuts
50 g light brown sugar
2 tablespoons butter, melted

1 teaspoon ground cinnamon
½ teaspoon ground nutmeg
120 ml water, or apple juice

1. Cut off the top third of the apples. Spoon out the core and some of the flesh and discard. Place the apples in a small Ninja Foodi cooker baking pan. 2. Insert the crisper plate into the basket and the basket into the unit. Preheat to 175°C. 3. In a small bowl, stir together the walnuts, brown sugar, melted butter, cinnamon, and nutmeg. Spoon this mixture into the centers of the hollowed-out apples. 4. Once the unit is preheated, pour the water into the crisper plate. Place the baking pan into the basket. 5. Bake for 20 minutes. 6. When the cooking is complete, the apples should be bubbly and fork tender.

Lime Muffins

Prep time: 10 minutes | Cook time: 15 minutes | Serves 6

1 teaspoon lime zest
1 tablespoon lemon juice
1 teaspoon baking powder
240 ml almond flour
2 eggs, beaten

1 tablespoon granulated sweetener
60 ml double cream
240 ml water, for cooking

1. In the mixing bowl, mix up lemon juice, baking powder, almond flour, eggs, granulated sweetener, and double cream. 2. When the muffin batter is smooth, add lime zest and mix it up. 3. Fill the muffin molds with batter. 4. Then pour water and insert the rack in the Ninja Foodi cooker. 5. Place the muffins on the rack. Close and seal the lid. 6. Cook the muffins on High Pressure for 15 minutes. 7. Then allow the natural pressure release.

Tapioca Berry Parfaits

Prep time: 10 minutes | Cook time: 6 minutes | Serves 4

480 ml unsweetened almond milk
120 ml small pearl tapioca, rinsed and still wet

1 teaspoon almond extract
1 tablespoon pure maple syrup
480 ml berries
60 ml slivered almonds

1. Pour the almond milk into the electric pressure cooker. Stir in the tapioca and almond extract. 2. Close and lock the lid of the pressure cooker. Set the valve to sealing. 3. Cook on High pressure for 6 minutes. 4. When the cooking is complete, hit Start/Stop. Allow the pressure to release naturally for 10 minutes, then quick release any remaining pressure. 5. Once the pin drops, unlock and remove the lid. Remove the pot to a cooling rack. 6. Stir in the maple syrup and let the mixture cool for about an hour. 7. In small glasses, create several layers of tapioca, berries, and almonds. Refrigerate for 1 hour. 8. Serve chilled.

Thai Pandan Coconut Custard

Prep time: 10 minutes | Cook time: 30 minutes | Serves 4

Nonstick cooking spray
240 ml unsweetened coconut milk
3 eggs

80 ml granulated sweetener
3 to 4 drops pandan extract, or use vanilla extract if you must

1. Grease a 6-inch heatproof bowl with the cooking spray. 2. In a large bowl, whisk together the coconut milk, eggs, granulated sweetener, and pandan extract. Pour the mixture into the prepared bowl and cover it with aluminium foil. 3. Pour 480 ml of water into the inner cooking pot of the Ninja Foodi cooker, then place a reversible rack in the pot. Place the bowl on the reversible rack. 4. Lock the lid into place. Adjust the pressure to High. Cook for 30 minutes. When the cooking is complete, let the pressure release naturally. Unlock the lid. 5. Remove the bowl from the pot and remove the foil. A knife inserted into the custard should come out clean. Cool in the refrigerator for 6 to 8 hours, or until the custard is set.

Butter and Chocolate Chip Cookies

Prep time: 20 minutes | Cook time: 11 minutes | Serves 8

110 g unsalted butter, at room temperature
155 g powdered sweetener
60 g chunky peanut butter
1 teaspoon vanilla paste
1 fine almond flour
75 g coconut flour

35 g cocoa powder, unsweetened
1 ½ teaspoons baking powder
¼ teaspoon ground cinnamon
¼ teaspoon ginger
85 g unsweetened, or dark chocolate chips

1. In a mixing dish, beat the butter and sweetener until creamy and uniform. Stir in the peanut butter and vanilla. 2. In another mixing dish, thoroughly combine the flour, cocoa powder, baking powder, cinnamon, and ginger. 3. Add the flour mixture to the peanut butter mixture; mix to combine well. Afterwards, fold in the chocolate chips. Drop by large spoonsful onto a baking paper-lined cook & crisp basket. Bake at 185°C for 11 minutes or until golden brown on the top. Bon appétit!

Chapter 9 Staples, Sauces, Dips, and Dressings

Hemp Dressing

Prep time: 5 minutes | Cook time: 0 minutes | Makes 12 tablespoons

120 ml white wine vinegar
60 ml tahini
60 ml water
1 tablespoon hemp seeds
½ tablespoon freshly squeezed lemon juice
1 teaspoon garlic powder
1 teaspoon dried oregano
1 teaspoon dried basil
1 teaspoon red pepper flakes
½ teaspoon onion powder
½ teaspoon pink Himalayan salt
½ teaspoon freshly ground black pepper

1.In a bowl, combine all the ingredients and whisk until mixed well.

Peanut Sauce with black pepper

Prep time: 5 minutes | Cook time: 0 minutes | Serves 4

80 ml peanut butter
60 ml hot water
2 tablespoons soy sauce
2 tablespoons rice vinegar
Juice of 1 lime
1 teaspoon minced fresh ginger
1 teaspoon minced garlic
1 teaspoon black pepper

1.In a blender container, combine the peanut butter, hot water, soy sauce, vinegar, lime juice, ginger, garlic, and pepper. Blend until smooth. 2. Use immediately or store in an airtight container in the refrigerator for a week or more.

Blue Cheese Dressing

Prep time: 5 minutes | Cook time: 0 minutes | Serves 12

180 ml sugar-free mayonnaise
60 ml sour cream
120 ml double cream
1 teaspoon minced garlic
1 tablespoon freshly squeezed lemon juice
1 tablespoon apple cider vinegar
1 teaspoon hot sauce
½ teaspoon sea salt
110 g blue cheese, crumbled (about 180 ml)

1.In a medium bowl, whisk together the mayonnaise, sour cream, and double cream. Stir in the garlic, lemon juice, apple cider vinegar, hot sauce, and sea salt. Add the blue cheese crumbles and stir until well combined. 2. Transfer to an airtight container and refrigerate for up to 1 week.

Gochujang Dip

Prep time: 5 minutes | Cook time: 0 minutes | Serves 4

2 tablespoons gochujang (Korean red pepper paste)
1 tablespoon mayonnaise
1 tablespoon toasted sesame oil
1 tablespoon minced fresh ginger
1 tablespoon minced garlic
1 teaspoon agave nectar

1.In a small bowl, combine the gochujang, mayonnaise, sesame oil, ginger, garlic, and agave. Stir until well combined. 2. Use immediately or store in the refrigerator, covered, for up to 3 days.

Italian Dressing

Prep time: 5 minutes | Cook time: 0 minutes | Serves 12

60 ml red wine vinegar
120 ml extra-virgin olive oil
¼ teaspoon salt
¼ teaspoon freshly ground black pepper
1 teaspoon dried Italian seasoning
1 teaspoon Dijon mustard
1 garlic clove, minced

1.In a small jar, combine the vinegar, olive oil, salt, pepper, Italian seasoning, mustard, and garlic. 2. Close with a tight-fitting lid and shake vigorously for 1 minute. 3. Refrigerate for up to 1 week.

Lemon Cashew Dip

Prep time: 10 minutes | Cook time: 0 minutes | Makes 235 ml

180 ml cashews, soaked in water for at least 4 hours and drained
Juice and zest of 1 lemon
60 ml water
2 tablespoons chopped fresh dill
¼ teaspoon salt, plus additional as needed

1.Blend the cashew, lemon juice and zest, and water in a blender until smooth and creamy. Fold in the dill and salt and blend again. Taste and add additional salt as needed. 2. Transfer to the refrigerator to chill for at least 1 hour to blend the flavours. This dip perfectly goes with the crackers or tacos. It also can be used as a sauce for roasted vegetables, or a sandwich spread.

Sweet Ginger Teriyaki Sauce

Prep time: 5 minutes | Cook time: 0 minutes | Serves 4

60 ml pineapple juice
60 ml low-salt soy sauce
2 tablespoons packed brown sugar

1 tablespoon arrowroot powder or cornflour
1 tablespoon grated fresh ginger
1 teaspoon garlic powder

1.Mix together all the ingredients in a small bowl and whisk to incorporate. 2. Serve immediately, or transfer to an airtight container and refrigerate until ready to use.

Pepper Sauce
Prep time: 10 minutes | Cook time: 20 minutes | Makes 1 L

2 red hot fresh chillies, seeded
2 dried chillies
½ small brown onion, roughly chopped

2 garlic cloves, peeled
475 ml water
475 ml white vinegar

1.In a medium saucepan, combine the fresh and dried chillies, onion, garlic, and water. 2. Bring to a simmer and cook for 20 minutes, or until tender. 3. Transfer to a food processor or blender. Add the vinegar and blend until smooth.

Red Buffalo Sauce

Prep time: 5 minutes | Cook time: 20 minutes | Makes 475 ml

60 ml olive oil
4 garlic cloves, roughly chopped
1 (142 g) small red onion, roughly chopped
6 red chillies, roughly chopped (about 56 g in total)

235 ml water
120 ml apple cider vinegar
½ teaspoon salt
½ teaspoon freshly ground black pepper

1.In a large non-stick sauté pan, heat 60 ml olive oil over medium-high heat. Once it's hot, add the garlic, onion, and chillies. Cook for 5 minutes, stirring occasionally, until onions are golden brown. 2. Add the water and bring to a boil. Cook for about 10 minutes or until the water has nearly evaporated. 3. Transfer the cooked onion and chili mixture to a food processor or blender and blend briefly to combine. 4. Add the apple cider vinegar, salt, and pepper. Blend again for 30 seconds. 5. Using a mesh sieve, strain the sauce into a bowl. Use a spoon or spatula to scrape and press all the liquid from the pulp.

Tzatziki

Prep time: 10 minutes | Cook time: 0 minutes | Serves 4

1 large cucumber, peeled and grated (about 475 ml)
235 ml plain Greek yoghurt
2 to 3 garlic cloves, minced
1 tablespoon tahini (sesame paste)

1 tablespoon fresh lemon juice
½ teaspoon rock salt, or to taste
Chopped fresh parsley or dill, for garnish (optional)

1.In a medium bowl, combine the cucumber, yoghurt, garlic, tahini, lemon juice, and salt. Stir until well combined. 2. Cover and chill until ready to serve. Right before serving, sprinkle with chopped fresh parsley, if desired.

Printed in Great Britain
by Amazon

16357805R00052